INDIANS, COWBOYS, AND UFOS

Stories of a Teacher on a Small Navajo Reservation

in 1970s New Mexico

INDIANS, COWBOYS, AND UFOS

Stories of a Teacher on a Small Navajo Reservation in 1970s New Mexico

∎

ANDREW SHOWS

SUNSTONE PRESS
SANTA FE

© 2025 by Andrew Shows
All Rights Reserved
No part of this book may be reproduced in any form or by any electronic or mechanical means including information storage and retrieval systems without permission in writing from the publisher, except by a reviewer who may quote brief passages in a review.

Sunstone books may be purchased for educational, business, or sales promotional use. For information please write: Special Markets Department, Sunstone Press, P.O. Box 2321, Santa Fe, New Mexico 87504-2321.
Printed on acid-free paper
∞
eBook: 978-1-61139-764-2

Library of Congress Cataloging-in-Publication Data

Names: Shows, Andrew, 1951- author
Title: Indians, cowboys, and UFO's : stories of a teacher on a small Navajo reservation in 1970's New Mexico / Andrew Shows.
Other titles: Stories of a teacher on a small Navajo reservation in 1970's New Mexico
Description: Santa Fe : Sunstone Press, [2025] | Summary: "This book is a romp through the history and cultures of Indigenous and local western characters who exemplified the independence and determination required to survive the evolving changes of the American frontier"-- Provided by publisher.
Identifiers: LCCN 2025002556 | ISBN 9781632937469 paperback | ISBN 9781632937247 hardback | ISBN 9781611397642 epub
Subjects: LCSH: Shows, Andrew, 1951- | Navajo Indian Reservation--Anecdotes | Navajo Indians--Social life and customs--Anecdotes | Navajo Indians--Folklore | Art teachers--Navajo Indian Reservation--Anecdotes | Ramah Navajo High School--Anecdotes | Ramah (N.M.)--Anecdotes | LCGFT: Autobiographies
Classification: LCC E99.N3 S53 2025 | DDC 978.9004/9726092 [B]--dc23/eng/20250320
LC record available at https://lccn.loc.gov/2025002556

WWW.SUNSTONEPRESS.COM
SUNSTONE PRESS / POST OFFICE BOX 2321 / SANTA FE, NM 87504-2321 /USA
(505) 988-4418

Dedication

This book is dedicated to Turza, my wife and my teacher.

Contents

Indians and Cowboys ▪ 13
The Placement Office ▪ 18
The Literary Society ▪ 21
My First New Mexico Driver's License ▪ 23
The Ramah Trading Post ▪ 26
Thirty Mules of Silver ▪ 29
Buffalo Chip Cookies ▪ 32
A Texas Chainsaw Massacre ▪ 36
Strangers in Paradise ▪ 39
Rod Stewart ▪ 42
Devine Bovine ▪ 45
I Write the Songs ▪ 48
Movie Wagons ▪ 50
Ramah Mormon Temple Santa ▪ 52
Tom Cummings' Black Oldsmobile ▪ 54
Saint Michael's Bowling Team ▪ 57
Cheyenne Autumn ▪ 59
Navajo Silversmithing ▪ 61
The U-Joint ▪ 65
Zuni Café Debacle ▪ 68
Christmas Festival at the Old School ▪ 70
UFO on McGaffey Road ▪ 73
Great Zuni Sheep Theft ▪ 75
Ladies in Waiting ▪ 77
Casseroles ▪ 79

Kaftan and Combat Boots ▪ 81
Mexico or Bust ▪ 83
Mama Cat ▪ 87
Old Gas Heater ▪ 89
Cowboy Saturday Night ▪ 91
The Great Escape to Albuquerque ▪ 95
KTDB ▪ 98
Apache Laughing Tears ▪ 100
Basketball ▪ 103
Cheese Please ▪ 106
Slaughterhouse-Five ▪ 109
Shalako ▪ 113
Lebanon, New Mexico ▪ 117
Chile Relleno ▪ 120
Ben Hur ▪ 123
Sheep ▪ 126
Photographs ▪ 131
The Last Buffalo Soldier ▪ 137
Sunday Beer ▪ 141
Navajo Divorce ▪ 143
Forty Below Zero ▪ 145
Ramah Rodeo ▪ 147
Buses and Telephones ▪ 149
Bar-D Ranch ▪ 152
Camel Cavalry ▪ 155
Flag Day ▪ 157
Patty Hearst and Richard Nixon ▪ 160
Tazhii ▪ 162
The Iowa Test ▪ 164
Rafael's Silver Cloud ▪ 166
Mongolian Spot ▪ 168
Hopi Basket ▪ 170
Western Pesto ▪ 173
The Weavers ▪ 175

"The Man Who Fell To Earth" ▪ 178
Yee Naaldooshii, Skinwalker ▪ 180
The Christmas Festival ▪ 182
Ammo Boxes ▪ 186
Blood Sausage ▪ 188
Hopi Bean Dances ▪ 191
Japan and Sweden Go West ▪ 196
Outlaw Country ▪ 199
The Rough Riders ▪ 202
Surprise Party at Pedro's ▪ 205
Devil's Highway ▪ 208
Beethoven's Fifth ▪ 211
Banditos ▪ 213
Elk Who Loved a Cow ▪ 217
Interscholastic Activity ▪ 219
The Old Man and the Sea ▪ 222
Ranchos de Chimayo ▪ 224
Zuni Witches ▪ 228
Coronado ▪ 232
Viva La Fiesta ▪ 234
Silversmithing ▪ 238
PTA ▪ 240
Substitute Principal ▪ 243
Ladies of Ojo de Gallo ▪ 245
The El Rancho and the Wigwam ▪ 248
Zuni Baseball ▪ 250
A Bear Story ▪ 254
Retreads ▪ 257
The Lost Sword ▪ 259
Alcohol and Pentecostals ▪ 262
Christmas Candy ▪ 264
Old Man Mirabal ▪ 266
Ramah Lake ▪ 270
Helicopter Johnny ▪ 273

The American Bar • 276
Ole Blue • 279
Satellite Dish • 282
Socrates • 284
Wrestling in Ramah • 287
Mexico With Stan • 290
The One that Got Away • 294
My Heroes Have Always Been Teachers • 298
About the Author • 300

The first person in my life is Turza Marie Shows. She is my inspirational coach and editor. No one could be as lucky as me to have such an inspiring muse to be married to.

Stephanie Baness is a constant friend and facilitator in all thing's computer as well as one of the most intelligent souls I know.

Pam Davis and Will Stripp are eternal friends though we need to spend more time together before it's all gone. Pam is a bank of local history of all things Ramah, and I treasure the time when we taught together. Will has also always been supportive and informative. I have always been grateful for his advisement.

Kristi Davis is a repository of family history in Ramah as well. I appreciated her historical references when I needed pertinent information.

I want to thank Ron Light, my old roommate, and Erick Nelson for the lost photos of 1974 Ramah, New Mexico. Just their existence on my bulletin board helped resuscitate indefinite recall to clearer memories. "I salute you, gentlemen."

Lastly, I want to thank Priscilla Henio, registrar of Pine Hill School, for helping me track down names of students I have been missing in my research. To anyone I have missed, please forgive me, and thank you.

Author's Note

At the time this book was published, fifty years have passed since these stories occurred. Though the memories feel as sharp as yesterday, it would be delusional to believe in the pure accuracy of one's recollections after so many years. Be that as it may, all personal memory is selective. These stories have been the ones that touched my soul and funny bone and demanded I honor their recall. There is one tall tale amongst the group. Can you find it?

Indians and Cowboys

Gallup is the history of the Wild West. The town was always a rough and tumble place where anything could happen. In the 1970s you could buy an old Winchester in a pawn shop, along with the choice of any one of a hundred saddles stored in the back rooms. You could then also purchase a Navajo horse blanket while you were at it. The point is, all the objects you envisioned as synonymous of the Old West, were at your fingertips in most businesses of trade in Gallup.

When I was a small boy of four or five, I wanted to be a cowboy. Even though I was an inner- city kid in Washington DC, we did have television. Gene Autry, Roy Rogers, Hopalong Cassidy, they all showed me how to be a cowboy.

I even dreamt of being a cowboy. I could see myself in dungarees, shiny cowboy boots, western shirts with those little pearly snaps for buttons, and of course, a really nifty white cowboy hat, 'cuz I was a good guy. My horse was a small red pony, and he loved me, and I'd ride him till the sun came down. The landscape had beautiful sandstone cliffs and grass meadows to race the bad guys on and on and on.

Patty was a little girl, who was staying with us, and I often availed my stories and ambitions of cowboy hood to her. I'd explain to her that I would soon be leaving for Texas to fulfill my dreams. Patty would study me, give me a snicker, and then say, "No, you won't."

She intentionally rocked my world, I staggered and replied, "Oh. Yes, I will."

Her return was, you guessed it, "No, you won't."

I stared at her, cold hearted and protested, "I will get on a bus and go to Texas."

To which she replied, "I dare you." Oh shit, did she say that? I was screwed. There was no escape, no alternative. I went to the bedroom, put on both cap guns in holsters, found my cowboy hat, fitted lanyard, walked to the apartment door, and after opening it, marched down three flights of stairs and strode into the early morning straight to the bus stop in front of our building.

Patty was watching me from the apartment's window. I waved goodbye to her and stood stoically, awaiting the bus. This didn't take long in a busy city like the District of Columbia. Finally a metro bus pulled up. I was the only one at the stop, the door opened. Hesitantly, I marched up to the driver, the steps were steep, and my guns were giving me trouble. Steadily I presented myself to the driver, looked him straight in the eye, and asked, "Does this bus go to Texas?"

"No," he says.

To which I replied, "Oh, thank you." I marched off the bus, walked straight back the way I'd come and meeting wide eyed Patty at the door, I said, "The bus doesn't go to Texas, so I can't go." I know she was astounded by my bravery and the new awareness that with that kind of determination I most likely would fulfill my dream and become one of the world's most famous cowboys. As far as I was concerned, that was close, too close for a five-year old. Maybe I should think about being a doctor.

In May of 1973, I was at Highlands University in New Mexico. It was early summer quarter break and I had been hired to work on a ranch in Folsom, New Mexico for the three-week break. This would give me a little money to get through my last quarter of school to achieve my master's degree. I was grateful. The woman who hired me was older, and she and her husband, who had been a copilot on the Doolittle raid over Japan, owned quite a spread west of Folsom. My new friend, my boss, was also a student and studying in a graduate program for children with special needs. I truly admired her.

So early one Saturday, after classes had ended, I drove us in her station wagon northeast to her home in Folsom. The ranch was beautiful. It had once been owned by an ex-governor of Colorado. Driving through the gates, up to the complex of house, bunkhouse, barns, and blacksmith shops, I became aware that this was a big operation. After meeting her husband, a good man, I then was introduced to the ranch hands and the daughter. Everyone seemed immediately friendly, and by this time it was late, and the dinner bell was sounding.

I slept well that night, I was happy, I was a cowboy. At four o'clock the bell suddenly rang, jarringly through my sleep drugged bones. All the hands were jumping from their bunks and proceeding to work, work? "What about breakfast?"

"Breakfast? Oh. breakfast is at seven, first there's chores."

The daughter found me stumbling outside the bunkhouse. She handed me a pail, and said, "Follow me." We continued down the hill to a lower barn and inside stood a young antelope and behind him six, large milking goats. The daughter told me the antelope's name was Sean, and he was orphaned by some hunters and was surviving on these goats' milk because the ranch was not licensed to sell it. Sean had become one of the family, and if I must say, he was joy incarnate. The goats were fine with my milking, that is, after I received my instructions, except for one. There are some individuals in life you are just not going to hit it off with. She was one of those. She kicked me in my side, on my head, stepped on my foot, and pushed me against the barn wall. Finally, I'd had enough.

I found a rope, tied her right front leg up to the corral, and then I tied her left back leg to the corral's other side. With her leaning to another corral side, I now had her pinned and milked away. But that look, oh that look, I swear I saw the flames of hell itself in those eyes. Oh well.

After other chores there finally came the seven o'clock breakfast bell, hot damn. There were pancakes and sausages and eggs and toast and enameled pots of coffee, who could ask for anything more.

After breakfast the owner, my boss, walks up and asks me if I can ride. "You mean a horse? Well, of course." After all, I had watched every cowboy flick ever made. I obviously knew, simply through the act of osmosis. One of the hands drove me down to the stable in a pickup that had no right to be running but was too stupid to die. We entered the stable, and I swear to God, there was my horse. The horse of my childhood dreams—she was full grown now and big and beautiful and red. After being refreshed of my obvious knowledge of saddling a horse, the ranch hand informed me I was to ride down to the south pasture and move twenty steers over to the west pasture, simple. So I ascended into the saddle of my red-dreamed beauty and proceeded to the south pasture. It was a sun-filled magnificent day, the birds were chirping, dragonflies were dodging us, and butterflies were thick as gnats. In a few moments my red beauty decided we were trotting a little slow, and we needed to pick up the pace. Okay, I thought, why not, and then she bolted. In less than a heartbeat, we were racing through the herd, passed them onto another meadow covered with huge blossoming sunflower stalks, and there was no slowing down. She would not obey the reins. Finally hanging on, I leaned over and banged on the side of her head with my fist, harder and harder. Something must have clicked because she inevitably slowed down, and I was able to regain control.

My arms and neck were ripped to shreds from the sunflower stalks. Then somehow between the burst of accelerated horsepower and fist banging, we returned to the corrals. Later that day I was informed the cattle hadn't needed to be moved at all, but that old racehorse, who could never be retrained as a ranch horse, needed the exercise, and I appeared naive enough to fulfill her request. I would be more aware of my assignments from then on, or so I thought.

Lunch was at two in the afternoon, sandwiches and chips. Work followed all afternoon, and I expected we knocked off at five. Ha, ha, you fool. We worked until dark, the kind of dark when you can't see anything anymore. The dinner bell rang at eight-thirty. Struggling up to the kitchen's dining hall, we sat to partake of our vittles. I don't remember exactly what we had that night because I slept with my head in my plate until someone told me to hit the sack.

The three weeks went by in a blur. Once the routine set in, the time went by quickly. Many people have illusions about ranch work. In my three weeks, and that is seven days a week, keeping in mind, full time cowboys get half a day off a month. They go to Clayton, buy necessaries, and raise hell.

I had many jobs. I changed wax seals and repaired toilets in guest houses; encased in veil and gloves, removed a wild bee honeycomb from an old bunkhouse's walls; I even had to capture a porcupine from up a tree with a net; then somehow deposit it into an old trunk for transport off the ranch. Then there was netting fish from a fishpond, which needed transferring. There are a million different jobs no one would ever consider pertinent to the running of a successful ranch, but there it is.

Finishing my three-week tenure as a cowboy, I received my pay of a dollar an hour, keep in mind room and board were included. The pickup truck, who wouldn't die, took me to Raton to catch the south bound train. I thanked my new friends for including me in their family for three weeks and boarded the train back to Vegas.

There was much to think about. I had been privileged to participate in the most romantic of American experiences—ranching. I'd damn well been a cowboy. No one could ever take that away from me. My childhood dream had really manifest, "So take that Patty." Still through all these trials and tribulations and all things considered, becoming a doctor did make more sense now.

The Placement Office

January of 1974, in Baltimore was hard. My car had been hit by a young girl during morning rush hour, who ran a stop sign. My Volkswagen Super Bug was totaled, and I was semi-crippled in the ensuing whiplash, the result of running into a brick wall. I was rushed to the University of Maryland Hospital, where I lay in agony for hours in the cold by the emergency room exit door.

A month later, thanks to my lawyer, Sidney Schlackman, I was on the street still in pain, but at least I had $600.00 a month from the insurance company to live on. In short, it was next to nothing.

The following months in Baltimore were a real struggle. Damp, cold, and unemployable, life evolved into playing pool at the Mount Royal Tavern to win free drinks, sometimes some side money, and then here or there a rumored poker game to cash in on. I was not proud of this life, but then it was all that I had.

Feeding my buddy, Socrates, had also become a real contest. Fortunately, I had found a damaged-goods grocery outlet, and at three cents a can I could purchase flats of cat food. This, of course, was not enough for a true son of New Mexico. Then I found a Greek deli around the corner. It had a steel-gate grating, which was impossible to penetrate, but with a twisted clothes hanger, I was able to stretch and reach sacks of stale bread. These loaves I took home, crushed into my dog's bowl, and then added the cat food plus a little water. I wouldn't wish this combination on my best friend, but he ate it anyway. We had a lot of mysterious food during that period.

March finally came, and there was some sunlight one day. My dog and I looked at each other and simultaneously thought, we have got to get the hell out of here and back to New Mexico.

A light burst into my meager cranium. With Socrates' help I remembered the placement office at New Mexico Highlands University, where I'd gotten my master's degree. My phone had not been disconnected yet for delinquent payment, so I discovered the university's number through information and called it.

In January of 1973, I had wandered into the placement office in search of a future employment opportunity after I graduated. Those who worked there were congenial and most helpful, but at that moment they were also honest enough to tell me what I'd already suspected—finding any job was tough. Evelyn, a pleasant older woman, tried to help me. Since everything came through the mail, anyone who happened to be in attendance, when the mail was opened, had the first shot.

Then Evelyn studied me and asked, "Do you play bridge?"

I said, "Not really, but I have watched some hands played and know the gist of it."

Evelyn said, "We lost our office fourth player. She went home to have a baby, and we're short a player. We close for lunch at noon, have our sack lunches, and play bridge. If you filled our fourth position, we could fill you in on all the new positions arriving in the mail."

How could I refuse.

I played every weekday afternoon for six weeks. During that time we discovered jobs in Australia, New Zealand, and Roy and Mosquero, New Mexico. The most promising position was teaching modern art history to nuns at Our Lady of the Lake college in San Antonio, Texas. Can you imagine me doing that?

Well, the office fourth returned finally, the baby was fine, and I was released from my bridge duties. The San Antonio position was a fellowship, and I had successfully won the position. Then the Dean of the art school lost a budget argument with the president of the school, who then cancelled mine and two other fellowships, oh well.

So after all this time, calling the placement office was a long shot, but what else did I have? Evelyn of all people picked up. Of course, she remembered me. I was the best partner she'd ever had. She said, "How are you doing?"

Filling Evelyn in on recent unfortunate events, I finally asked, "Evelyn, are there any jobs in New Mexico education, anywhere? I'll take anything. I mean anything. I need to get back home."

She took my number and said she'd get back to me, but I'd heard that before. So I told Socrates, and we went on with the enduring day-to-day hopeless survival of the inner city.

One day returning from the Greek deli with bags of stale bread, I heard the phone ring as I opened the door of our old, iron factory residence. I made it in time to get the call, thank God. They hadn't disconnected it yet.

It was Evelyn, "Andy, I know we owe you, and we have put a priority on your plight. We have something. It's not great, but it could at least get you back here." She filled me in about a small Navajo Reservation in Ramah, New Mexico, who needed an art teacher for this summer school session of 1974. "What did I think?"

"Of course," I responded. "Evelyn, thank you, of course I'll take it." Later I was contacted by Mary Cohoe, the counselor and director of summer school. Thanks to records and recommendations from Highlands University, I had the job.

I told Socrates. He seemed more elated than me that we were finally going home. It couldn't be soon enough for him. I was certainly beyond ready, and lately my dog had even been acting squirrely. He was rubbing up against me and making funny mewing sounds. Humm, I thought—is that the cat food?

The Literary Society

Some think of the game of Poker as the gamblers' highest test of courage. I didn't find this true. For me it was only a source of job security. How, might you say? Let me explain.

In the summer of 1974, upon the start of my new employment as a summer school art teacher at the Ramah Navajo school, I was fortunate to be invited as seventh in what was called the literary society, a poker game. The society met at seven in the evening on Wednesdays and Saturdays during that summer. The only problem was you had to have five dollars to buy into the game. That first game I was so strapped for cash I actually borrowed money from my Navajo students to get into the game.

There really was nothing going on that summer, so this distraction gave us a breath of fresh air in an otherwise fairly restricted environment. The game needed seven in order to play the maximum number of games possible in the full poker curriculum

The players—three Navajos, three old white guys, and me—were a varied mix of school administrators, including the director, and the high school principal. It was obvious from the first that this was one thing that made life here worthwhile for these guys. By the end of that first night playing, I walked away with twenty-five dollars in winnings and no lack of respect showing in those boys' eyes.

The next day I doubled my student's investments and was now cash set to continue playing. My salary that summer was a hundred twenty-five a week and for only six weeks. I was on the clock.

What my fellow society members hadn't known about me was that I had spent the last eight months convalescing from a car accident. Being wrapped up in a couple of body braces, I hadn't been able to work until this new job with the Ramah Navajo. My time hadn't been wasted though. Somehow I had scratched out a living playing pool in bars in Baltimore and through mysterious means found underground poker games that were not supposed to even exist. During this time I had the most unbelievable run of luck. Gratefully the money had carried me through those months of mending. I wouldn't have made it otherwise.

So now I'm in the literary society counting the days until my contract's termination and fleecing my fellow players of every dollar I can. Soon I was starting to match my teaching salary in cash from poker winnings.

Finally the last week of teaching was arriving, and I'd been preparing to leave. One day while I was packing things into my car, Larry, the school director, happened to be passing by and ask what I was doing. I told him I was preparing to leave since my employment would soon be up. Larry looked straight into my eyes and said, "You're not going anywhere, you took too much money off of us, and we need to win it back. You have an interview at nine tomorrow morning with the school board."

It turned out the permanent art teacher was not too keen on the part where you have to teach kids and wanted a promotion to a Title Program instead. After the interview with the school board the next morning, I walked out as the new head of the art department of the Ramah Navajo School System. To have a permanent job in the 1970s was not an easy quest, and I was woefully grateful beyond words.

When the regular school year began, so did the literary society but only on Wednesday nights. My performance at the games was never so stellar as that previous summer. Once in the middle of a deal, Marshall Plumber, said to me, "You know, Andy, you were hot as a pistol before now, what happened?"

I smiled at him and calmly responded, "Marshall, I didn't have permanent employment before, so I couldn't afford to lose."

My First New Mexico Driver's License

Driving on the reservation is an unknown joy to all but the residents themselves. The landscape is vast, beautiful, and at times seemingly endless. There is generally no hurry or incentive to speed, unless it is payday and on one payday I got stopped by the police.

The Ramah Navajo Police usually are concentrating on their own Native people but this one time for some reason, I caught their eye. The exchange with the officer was pleasant. I informed him I was a new teacher at the Navajo High School and was unfortunately distracted thinking about Pedro's endless rellenos in Gallup. He laughed at that and said he would just give me a warning, but then he notified me that my Maryland driver's license was due to expire in thirty days, and I'd better drive to Gallup sometime in the future and get it replaced with a New Mexico driver's license.

I was taken completely unawares and was thoroughly appreciative of his attention to this detail. I would never even have thought to check if not for him. I had been simply overwhelmed settling down into my new job.

The following week I called Gallup Department of Motor Vehicles from the school office and found their hours—Monday through Friday nine to five, but Thursday was the only day for the actual physical driving test itself. So that Thursday I got through their doors at four in the afternoon, took the written test, got 100%, and proceeded to the counter for the actual driver's test. One must be aware the only reason for the test in the first place is that my previous license was from out of state.

At the counter a Zuni woman greeted me and asked if she could help me. I stated I was here to take the physical driver's test.

She said to me, "Do you want to take the driver's test?"

I responded, "Yes, of course."

To which she answered, "Well, the man who gives that test is not here, but he'll be here next Thursday."

In frustration I left, disappointed, and I drove back home.

The following week I returned on Thursday again at four o'clock, went directly to the same woman, and stated I was here for the driver's test. She said to me, "The man who gives the test is not here. Do you want to take the test?"

I said, "Yes, of course, does this happen often with this man?" She just shrugged.

The following Thursday I was decidedly frenzied by all the inconveniences Gallup DMV had caused me. I'd had it. I went to the counter. The Zuni woman was waiting for me. I said, "I'm here to take the driver's test."

She looked at me and I swear to God, she said, "The man who gives the test is not here. Do you want to take the test??"

Suddenly a bright light illuminated in my meager cranium, awareness became apparent, and I hesitated and said, "No, I don't want to take the test."

She smiled and said, "Fine , which classification of license would you like?"

There were seven classifications starting with #1 being a motorcycle. I chose #7 which allowed me to drive anything, from a double semi to an

Abrams tank. The nice lady processed my paperwork, and I walked out with a spanking new driver's license, which permitted me to drive anything outside of a space shuttle.

For years after, that license served me well, whether I was driving the school bus in an emergency or substituting for a sick truck driver in a pinch. The State of New Mexico did finally cancel that driving classification fifteen years later when I couldn't prove I owned a semi-truck.

The Ramah Trading Post

The original Ramah Trading Post was built by the Masters brothers, Bob and Giles. They came from England in the early 1900s, and after a temporary commercial structure on the west side of Ramah was built, they finally settled in and built the beautiful, stone edifice that has resided in the center of the village ever since. This building became the hub of commerce for Navajos, Mormons, Hispanics, and even Zunis. Everyone had traded here, even John Miller.

Miller was always suspected by a few locals of actually being Billy the Kid. Why? It seems John only came to trade in the middle of the night, he often disappeared to Colorado for periods of time, and then he would reappear flush with gold and silver dollars. Outside of that, his only recognizable income came from bronc busting. His wife/mistress was Hispanic from Fort Sumner and only spoke Spanish. But the real clincher was his best friend, Bushy Bill Roberts. Bushy even claimed his identity when John finally died at the Prescott Pioneer Home in Arizona. Roberts even went before the Governor of New Mexico in 1951, claiming to be Billy the Kid. Bushey had all the stories, but John Miller took the real evidence to the grave.

The Ramah Trading Post glided through history with all the charm of an old dame and the day-to-day business of trade and credit that supported multiple communities was faithfully attended to with grace. The establishment was as much about families as it was commerce. The old potbelly stove was always offering respite from the cold or winds in winter, and the coffee pot was always attended to. A later owner, Mr. Lewis, added a popcorn machine to keep the kids occupied as well. This was the community center before the Ramah Navajo Chapter House was built. All neighborly gossip and tribal information often traveled here first. You must remember the Navajo were nomadic, they lived in separate homesteads, and often only heard from their neighbors at the trading post. This was the normality of life in the Ramah Community, when our school was established.

In 1974, I arrived in the village. One of the first things I was instructed to do was to establish credit at the trading post. This I did since I was flat broke, having traveled from the East Coast with my few meager possessions. As I said, the present owner of the store was Mr. Lewis. There were a few Mormon Lewis's, but this one owned the trading post. He created an account in my name in an index file, and in the years to come I charged gas, oil, groceries, medicine, and any other vital piece of hardware or doodad only an old trading post would procure.

Come payday, Mr. Lewis would cash my check, minus the past items charged on credit, and hand me a cash balance. Not a bad arrangement for a hungry teacher even at his prices. We were a family of sorts in those early days. We knew everything about everybody and if we missed something, we could just go into the store, pour a cup of coffee, browse the aisles and listen to catch up.

If someone died on the reservation, Mr. Lewis was often asked to officiate the funeral. Even though he was a Mormon, he was family and could always be depended on. The only problem at such events was, he insisted on wearing a ratty, old toupee that had seen better days an entire generation ago. The congregation was always distracted during these solemn affairs as they stared at him, wondering if the toupee would finally slide off. Why we never took bets is beyond me. Mr. Lewis wore a hat all the rest of the time, and he had that toupee obviously hidden in a secret location, maybe the safe.

The old trading post is closed now. The Ramah Navajo bought the old building and are planning something eventually. In my mind's sweet closet of particular memories, I can still hear distant laughing, and whispering and cajoling in Navajo, English and even Spanish in the Isles of the store.

The local politics may have changed as everything in life changes, but I remember my first day in Ramah with a growling stomach and no money. It was the trading post that fed me and reassured my faith in the goodness of strangers. But much later it became apparent to me that business is business. After all, if they would take Billy the Kids' credit, they certainly should take mine.

Thirty Mules of Silver

There are many stories of lost treasure throughout New Mexico's history. These stories often follow disruptions in historical events such as the Mexican American war and before that the ascension of the new government of Mexico over their previous Spanish overlords.

The movement of gold and silver specie would often be a frantic and desperate effort for previous territorial administrations and chances not normally imagined would become the only obvious solution to escape with the goods.

Eileen Eshner, the Carnegie librarian in Las Vegas, New Mexico, and I were friends and dreamers of lost treasures. Victorio peak was at that moment in 1972, we believed, being purged of its secret treasures by the US army. Since the discovery of the site resided on White Sands missile range, who could ever contest their authority. Needless to say, all this was disheartening to say the least.

There was another treasure that Eileen and I researched. This one was a product of an 1820 dash from a Spanish Colorado silver mine and was borne on the backs of thirty mules. This last absconding group of Spanish miners and soldiers left Colorado following a long- established mule trail South to Laguna Pueblo.

At Laguna they refitted and resupplied and exited South for friendly Spanish governors still ensconced in Mexico. Their escape south though, was intercepted on the trail by attacking Apaches. After a brutal and bloody exchange, only three Spanish soldiers of the mule train survived.

One, badly wounded, didn't make it long further on. The two remaining soldiers traveled west to escape further Apache confrontation. Later out of desperation, the two found some numerous lava chasms south of what is now Grants, New Mexico. They slaughtered the mules still packed with silver ore and shoved them down these flues figuring on returning later with the contingent of soldiers.

From there the two survivors headed directly south. Only one made it home alive to tell the story. Unfortunately, during the period of this soldier's incredible ordeal, Mexico had achieved its independence, and the Spanish crown now had no claim on the lost treasure of the thirty mules of silver. As a result, the story fell into the pantheon of lost legends of the Southwest and was hitherto forgotten.

Years later I found myself hired by the Ramah Navajo school board as their art teacher. One day it dawned on me that I was in the vicinity of what I remembered was the legend of the lost treasure of the 30 mules of silver. How fortuitous, this could be no coincidence, something must be waiting for me.

I started talking to Navajos I worked with and fortunately befriended a couple, Marty and Roy Garcia. They were possibly interested in a "get rich quick" treasure scam that I was selling convincingly. On a lark, we drove around to areas of the reservation that looked like serious possibilities and made a plan for the following Saturday to investigate.

When Saturday came, I had a flashlight, ropes and shovels I had borrowed, some canteens and snacks also. They picked me up and we were driving to the area we had targeted as the best possibility. On the way there we met another pickup of old Navajos and when they asked what we were doing, Marty told them. They hesitated, then proceeded to recount a 1947 escapade of a group of Belagaana (white people) treasure hunters who came on the reservation and were searching for an elusive legendary treasure. After some search time a few of these men just up and disappeared. They were never heard of again and the others made a brisk exit. Something had gone terribly wrong.

After Marty relayed this story to me there was a shadow of unfortunate foreboding over our quest. Still, we had the ropes, so why not try at least something. Roy found a lava fault that looked very promising, and we all agreed to try it. Marty and Roy did not volunteer though to go down the fault, they said, "It was your idea." So I lassoed up and using the tow hitch on the truck, they lowered me down, down a dark treacherous crack in the earth.

Landing deep and operating my old flashlight, I was met by tumbleweeds, old juniper branches and a few old sheep skeletons/no treasure, no mule bones, no old leather remains, no nothing. Oh well, it was worth a shot, and we had tried.

So I called up to my compadres and said, "Pull me up." Nothing happened. "Pull me up, please." Well that didn't work either, so finally I started screaming. Maybe they couldn't hear me. After a long while and going nearly hoarse, the rope was finally moving and eventually I was pulled up to the surface. "What the hell happened?."

They looked at me in shock and said, "What do you mean?"

I said I had been screaming for retrieval for what seemed like an hour, and nothing happened. I was freaking out.

They told me they'd heard nothing and were finally tired of waiting for me and just decided to finally drag the rope up with the truck and there I was.

Now I'll never know if the ghost of a lost treasure was preventing my pleas from reaching the surface or were my new friends, Marty and Roy, teaching me a lesson in humility. If so, they truly had the last laugh. I'll never comprehend the inscrutable mind of the Navajo and in the end I was perfectly fine with that. Ha. Ha.

BUFFALO CHIP COOKIES

My first PTA was such a casual affair in the fall of 1974, I vaguely remember any attendance at all of my students' parents. I had brought a platter of chocolate chip cookies for my guests, and nearly all were still on the tray come the end of the conference period.

Submitting to my impatience I decided to go home. Suddenly as I was preparing to leave, one of my female Navajo high school students appeared with her grandmother. This was unusual to say the least, but circumstances on the reservation created its own conditions, and one needs to flow with its stream. This student lived with her grandmother, who wanted to see her classrooms and teachers. Curiosity, I guessed. I offered her grandmother the platter of cookies, and she thanked me in Navajo for what was translated as the buffalo cookie. I corrected my student to translate to her granny that these were chocolate chip cookies. After a short talk with grandma, my student informed me, according to her grandmother, these were Apache, buffalo chip cookies.

Perplexed by this, I asked my student why and if her granny knew of the story behind the buffalo chip cookie name. She was obliging and delivered this, translated by her granddaughter, legend of sorts.

Surprisingly, the story didn't start in New Mexico, but rather in an upper Chicago high school in Illinois of all places. It appears there was a tiny, home economics teacher named A. McGillicutty, the A. was for Alice, of course. Alice taught high-brow upper Chicago girls the fundamentals of cooking, sewing, place setting, and in short all the things these kids' servants did for them at home.

But Alice had a dream, so she worked hard, tolerated her situation, and pinched her pennies until she had a grubstake to go west, where people strove for a new life of adventure. You see, Alice dreamed of living in New Mexico, where woman were woman and men were glad of it.

Soon with her money saved and her trunk and an old iron stove to boot, Alice hopped the train from Chillicothe and traveled the rails southwest to a place called Belen, New Mexico. There she found a land office and purchased a property further south near a village named Las Cruces. Alice hired a wagon with a Mexican driver and proceeded to her "promised land." This diminutive figure of femininity had the heart of a giant and the drive of a locomotive, she had a lot of spunk too.

Anyway, the old Hispanic driver found the property's location. It was a sad, old terrone, a sod brick house with vegas fallen to the floor and the roof half burned. Now Alice had understood the Apache had been pacified, and it was safe for her to venture south and establish a new homestead. So with the determination of a high school spoiled debutante teacher, she proceeded to clean and organize. With the driver gone Alice was on her own.

Eventually she met other "sod buster" homesteaders, and with their help she was able to put her new home to rights. With her stove in place and operational, Alice started baking. She repaid her distant neighbors with the warm bread of gratitude. As time passed Alice was more than content, she was finally happy in her new home in the New Mexico Territory.

Then, turbulent times returned. Geronimo was loose, and the Apache were on the rampage. No one was safe, least of all a home-ec teacher alone in the wilderness, but Alice wasn't leaving. She had worked hard with no man to build a life for herself in a place that made her truly happy, and she wasn't leaving. All her neighbors tried to convince her to go with them, but Alice said, "No go," and waved goodbye.

All alone out on the New Mexico plains, Alice continued her day-to-day life like nothing had happened. She watched the beauty of the sunrises and sunsets. At night she'd take her coffee cup outside and sitting on a stool, ogled at the stars that looked after her. Alice was in love, and she wasn't leaving for any reason.

One morning though, while feeding the few chickens she had outside the house, she heard some distant shouts and cries. Her instincts warned her this was no time for questions, these were guaranteed to be Apache, no one else was around.

Alice ran into the house, barred the door, and added wood to the stove. She pulled down her mixing bowl, found flour, sugar, and other ingredients and started stirring. At the last moment Alice found some chocolate she'd been saving and chopping it up, added this also to the mix. Now any woman, who has her druthers during those crucial times in life, will verify that in periods of extreme stress, cookies are the only way out. A good cookie will get you through some of the toughest of times.

The Apache had arrived, they were hooping an' hollering as they rode horses around the house, the end was near. Finally, the warriors jumped from their horses and attacked the front door. Chop, bang, chop, they clobbered the old door with tomahawks until in splinters, it collapsed on the floor inside. Entering the house, fierce in their war paint, they strode in for the kill just as Alice turned to them with a steaming hot tray of fresh cookies. Now what are you going to do with the smell of the oven and cookies? You've been working hard all morning, raping, murdering, rampaging up and down the territory with never a break. The Apache decided what's wrong with a little break for themselves anyway, so instead of the expected murder/rape thing, they decided to sit down at the table and partake of Alice's magnificent culinary treats. The cookies were a smash, and with coffee served they were near perfect. Did you know Apache loved to dunk their cookies just like everyone else?

Alice kept baking cookies for these hungry gentlemen when there was a ruckus outside, coming from a rider just arrived. An older warrior strode in indignant and angry; it was Geronimo himself, and he was, to say the least, pissed to see his cutthroats having coffee and cookies at their leisure. As the moments passed the aroma of the food assaulted his senses, and he was also a captive. Sitting down Geronimo saw a fresh platter of cookies and identifying the shapes as those of the buffalos' prairie deposits, dubbed them "buffalo chips."

Well everything went swell from there on, the boys filled up on these good vittles and coffee and after some discussion settled on an agreement with Alice. If she would bake buffalo chip cookies anytime the boys were in town, she could stay on her homestead indefinitely.

They even fixed her door on the way out. So there you have it, the original chocolate chip cookie was actually a buffalo chip cookie.

We were the last ones out of the school that night. I thanked my guests for straightening me out on the origin of this cookie and bid adieu. It had been a long night, and walking home it occurred to me that Keebler and any other company who created their variations of the 1930s Tollhouse cookie should hire private investigators to explore into this story or there could be sweet repercussions from the Apache someday.

Now I know this story sounds farfetched and absurd, but I am willing to swear on a stack of bibles that from the reliable information I possess that this story could or could not be true. What do you think?

A Texas Chainsaw Massacre

It is a cruel and heartless thing when you receive an auto insurance cancellation. You ask yourself, was there no loyalty? Was the significance of this mutually extended relationship meaningless? Had I meant nothing to them? Was it, in the end just simply flirtation and usury? What was I after all to them, just chopped liver?

GEICO had dropped me. But I wasn't prepared for this and had too much else on my plate at the time. Back then in the 1970s, I doubt I'd have had very good coverage in the Southwest anyway. They at the time were a government employees' insurance, based in Washington DC. The point is—it was bad timing all around.

Early October of 1974, I was still a new-hire teacher with the Ramah Navajo, and of course, there were several catchup bills from some of the previous year's study unemployment I had to contend with. It was just a bit much at the time.

This now meant I was driving uninsured, not a pleasant happenstance. I didn't know what to do, so I decided to go to the movies in Gallup. There was only one theater at that time in Gallup, the El Morro. Driving the fifty or so miles to town thinking about insurance, all I did was worry, worry, worry. What if I had an accident? What if I got hit by another driver? Many drunk drivers had taken company with them on their trek to the pearly gates. Anything could happen.

Arriving at the theater and having no idea what feature would be playing, I observed the marquee. *A Texas Chainsaw Massacre* was presently showing, huh, what's that? I paid my dollar and a quarter admission and proceeded into the theater.

The El Morro theater, built in 1928, was old when I had entered it. Its history covered the travelling vaudeville circuit with the likes of WC Fields and even Mae West. They would come from the train, do a show, and leave. The railroad tracks were only three blocks away. Later silent films would graduate into talkies and dominate the entertainment venue from then on. This relic of Spanish Colonial design served generations of Western New Mexicans. It's all there was in this region after all.

Mexicans, Hispanics, Navajos, Zunis, Hopi and, of course, railroad men stranded in a strange town along the tracks, flocked to the welcoming doors and bright lights of the El Morro. It was a respite from the coal-polluted rails of the train depot and the town itself.

There is a story, a legend really, with no validation to back it up of a train chartered by The Band that stopped in Gallup. The hippies riding it, jumped off for break, and as if locusts were swarming, proceeded to empty every liquor store and bar near the tracks. By the end of the twenty-minute delay, the train proceeded on. Supposedly, quite a few treasured musical hits of Robbie and the boys were birthed on that locomotive journey.

Robert Zimmerman lived in Gallup as a boy. His father was a salesman, and he played with the local kids like any normal youth. Later, the family moved on to greener pastures. Many historians argue this claim about Bob Dylan. But really, who would lie about spending part of their childhood in a place like Gallup, New Mexico? The tooth fairy?

A Texas Chainsaw Massacre was precisely that, how unfortunate. But, unexpectedly it did the trick. Now I am not some sort of sissy, who avoids thoughtless, stupid, idiotic, bloody, cruel horror flicks, but they're not on the top of my list. This was the one and only movie feature in town that day, and it had deeply disturbed me. I walked out shaken uncontrollably to my very core. Okay, I am a sissy. Anyway, standing there recovering at the entrance of the theatre, I eyed a telephone booth down the sidewalk. It was time, I knew it, there was no turning back.

I marched to the phone booth, entered, and with a pocket full of change I'd acquired from the ticket booth, dialed 411 for information. Hello operator, could I have the number of Horace Mann teacher insurance in Albuquerque, New Mexico? Yes, would you direct dial me through, thank you. I had acquired the name of this insurance company via another teacher at the school for future use, not knowing how soon that would be.

After receiving an insurance binder number over the phone, the tension I had accumulated the last two days, rolled off my body like an undertow in a sea suddenly releasing a swimmer caught in its deathly clutches. The drive home was quite pleasant, and with my predicament resolved I became aware of what a beautiful day it had become.

So if you ever experience lapses in judgment or moments of indecision causing you great strife resulting in back-burner unrealities flaming and smoking in your subconscious, may I suggest renting, *A Texas Chainsaw Massacre*. It will clean you right out

Strangers In Paradise

Few people know W.C. Wyeth lived and worked with the Navajos in 1904. At twenty years old, he came on the westbound Super Chief Train from Albuquerque to gain experience for western illustrating. Living in a Hogan with a family of Navajos, who somehow befriended him, he also rode a pony to deliver the mail between trading posts near Two Gray Hills on the reservation. Now the sunlight between 7,000 to 8,000 feet altitude can be quite breathtaking in the Southwest at sunset. The light shoots horizontally across the plains and explodes into a 100,000-watt spotlight-like glow that no words can truly describe.

I know this light affected Wyeth immensely after I surveyed his painting and illustration catalogs. The light behind *Treasure Island* illustrations makes it so apparent to me, as well as numerous Saturday Evening Post works. Maxwell Parrish was not the soul possessor of the glorious golden sunset. WC, more so I feel, actually brought the light into a reality relatable to most painters and laymen. After a year with riding and delivering the mail, eventually WC had enough money to get a ticket back home. The rest is history, but seldom is it ever mentioned of any gratitude directed to the dear old Navajos who helped WC see the light.

Somewhere and somehow in the early 1970s, a black man was found, hitchhiking with a saxophone case on the Navajo reservation. He luckily was able to hop a ride with an old sheep herder on his way to the trading post. Being nearly frozen on the early December morning, the warmth of the wood stove in the trading post revived him sufficiently to answer some questions by the local trader. His name was Jimmy, he was from Chicago, and he played the saxophone. After a while, having recovered somewhat,

Jimmy struggled and opened his sax case. To the eyes and ears of staring Navajos with the saxophone to his lips, he started streaming a melody of magical proportions, which stunned his audience into silence. On he played with their approval into the afternoon 'til it soon became apparent the sun was starting to low towards an early winter sunset. Suddenly as Jimmy completed his set, he became aware he had not eaten it seemed forever or had a berth to stay in for the night. After some discussion a Navajo family, who spoke some English, volunteered to take Jimmy to their hogan to spend the night.

It turned out Jimmy actually stayed with this family quite a while. The little money he had he contributed to buy stores at the trading post. Jimmy would also split juniper for the burning tin sheepherder stove in the hogan. What Jimmy did most for his host though was play sax, beautiful, full throated, honest, loving sax. Friends of this family would travel to visit and hear the black man who played to the gods.

One night the real winter finally visited and decided it was staying. Jimmy continued to collect juniper for the wood stove, but now food was running scarce. The Navajos had no more money; Jimmy had no money. Things were looking kinda bleak, well at least Jimmy would soothe them with the saxophone and send them off each night to dreamland.

Soon time was beginning to run out for Jimmy and his dear friends. In desperation, through blowing snow he drudged through the deep powder and somehow made it through the long distance to the trading post. The trader spied him struggling and had the door opened for him. Reviving Jimmy with a cup of coffee and heat from the wood stove, the trader patiently got the dire story out of him.

In a while Jimmy pulled the saxophone from under the blanket he had made the trek with. He begged the trader to take it in exchange for the desperate stores he needed to save the family, who was sheltering him. How could the trader refuse. He bundled up all the supplies, packed Jimmy up as best he could, and sent him back out into the storm. Now they'd have food at least but no music.

Jimmy left that spring. He hitchhiked out alone and moved on. But that saxophone hangs from the ceiling of the trading post in a place of prominence still and will never be sold. Why would they ever want to forget that black Belagaana sax player who was sent from heaven?

Rod Steward

In 1974, my first summer school term was coming to a completion. Having secured full-time employment for the next year, I was feeling for the first time in a long time like I might have a future after all. Things were looking up.

To celebrate the conclusion of the summer program, our principal had purchased tickets to see Jerry Lee Lewis in concert in Albuquerque. We would have to drive there separately, but once we were there—drinks, dinner and "Jerry" were ours. This was a great morale booster, and we teachers were ones not to forget a kindness of appreciation. I missed that principle; he understood.

Jerry was playing at the Rancher's Club downstairs at the Hilton Hotel. Conrad Hilton's actual roots were first set in New Mexico. His father ran a very small hotel for railroad employees in San Antonio, south of Socorro, New Mexico. Conrad must have seen some possibilities in the business as a kid and ran with it to create a new vision of hotel hospitality for the future.

The Rancher's Club was a boutique performance venue that revolved guest artists from around the country. Jerry was just a one-night stand, and we obliged him. Jerry started slowly, played coy and disinterested, and baited us with sarcasm and piano riffs. Yet in a blink of an eye, Jerry caught on fire. We couldn't even see his fingers as they played in the flames ascending from the ivories, how was that possible?

My future wife was in the audience that night. Turza was with a date. She had a lot of dates. She was a popular girl. Anywho, the evening was a spectacular success, and a great time was had by all. Afterwards, I prepared to leave, but there was no money to stay at a motel, so home I proceeded. It was now one o'clock in the morning, and that meant a three o'clock arrival home at the earliest. Driving was hard in the exhaustion and the adrenaline spent at the concert. The car's tank was full, but personally I was out of gas.

Somehow I made it to Grants and continued driving on south Route 53, a lonely dark narrow road. There was no traffic, so there weren't even interruptions of passing cars to arouse me. Sleep was beating me mercilessly with a baseball bat, and every mile was a battle for my consciousness, but I kept going. Soon, I knew I was close to my destination. I was near the outskirts of the village; everything would be okay now.

Suddenly, in the haze of my sleep oppressed mind, I became aware of a disruption in the clarity of my vision, was I blacking out? In a heartbeat my brain finally registered what was interrupting my consciousness. Three Black Angus cows were spread out across the road on both lanes. Somehow they'd become loose and were straying across the blacktop at the village limits. In a microsecond I realized the closest one was to the right, passing that one the next was centered further down the road, passing that one, and the final one was further down in the left lane. Due to this staggering of their arrangement and the fact that they were all moving to the right, I miraculously avoided them all. Crowning the edge of the left lane's curb, I was able to retake the pavement and get home. I was awake now.

That fall I had a date with a nice young lady in Albuquerque. We had been seeing each other for a while. Departing at noon on Sunday, I became aware of my long trip home and realized a bit of lunch would make sense, so I stopped. The Hilton had a well-run cafe, and the food was good. Entering the lobby I quickly proceeded to the cafe, it was empty. Taking a seat at the counter, I sat and awaited a server. In a while, a wide-eyed woman appeared, and I requested a menu. She hesitated, then she gathered her wits, grabbed me a menu, and brought me coffee. While placing my order there appeared a couple of men at the cafe entrance, creating a sort of human barrier, well so what. My food arrived as also a young couple appeared and seated themselves to my right. I thought nothing of it; I was engrossed in my Rueben. Nothing was going to disturb me, or so I thought.

Then there came a whining, wheering sound of a squawking noise, coming from the couple's table. I tried to ignore it and kept eating. Then the sound changed to a machine-gun monologue that baffled human consciousness. Was that even language spoken? Slowly I turned around, trying not to be caught spying, and was shocked to be staring into the eyes of Rod Stewart. Next to him lounged Britt Ekland, and I believe there was smoke emitting from her lips from the friction, created by the speed of her mouth's locomotion. Rod never said a word; he just sat there. He had finished a big concert the night before at one of the university's auditoriums, and this was his reward for a good night's work.

Looking in his eyes I saw a dedicated musician, who never anticipated all the rewards of fame. Be careful what you wish for. Anyway, as I finished eating and paid my tab, I glanced one more time at my ole buddy Rod, and with a quick glance of mutual understanding, I believe I could hear him, clear as a bell, in my head say, "Wanna be a rock star?"

DEVINE BOVINE

In August, at the beginning of the school year, my roommate Ron and I were ensconced in our new digs on a hill above the public elementary school in the Village of Ramah. The house I had found was built of World War II ammo boxes. They were surplus from the war via Fort Wingate. After the framework from this lumber was complete, the buildings were then papered and plastered with cement, then stuccoed, and roof shingled.

Our house was built dead reckoning on a hill peak, and eventually, it would settle with a high point in the center of the living room. From this point the remaining structure sloped downhill in every direction—all 360° of it. You didn't need a Stairmaster to stay in shape either. Simply walking up and down the house's floors kept you in tip-top shape. All things considered it still served our purpose as well, and we were content.

My bedroom window was facing north, and from there I could see the old Bureau of Indian Affair's dormitory where Navajo students used to reside during the school year. Now that the Ramah Navajos, thanks to the US Congress, had been able to contract their own school system, the kids had finally escaped the dormitory's entrapment. It was now an empty, sad shell of a building.

At this point in New Mexico history, the one absolute about cattle grazing was, if you weren't fenced, any cattle had the right to feed off your grass. They always, had the right of way, and if you were in doubt of this maxim, you could be certain the alternative was a jail cell and a hefty fine. That is if you weren't simply shot outright to begin with.

Having been schooled in these intrinsically, territorial commandments of cattle ranching, I was aware I would now never even speak to these freeloading free-range cows. Nor would they ever be asked to a cup of tea. They were simply too uppity and inconsiderate of other people's feelings yet tolerated to be hopelessly condoned.

Thus, one evening midweek with school the next morning, I found myself befuddled by a moaning outside my bedroom window. It was past midnight, and I was now awoken and disturbed. What the hell?. What could it be? I ran outside since I couldn't see through the darkness out the window. Lo and behold, a female Hereford, in a most motherly way, had settled on the outside of my bedroom to fulfill the miracle of birth. Oh joy. Oh joy. How could I express my excitement.

Patiently I tried to convince my bovine friend that the grass was greener down below next to my landlord's house, but she feigned ignorance to my suggestion. She wasn't going anywhere. Her look told me, we're in this together, so get used to it buddy. Dejected, I reentered the house and slipped beneath the covers. There was no justice. All night long the strain of her agony echoed through the village and vibrated at the wall of my bedroom. The octaves of her birth song of cataclysmic eruptions, rippled through my brain in my foolish desperation for sleep. This went on and on and on and on and on, well you get the idea. Somehow in the fever of the nightmare of that evening, there was finally silence. Now I really couldn't sleep.

I grabbed a blanket, covering myself, went outside, and followed the exterior walls of the house to my bedroom. There she was, beauty incarnate, the prettiest calf, wet and shiny and being made presentable by her mom. I only stayed a few moments to appreciate the event. I was not needed, so I returned to bed. In an hour it would be time to awaken by the village's morning roosters. The next school day was a daze at the most. I don't remember leaving the house or much less teaching all day. I was thoroughly useless.

If you are mystified by the miracle of life and are intrigued by the majesty of the event in order to fulfill your reassurance in another world, please, the next time a cow decides to deliver by my bedroom wall, would you bring a trailer to my house and I will for free help you load her up and wish you both a bon voyage to life's mysteries.

I Write the Songs

Being an early bird has always suited my personal teaching schedule. Having the keys to the school always allowed me early access, hot coffee and a jump up on preparation for each new school day. When the adolescent hordes attacked, my defenses were in place and every attempted breach had already been foreseen. Well, at least that was the hopeful intent.

There was only one stumbling block to my early morning harmonious routine. That was an ancient electric clock radio that appeared in my old Mormon residence before I even got there. No one had laid claim to it. No previous renter came to retrieve it. My landlord had never seen it before I moved in. It was just there. Fortunately, the radio alarm clock did work, but only at five o'clock in the morning for twenty minutes. Then there was nothing but static the rest of the day. Even so, I had a functional early riser wake-up song every morning. Who could ask for anything more.

Now this gets strange. For the next two years every Monday through Friday at five o'clock in the morning, Barry Manilow's "I write the songs," played exactly that time every morning. Imagine being abruptly awakened out of some marvelous dream by Barry's song, and wondering how could the DJ or the devil as well possibly stand for it one more morning of this abuse, and yet, there it was every morning Monday through Friday.

Radio reception for any other station simply didn't exist on the reservation. Only this lone station out of El Paso, Texas, connected with us for only twenty minutes from five o'clock to five-twenty, Monday through Friday, and it always, always played, "I write the songs that make the whole world sing." What was I being punished for? Was this the station from Hell? I never found out.

In later years I would see Bill Murray in "Groundhog's Day" and think Bill didn't know how good he had it. All I could think of was where was Dylan when I needed him?.

Movie Wagons

Once upon a time in the 1930s, there were three Mormon brothers. Two of them had decided to start a truck dealership east of Gallup at Fort Wingate, New Mexico. The third brother traveled to Los Angeles to find his fortune.

The first two brothers soon found a conundrum to their present plans. It turned out most of their future clientele would be Navajo sheep ranchers. Now these folks came into cash only twice a year when their sheep were sheared. The rest of the time they were mostly flat broke, so the problem for the brothers was, what could you take in trade as a down payment to sell a truck to these prospective customers.

The Navajos had been given buckboard wagons by the Bureau of Indian Affairs, which allowed one wagon per family. These wagons became the universal mode of transportation on all reservations at this time.

The brothers cogitated a solution—what if we traded the wagons for the down payment on a new truck and then collected cash at shearing times? This was what the two brothers decided to do and "Voila." They were in business.

After time passed stacks of wagons overcame the capacity of the brothers' commercial property. This was a problem.

About this same time the youngest brother got a job working for a movie set supplier, which was a good job, and he was mighty happy. One day a movie director, named John Ford, stopped by to complain to his manager. He needed buckboard wagons and plenty of them for something called "Westerns" that he planned to shoot. Ford couldn't find any of them anywhere in Hollywood.

As luck would have it, the third Mormon brother overheard this conversation and gently interrupted, "I know where there are all the wagons you'll ever need." He stated the fact that his brothers in New Mexico had all the wagons, stacks and stacks, and at darn good prices.

With the solution at hand, a train of empty flatbeds was sent to Fort Wingate, and every old BIA wagon was loaded up and shipped back to the movie studios in Los Angeles. Who would have guessed the Navajos supplied the hinge that cowboy westerns were hung upon.

RAMAH MORMON TEMPLE SANTA

Ramah is a very small place as small places go. In a week you could meet everybody, and everybody would know you. While teaching at the new Navajo school and living comfortably within this close-knit Mormon community, I became friendly with an older knowledgeable woman named Flora. She ran the Cowboy Stopover, often confused with its other given name the Cowboy Stoop Over by non-Mormons. Flora was the motherly type and took my tall blonde self under her watchful eye. In time I learned to be dubious of my new friendship with her. It turned out she was also the local matchmaker and was stealthfully promoting me to the Mormon bishop's daughter of the Ramah Temple.

I would learn to be incredibly cautious and polite in dealing with this situation. My first Christmas in Ramah in 1974 was months away. One day while getting gas for my car, Flora mentioned that she was Christmas program director at the Mormon Temple, and she needed a Santa Claus for this year's program. There would be small Zuni and Navajo children in attendance. "Would you please do this for me? I would consider it a personal favor," she said.

I don't know if I was mostly honored or just plain afraid that she wouldn't let me pump gas, so, of course, I said, "Yes."

When the day came, the decorations were wonderful, and the temple was arrayed beautifully. All was complete in the preparation for the children. My Santa outfit appeared comfortable, and I proceeded to suit up. I considered my performance impeccable. The children were adorable, and awe filled. Who could ask for more? While the little ones were attacking tables of sweets and presents, I hastened to the temple's restrooms and started undressing. Soon though, there were children at the door, who refused to let Santa go. Or were they just trying to uncover the identity of this alien Santa from nowhere? Who the hell was he? Where'd he come from? North Pole. Right.

I was trapped in that bathroom for an eternal hour. Finally I could hear the children were being transported home. Then Flora came, knocked on the door, and said, "Andy, they are gone, I'm sorry about that."

The end result was those little monsters never did uncover my identity, and I was certainly never being Santa at the temple again. I had done my duty, but the bishop's daughter was another story.

TOM CUMMINGS' BLACK OLDSMOBILE

Tom Cummings always wore a bright, white starched shirt. It may have had a frayed collar and sleeves and in need of extensive mending, but "Damn it, it was bright white and starched." The rest of his suit and tie ensemble didn't seem to retain nearly as much care as that white shirt did. Oh well, that was Tom.

Tom was originally a boy from "Southy," Boston. He was a brilliant Irish boy, who went to Harvard, and then answered the call of JFK. I always thought Tom reminded me of Will Rogers, in that he liked everyone, but he worked with some better than others. He was a people person through and through.

Tom was instrumental in leading me to possible funding for a school trip to Mexico. It was his prodding that inspired me to that notorious misadventure.

Before I knew Tom, a legend had circulated about Tom and his beat up old black 1962 Oldsmobile sedan. The story, if it could be true, was unbelievable, and yet every time you saw this car you had to wonder.

Around 1970 Tom had a fellowship to teach in Taiwan. That same year his father died and left him ten thousand dollars. Tom arrived in

Taiwan flush with money. While teaching, he endeared himself to the Chinese faculty and students alike. The parties, knowing Tom, must have been sensational to say the least. Anyway, time goes by and eventually Tom completed his fellowship.

Before Tom left for Taiwan, he was working for the Navajo reservation education fund, trying to get young Navajo students into early engineering programs at colleges across the country.

When the opportunity for Taiwan came about, he took a sabbatical from his reservation job. He had only one possession that he was concerned about, and it was his beautiful, shiny black 1962 Oldsmobile 4-door sedan. There was a young Navajo couple, who he apparently trusted, gave them the keys, and told them to use it until he returned.

Two years later Tom returned; the couple and the car were gone. After some extraordinary luck he found them and asked for the return of the car. Tom's friends said that they visited friends for a while, and when they returned, the car was gone. The keys had never been removed from the ignition, and eventually someone drove off with it. That was over a year ago.

Tom, by word of mouth and flyers posted at trading posts, spent another year trying to recover that car. He hitched rides everywhere, and he was determined not to buy another car until he found it. Eventually, miraculously, a Navajo policeman out of Window Rock, called him one day six months later and informed him there was an old car, possibly an Oldsmobile, lying in the creek bed of an arroyo near Tohatchi.

Tom bought a new car battery and five gallons of fuel, just in case and hitched a ride to Tohatchi. Hallelujah, yes it was his car. But the windows were open, and half the desert was living inside it now. Even so, Tom was a loyal lover, and he cleaned her up as best he could, replaced the battery, and filled the tank with the five gallons. With the extra set of keys he had, he tried the ignition. The witness, who gave Tom the ride, observed a hopeless sound from the starter, then there was a funny whirl, followed by a stuttered cough in the engine, and then with all the Irish Saints in heaven watching, the engine growled to life. Well, as much life as an old, abandoned Oldsmobile can give.

Tom slowly drove his lost beauty to a dealership in Albuquerque and asked for a miracle. They were quite hesitant, but the look in Tom's eyes convinced them to operate and hopefully bring this patient back to life. Some weeks later they told Tom she was ready.

Tom had that car all the time I knew him. He was just as faithful to his friends as he was to that Oldsmobile. If you were Tom's friend and there was any hope for you, you could bet Tom would always be there.

St. Michael's Bowling Team

The monastery school of Saint Michael's was west of Gallup and one or two hours from Ramah. This school is one of the few Catholic establishments that has specifically benefited the Navajos. In years past, RC Gorman, the famous artist, went to school there. This Catholic school served the community faithfully, and surprisingly it also was the only source of printing on the reservation. Almost all the local schools used their generous services, we certainly did.

The priests who ran the school and print shop were quite a unique bunch. Tell me—who would volunteer to serve a community so far in the vista that even God sometimes forgets where it is? I often wondered if these priests were being punished for some indiscretion too horrid to conceive. Why were they there? What had they done?

Once I was sent out to pick up some school printing from Saint Michael's. I found the print shop on the further west side of the school and went inside. I could smell the addictive scent of printing benzene that permeated into everything. A large man, who was wearing a bowling shirt, was sitting on a stool next to an operating printing press with a Benson and Hedges 100mm cigarette protruding from his lips. I remember specifically, because the ash hanging from that cigarette was the longest I'd ever seen. In time I spoke to this man and found him to be one of the senior priests, and he oversaw the presses. In our conversation we checked on the school's order, that I wanted to pick up and other details concerning this and that. Before I left, out of curiosity, I asked about the bowling shirt. The priest laughed and told me it was one of their team shirts, and all the priests were part of a bowling league in Gallup.

It became very apparent to me that priests were often placed in special locations, sometimes for good or bad things they had done, and it seemed clear to me these priests were bowling junkies.

Now, it was well-known in Gallup at the time that every Wednesday night, these priests would pack into a couple of church sedans and beeline it, a two-hour drive, to the bowling alley and league night in Gallup. It was apparent that they were notorious and passionate about the game. The fact that there was a full bar in the bowling alley didn't hurt either, and it certainly eased the pain from missed strikes or spares. The moral support from the bar alone was also a blessing. These God-fearing men were an inspiration to all, and their faith in bowling was second only to Jesus Christ himself.

By the end of the evening, with all the dragons and competitions slain, these fine pious men of God would pile back into the churches' cars and with their regular police escort, courtesy of the Gallup Police Department, they would proceed on down the road to their sanctuary of Saint Michael's until the next Wednesday.

I have fond memories of these fine representatives of the Catholic Church and sometimes thinking of them, I believe I can almost hear the flying of pins in a special bowling alley reserved for them in heaven. Bottoms up.

Cheyenne Autumn

John Ford finished filming "Cheyenne Autumn" in 1964. The movie's release was that October. It was a big budget movie with big budget stars, among them were Jimmy Stewart, Richard Widmark, and Ricardo Montalban to name just a few. The screenplay was based on the true story of a starved band of Cheyenne, who escaped their repressive reservation confines and made for their ancestral homelands in Wyoming.

Ford liked filming westerns near Gallup, and he was especially fond of Navajos and they of him. He would often hire huge numbers of extras especially for battle scenes and other necessary historical film filler. Of course, this was hysterical, given the Navajo were a Southwest desert people and had not the slightest notion of how a Northern Cheyenne should act at that point in time, but hell, wasn't this all part of movie magic? The point is these Navajos, recruited from bars and trading posts, took time off from sheepherding and silversmithing and went to join up with Uncle John to become movie stars. They made some money, had some fun dressing up like ridiculous caricatures Hollywood expected, and probably caught up with some relatives, who were there for the same reasons as they were.

Later the film did well, was well-received, and was forgotten as soon as the next colossal hit left tinsel town's studios. It wasn't forgotten in Gallup though because Gallup had a drive-in movie. "Cheyenne Autumn" came to it in the summer of 1965. "You'd say, oh, just another Indian movie to make the red man feel good," but you were far from the actual mark. You see "Cheyenne Autumn" came as a close to a collective family home movie as you could ask.

Remember all the movie extras, and there were hundreds of them. The question would become what Navajo family didn't have a family member in it. After the first night's premiere at the drive-in, the word was out to the reservation to come see, come see. Those extras would regale their experiences, filming with the famous director, John Ford. Then they would reveal stories and anecdotes associated with his true ignorance of Indian ways.

For years, I mean years, the Gallop drive-in faithfully showed "Cheyenne Autumn" every summer. By now generations of Navajos spent balmy summer evenings having their elders point out a father, uncle, grandfather, or other relative. Then as they listened to the Navajo language spoken during the filming, which, of course, Ford had no idea what they were saying or what the translation was, the soundtrack would have the entire drive-in in belly laughter and the most joyful hysterics of reactions.

It seems no one had told John what the Navajos were really saying. During a battle scene with shouting and the attacking cavalry, they were actually saying on soundtrack things like "John Ford, you cheap bastard, you need to give us more money," or "I'd rather be drinking beer in Little Bears than sitting in this hot sun waiting for that little shit to get his perfect shot." This went on and on. Now think about it, who gets to see family, some long dead, but still on the big screen like it was yesterday, bitching through their doleful movie parts, and leaving posterity a piece of their soul.

I don't think the Gallop drive-in still exists. It probably doesn't, but if it does, I guarantee "Cheyenne Autumn" is going to play this summer. If you're smart and need your spirit uplifted, you'll get your tickets now.

Navajo Silversmithing

John Adair, who wrote *Navajo and Pueblo Silversmiths*, visited my roommate, Ron, and me in Ramah in the fall of 1974. Ron knew John through past ethnographic connections and since we, being the possessors of the only guest room on the reservation, provided John with our all so humble accommodations.

Thirty-six years earlier Adair had resided in one of the three stone rooms rented by the trading post in Ramah. From here, he researched his book through live interviews with Navajo and Zuni silversmiths. That was in 1938, and most Native jewelry making was solely and specifically manufactured by these two tribal entities at the time.

Ron and John spoke throughout dinner at the house; I mostly listened. There was in-depth family and academic politics discussed, but nothing profoundly interesting for me. But the little I learned of the situation in the 1930s, did interest me including the great sheep culling, which created a rift between Roosevelt and the Navajo that has never been forgotten.

Then, John left in a couple of days, having completed his homage to his old native stomping grounds.

In 1974, the Ramah Navajo art department was in an old, very small, stone schoolhouse, the Ramah village's first schoolhouse. The facilities and art mediums were very limited, but in 1975, our new school would be built, and silversmithing would be included in the curriculum. The problem was, as head of the art department, I had nil skills in this future department. I was in trouble, but I did have one year's grace to get some experience. If not, at least I could get some live observations under my belt. So I started asking questions and followed the breadcrumbs of two jewelers, who were still working within the community.

First, I found a family of fabricators, who lived on the reservation in a trailer and created simple half round wire bracelets with a turquoise cab set in the center with a funny stylized curve to the bracelet. None of the pieces, these individuals made, impressed me, but their soldering skills did, so I watched carefully and learned. This was the most important lesson of all in assembling individual silver pieces.

Next, in the village of Ramah of all places, I met an oddball, stick-skinny, overly talkative, young Mormon father, who had a shed next to his house full of kids. In the shed, obviously his escape from the wife and kids, he was supposedly making money for the family. This man cut turquoise and made cabochons to trade or sell. He invited me to watch him cut stones and then set the stone slabs on AL40, an aluminum glue that offered a backing to an often too thin slice of turquoise. A high silver bezel could cover all the base of the stone, so you'd think under the slab was pure stone, phony. Still this friendly crackpot gave me low grade green turquoise stones out of the generosity of his heart, and I have no right to disparage him. Still, he was very odd.

My next schooling was from a Navajo adult education teacher named Roger who was from Coyote Canyon on the main rez. Roger, in his spare time, was a tufa caster, one of the very first forms of Navajo jewelry making. One day, Roger invited me to his trailer to observe him casting a silver buckle with the traditional corn blossom design. I saw the already-carved design in the tufa stone and the air vent lines for casting. I also observed how he used old car motor oil to burn a carbon release, coating on the mold. Then I watched him tie the mold to another smooth stone. Then tilting the whole setup at a 75° angle leaning on a brick, he was ready to pour the molten silver. Roger had his silver melted in a hand-held crucible and poured it directly into the mold's opening. Within a few moments the buckle mold was untied, and the casting was released and quenched in sulphuric acid pickle. But here's the thing, when Roger was melting silver into the crucible, he was also dropping copper pennies in. I had always wondered why his silver was more blue than white. His pieces looked more like stainless steel or nickel silver, sometimes called, German silver.

What became of all this observation and local education, led me to confusing conclusions. Was I to teach my students the fabrication of tiny, small shapes in silver that would never add up to much income as a working jobber? Was I to teach them cabochon making that might get them arrested for making false cabs and swindling stone from the trader that supplied them. Or was I to teach my students how to melt silver and copper and whatever else was at hand to cast beautiful monstrosities of Frankenstein silver? I was grateful for all the lessons these casual instructors afforded me. Without them, I'd have had no idea of the short cuts, desperate or not, these individuals would resort to in the name of profit. None of them went on to any success in the art form, but they had instructed me on everything you could do wrong. Without them, how would I have known.

Near the end of the summer of 1975, I was driving to New York City to see friends. One last jaunt before school started. While filling up at the Cowboy Stopover (commonly called Stoop Over), Flora, the manager, asked me if I had a sec.

I said, "Sure."

Inside the owner, her son, showed me a large sack of Zuni heishi, necklaces, and earrings. Knowing I was journeying to New York, he asked if I'd be willing to try to find a market for them in the big city.

Well ,why not. So I said I would. Taking the inventory with me, I went on my merry way. Having had a pleasant stay with my dear friends, Debbie and Burt, I made an appointment with Saks 5th Ave. to speak to the jewelry buyer. A couple of days later, arriving on time I sat in an office in downtown New York City and spread the array of items on the counter. None of it was high-end, yet it was still appealing in the present market. But it was the buyer's response that took me for a loop.

"This is all fine and dandy stuff, but we at Sack's go right into the teepees of Navajo royalty and buy our jewelry straight from the king and queen," he said.

In a stolen moment of shock, I became aware of what I was dealing with—these buyers were hilariously naive and full of themselves. They didn't even know that Navajos now lived in trailers. Ha.

The U-Joint

Following the episode of the Great Zuni Sheep theft, the old light blue 1963 Ford pickup, that allegedly may have played a part, predictably started having a vibrating shimmy and was difficult to maneuver on the road. After what this old girl had been through though, who could blame her.

Hearing her obvious distress, I drove her down to the Cowboy Stoop Over, where a kindly young Mormon mechanic took a patient survey of her innards and gave me his prognosis. "U-joint's shot." He pointed out the part that connected the drive shaft to the rear axle and, moving it up and down, showed me the problem.

"How much?" I asked.

After he quoted me a perfectly reasonable price and me realizing that that still was a whole lot of money to a young teacher, I asked him, "How much for the part?"

To which he responded, "Nineteen dollars and fifty cents."

I said," I'll take it."

Now I, through the necessity of poverty, tended to learn on the hoof, so to speak. I would figure it out, do the repair, and on completion, drive off into the sunset. That is what I thought.

Only it wasn't a sunset, actually, as I recall, it was a cloudy day. Unlike the public schools we had a different schedule at our school, and for some reason that week there was a free day available to do the repair. I had the part, had my tools ready, and was prepared for surgery. The first part of the operation was the removal of the O-rings which held the U-joint in place. This was awkward, keeping in mind, I was situated on my back under the truck. Eventually the last ring was removed, and the joint was free at last. It, of course, was stuck holding the drive shaft to the axle still, so with the assistance of a large ball peen hammer, I hit it free from its encumberment.

All of a sudden there was a movement. Did you know that if you release the U-joint from the drive shaft, the car will inevitably be in motion if you live on a hill? I didn't. I had not even blocked the tires. Of course, this was most unfortunate.

The truck now moving faster ran over my lower leg. That really hurt. The worst part was it was travelling back toward the public elementary school still in attendance at the bottom of the hill. Screaming in pain and shock, I somehow stood on my damaged leg and struggled to chase my marauding patient. I was not going to make it.

As I torturously ambled towards the escaping truck I spied children's faces at the windows of the school as the truck zeroed in on their specific location. There was no hope, I was surely going to Hell.

Something happened, the patient was slowing a little. Miraculously, I grabbed the driver's cab door, and with the superhuman strength of a Hercules himself, I swung myself into the truck's cab. Hitting the brakes, the truck came to a jolting halt.

Well, it seems hell would have to wait for another day. A steel barbed wire fence post was hit dead center by the rear of the truck, and this sole obstruction gained me my miracle.

I staggered out of the truck, proceeded to block the tires, and said a prayer of gratitude to any gods who might be listening. The kids at the classroom windows appeared disappointed. The afternoon's entertainment had ended. On the other hand, I'm sure they had no idea that "The End of Days" had been so near for some of them.

Somehow, I completed the repairs right there on that spot on the hill. I now knew how to change a U-joint and prayed I'd never see one again. My leg took weeks to finally heal from the bruising. How had I not broken it? All I know for sure is, if you ever have a nice young Mormon mechanic give you a good price on a particularly difficult repair that requires some smarts, just ask him one thing, "Cash or check?"

Zuni Café Debacle

Much of the Zuni jewelry trade went through Palestinians in the 1970s. They owned and controlled the major trading post concern in the village, and like it or not, they probably organized the fetish carvers and jewelry inlayers into a credible and viable group. The early 1970s were the beginning of the heyday for these Native artists, and the Palestinian traders made sure they got a piece of every dollar acquired in sales.

A friend of mine familiar with the Zuni, informed me of a delightful new cafe in the Pueblo and asked if I would be interested in trying it out along with a few other teachers. "Sure," said I, since there just weren't any cafes or restaurants closer than 50 to 70 miles in any direction, so anything with a tin roof and a sign advertising food was fair game, and we were quite willing.

Zuni is 30 miles from the Ramah Navajo, so even this still was a trek. Later we arrived on the main road into the village, slowed down to the always constant 25 mph, and in a little while discovered the cafe. It was adjacent to the Palestinian's trading post.

Entering the establishment it appeared like any other Zuni Pueblo residence, plastered stone and adobe walls, vegas supporting the ceiling, and flagstone floors. There was, of course, an adobe fireplace in the corner, where a substantial fire was sharing its warmth with the customers. The dining room was pleasant, welcoming, and expressing an aroma of red chili too delicious to describe. We did not regret our long journey.

Upon sitting, addressing the limited menu, and relaying our selection, we settled into a relaxed state of anticipation.

While resting comfortably, an Arab looking fellow stepped in and surveyed the restaurant's attendees. He saw our table, recognized our friend, and proceeded within to say hello. After introductions he settled down and to joined us.

This man was ingratiating and regaled us with village gossip and stories, and he hinted at possible Zuni dance dates as well. Unless you knew someone from the Pueblo, it was impossible to discover when rain and other dances would be held. This kind fellow was one of the Palestinian traders and full of fascinating information about the Zunis. He was convivial and charming, and we felt privileged to make his acquaintance.

Then came a shout from outside, and our new friend battered out some Arabic in response. A young man waving a gun ran into the restaurant, also of Palestinian descent, and crashed into our table in the café. Then he charged our newfound friend.

The gun was a monster of an old Army 45, and this was no joke. He had come to kill this guy. There was screaming in Arabic back and forth. After a while, there were also tears and vicious anger, insinuating inevitable murder. We knew someone, if not a few of us, was going to die. It was a certainty.

Then there was silence, then hugs and kisses followed, and then small mutterings of what must have been apologies from both. In time our new friend invited the young Palestinian to join us, and he wholeheartedly accepted. The young man then placed the 45 on the table next to his plate and joined us in the feast. Our meal was "Multi Bene." Let's be honest you can't get a floor show like that anywhere.

In retrospect, may I suggest that anytime you find a restaurant, no matter how great the food, that allows firearms on the table, you might seriously consider a change of venue. It's just a suggestion, but I sincerely believe you might live longer.

Christmas Festival at the Old School

Christmas of 1975 was quite an event at the old schoolhouse, which was the temporary location in Ramah as our new school was being built on the reservation. That fall I came up with a harebrained idea of a school Christmas program. The only trouble was everyone loved the idea.

The art class built a giant Christmas pinata that would be filled with hard candy donated by merchants in Gallup. There would be cakewalks, which were always popular. Basketball hoop shoot contest, and other games for all, but the creme de la creme was the "ho, ho, ho" contest amongst the older Navajo men, including school board members—my idea of course.

To obtain the ten Santa suits, I drove to Disco Display in Albuquerque to rent them. Disco informed me the suits must be returned by 8am the day after the event. Not thinking about it and grateful to have procured ten Santa suits, I said fine.

The festival went off without a hitch. Fun was had by all. It was a total success. I even realized, just in time, that 100 pounds of hard candy falling from the pinata might cripple or crush a child, so I swooped in and saved everyone from the unexpected catastrophe. The ho, ho, ho contest on the stage was wonderfully endearing. These old men cheered on by the children was the most special of moments.

Later my roommate, Ron, and I were celebrating the evening's success with my special spiked eggnog. Then it dawned on me that the Santa suits needed to be returned to Albuquerque by eight the next morning. Now

I knew a woman who worked at the Louisiana Restaurant on Central Avenue, and she invited me for a drink anytime I was in town. With that in mind I decided to drive the two hours to Albuquerque and get to the restaurant before closing time.

I arrived at the restaurant and walked into the bar five minutes before two in the morning just as my friend and another woman were closing up. I received a cold shoulder and realized I was an inconvenience. They were not rude to me but asked what I was doing in the city. I described the Christmas fair at the school in detail, while they worked and explained I was there to return the Santa outfits to Disco Display by eight.

Suddenly they abruptly stopped and stared at me and said, "Are you telling us you have a trunk full of Santa suits?"

"Yes," I said.

They looked at each other and then at me and almost simultaneously said, "Would you like to go to some Christmas parties tonight?"

To which I emphatically responded, "But of course."

Within minutes of locking up the bar, we were dressed in our individual Santa suits and prepared for an evening of chimney crashing. We attended so many parties that I cannot possibly remember any of them. At each one though, the trio of Santas were an instant hit—a trifecta of celebration. We spread joy everywhere we went. It was an ecstasy of surprise and magic. We were the spirit of the season.

Eventually one of us noticed the time and realized that dawn was nearing. One of the girls suggested breakfast at the airport, which had a restaurant that was open 24 hours. We arrived as the light of the horizon was just beginning to blink and went inside. We were so hungry we forgot we were still dressed as Santas, oh well. Those customers who were still awake and aware, stared as we marched in, chose a corner booth, and proceeded to order breakfast from an amused waitress.

After ordering and regaling the evening's memorable episodes, we were finally calming down until he showed up. A tall Albuquerque Police Department officer marched into the restaurant, searched the premises, and then made a beeline directly to our booth. There was no smile, no crack of a joke, just the look. He said to us in a dead steady voice, "Is that your sleigh double-parked out front?"

After the shock of his inquiry, what could we say, "Well, yes, officer and we're extremely sorry."

With an unanticipated look of funny, blissful kindness, he responded. "Well, I'll overlook it this time, being the season and all, but next time park it on the roof where it belongs." After reassurances from us all he wished us, "Merry Christmas." And marched back out into the dawn.

Later I dropped the girls at their respective apartments after breakfast and made it to Disco Display in enough time for a whole half an hour's night's sleep before they opened. Still, it was a merry, merry Christmas, and who could ask for anything more.

UFO on McGaffey Road

Sometime in the late 1960s, there was a major aerial crash on the upper McGaffey Road north of Ramah, New Mexico. Now the locals can tell you that the US government regularly launched a variety of undisclosed, experimental aircraft within that area.

Anyway, the crash on McGaffey Road was very close to the road itself, and soon a few locals arrived to investigate. They had heard an extraordinary boom so close to home and went out to find out what was going on.

Later, their observations concluded the following—the object was somehow metallic and shaped like a large peach pit. The size was equivalent to a couple of car sedans side by side. One rancher got close enough to observe some figurative symbols that appeared on the upper body of the object. The rancher had a pencil and paper in his truck cab, retrieved them, and reproduced the symbols and shapes, as best he could.

All those gathered there were speechless as to what the object was, and where it came from. It was unmistakably obvious that it was alien, a UFO.

Then a helicopter appeared from nowhere. A loudspeaker demanded all spectators leave the area immediately and go home. Twenty minutes later a squad car and a huge army flatbed truck showed up and proceeded, with the help of a crane, to load the object onto the trailer bed and exited McGaffey like magic. An army officer from the government remained behind and talked the remaining locals into forgetting everything they had just witnessed.

Even so, years later, rumor has it that the rancher, who had copied the hieroglyphics, never revealed the drawings to that army officer. Most likely they are probably still safely hidden away and now long forgotten.

GREAT ZUNI SHEEP THEFT

For my birthday in the spring of 1975, I decided I would grill a sheep on the spit outside and invite my new-found friends from the community. Having no experience in this realm, I needed to find out how to procure a sheep, and how much it would cost. The logical solution presented itself when I asked my Navajo students about my birthday predicament. Soon two of my high school seniors readily volunteered to help me, Bradley and Lancaster. Lancaster assured me his uncle had an ewe (castrated male sheep) that would fit the bill. The price was $25.00. Two days before the event, we set off in my old light blue 1963 Ford pickup to get us a sheep.

Now Lancaster seemed vague in his exact directions to his uncle's sheep camp, but he appeared certain the camp was somewhere to the west. We proceeded down old rancher roads, constantly opening and closing barbed-wired gates behind us. Finally after an eternity, we found his uncle's flock. For some reason his uncle was not to be found or seen anywhere. Lancaster told me it was okay; he'd give the money to his uncle later.

Now the flock was perched up on the hillside, and it was quite a huff just to get to them. When we were finally close enough, Bradley and Lancaster pointed out the ewe we were to take. They led me to him, and when I asked for help carrying him, they both refused to help. Telling me if it's your sheep by tradition, you are required to carry it. That ewe was not small. Somehow I carried him down from the hill and secured him in the bed of the truck. Then we were off. For some reason the boys were in a hurry to get back home to dinner, so I pushed the pickup faster than I should have on those last miles home. The washboard condition of those rocky tracks called roads were terrible, but eventually we got back in one piece. I dropped the boys off and continued in the dark to my old Mormon rental. When I parked and looked in the truck bed, I was horrified. The ewe had died of a heart attack from the rough trip back. This meant I had to tie his back legs, and with a rope haul him up into the tree outside my house, and gut and skin him that very night. There was no other alternative. With the headlights of my truck, I was able to illuminate the tree and eventually completed the filthy deed. I was exhausted. This was too much and more than I ever bargained for.

Everything went well for the celebration, and everyone thoroughly enjoyed the lamb meat. I was very happy. I had fulfilled my dream of roasting a lamb, and my birthday was a huge success.

A week later I was collecting mail at the Ramah Post Office. I saw a flyer newly pinned on the FBI's most wanted poster board, informing the community there had been a sheep theft on the Zuni Reservation. Anyone with any information, please call this number. I never did call that number, and I never bought a sheep again from a student's uncle. First time you fool me, still that sheep was awfully tasty.

LADIES IN WAITING

Dating, as a teacher on the reservation, was nearly non-existent. Our community was too small, isolated, and focused into the day-to-day activities of establishing a new school system. The fact that these young educators were probably building their resumes with this scholastic experience and weren't planning to stick around long anyway, was probably the major factor. For them there really was no future in any intimate relationships.

I had a Hispanic girlfriend in Las Vegas, New Mexico. Her name was Maria, and she was an emergency room nurse. The drive to see her was four hours though one way—quite a long trek. I had met her when I was in graduate school; and somehow later we had reinvented our relationship now that I was teaching with the Ramah Navajo. Still, the drive was so long that it was infrequent at best.

While teaching ceramics for the University of New Mexico extension school in Ramah, I was once strategically cornered by two short young Navajo women, who had unfortunately taken a hankering toward me. This was a problem. The fact that the two were lacking any pulchritude only compounded my predicament. God forgive me, they scared the hell out of me. I was a total adherent of adoration of St. Sophia Loren, and this had stunted my awareness of inner beauty.

Now these two girls were a determined pair and like true team mud wrestlers, they knew all the moves. Extricating myself from their attentions, was a contest every time they confronted me. "Hi, Show, you got a girlfriend? You like girls? What you doing after class? Want to go to Tinaja?" It never stopped.

Fortunately there were other students to attend to, and the girls would slowly fade into the background. They were always there, staring though. Somehow the semester was eventually over, and I had survived their insistent insinuations and bodily remonstrations. The girls had been single-minded from the start and determined, but I had somehow survived.

Months later during the school year, while visiting Tinaja Bar with some other teachers, I stepped outside to escape the cigarette smoke. The air was crisp and welcoming—just perfect. Suddenly a car pulls up and out tumbled these two Navajo women, their eyes zeroed in on me, and I was a deer in their headlights. "Hi, Show, waiting for us? Funny meeting you here, let's party. Don't be shy." They must have seen the infinite terror in my eyes and knew they had me, I wouldn't escape this time. This wasn't class. I was a goner.

All of a sudden the bar door banged open, and one of the teachers came out and asked what was keeping me. Angels are everywhere. I begged to be excused from my two captors and escaped back into the bar smoke and joined my friends. That was close.

A year later, I heard a Ramah Navajo police officer, name Jamaica, was caught with his pants down, literally, in the back seat of his squad car by another officer, patrolling the Ramah village. With him was one of the mud wrestling girls, and he would never live it down. It became an incident of legendary proportions. The resulting laughter of the community echoed down through the canyons for years. I pray that he recovered someday.

Casseroles

Teachers were poor, economically speaking in the 1970s. My salary in the new school year of 1974 was $7,200.00, and I was the highest paid teacher because I had a master's degree and three years of teaching experience on my employment file. This salary only covered the school year, so with no recourse, I worked every summer, teaching summer school.

New teachers always arrived in September for the new school year. Many were individuals who would contribute to this unique experiment with their own varied experiences. Some were newly minted educators, while others had solid backgrounds and were exploring further dimensions in cultural awareness.

To welcome them into our little fold, we, of course, always had a potluck party for them. At this time in the economy of the 1970s, the potluck celebratory solution was always the "casserole." It was the bedrock of scholastic acceptance. If you were not familiar with it, then why the hell were you on an Indian Reservation claiming to be a teacher? The casserole was our bond of solidarity, our unification, our declaration of economic educational survival. No one in their right mind, even once, ever asked, "Is there something else to eat?"

The answer would have been a swift and emphatic, "No, asshole."

Now, casseroles could vary in ingredients, so long as they had canned tuna, cream of chicken soup, noodles, and if all reserves were not eliminated—potato chips. They were lovingly prepared and baked by teachers, overworked and hurried to accomplish the task by the seven o'clock celebration's scheduled deadline. No one ever missed a potluck, ever.

For all the teachers of the 1970s on reservations throughout New Mexico, "Casseroles, we salute you. You got us through hard times, and yet supplied many fond memories for us to take with us. Thank you."

Kaftan and Combat Boots

There was a ceramics kiln in the old schoolhouse art department. It was so old the instructions stamped on the side were in Sanskrit. Still, miraculously, it worked and functioned beyond my greatest expectations. The kiln was used for various classes who worked in clay, including two University of New Mexico extension classes I ran after school.

If any of you remember the old kilns, they operated with the gradual cone system. Essentially what happened is, when a kiln gets hot enough, the standing cones start bending over when the correct temperature is reached. This means the clay has been fired, and the kiln can be shut down.

Now here was the problem for me—I could only run the kiln at night after classes. While firing ceramics with glazes, many different gases are released. This kiln was in the classroom, so firing at night was the only safe time to do that.

My house was a quarter mile from the schoolhouse. This meant at approximately three in the morning I would have to hike through the village of Ramah, shut off the kiln, and open a classroom window to clear the air before classes the next day. This was not a cherished requirement of my position as basically the whole community's art teacher.

Setting an alarm for three, I would drag myself out of bed, dress in my old green and pink kaftan from my trip to Spain in 1971, pull on my Air Force combat boots, which were my only shoes, and leave, marching in the dark though the village in starlight.

I never thought much of this, but the neighborhood dogs certainly did. As soon as they started howling, lights went on, and people peeked out windows. One man even stood in a doorway with a rifle in hand, preparing for an attack. Even so, none of this phased me. I was half asleep, and I just didn't care. Only later did I realize, the kaftan and combat boots were asking a lot of a small Mormon village in the middle of nowhere.

In time, word went out it was just that crazy art teacher, going to shut down his kiln. It also didn't hurt that a couple of the local Mormon women were attendees of my extension classes.

I kept that kaftan for many, many years afterward.

Mexico or Bust

Jessy O'Leary was a math teacher at our school long before I arrived in the summer of 1974. He was part of the original cadre of teachers, who filled the rosters for the original Ramah Navajo School. Jessy loved, outside of teaching, Cheetos, Pepsi, and motorcycles. I don't know the chronological order, but these were the dominant three I remember.

At the beginning of Christmas break in1974, Jesse dropped by the house one morning and inquired if I would be interested in a trip to San Carlos, Mexico. I did not know where San Carlos was, but I did know where Mexico was, and I had never been. I spent a long enduring fifteen seconds, deciding and promptly replied, "Why yes, of course, how do we get there?"

Jesse pointed to his BMW motorcycle and that was all that needed to be said. Never in my life had I travelled long distance on a motorcycle, so this was certainly to be my first.

One must imagine our Mutt and Jeff's appearance on this journey to old Mexico. I was six foot three inches, Jesse not so much. Jesse had a front windshield to protect him on the motorcycle, I was too tall. The only advantage I had, was the fact we were having some amazing weather, free of inclement overtures. It was warm and beautiful that December.

Keep in mind now, there is only so much you can carry on a cycle, though Jessy did have solid side saddle carriers. In one of these we stowed our few clothes and in the other went the tent and a few camping supplies.

The drive south from Witch Well, Arizona, took us through St. John's, Show Low, and on to Globe. In Globe we stopped at an old mining bar

Jesse knew of and had a pickled egg and a draft beer. On a motorcycle it is wise every couple of hours to stop and stretch if you know what's good for you.

Continuing, we cruised through the Salt River Canyon. With the winter sun arcing, the Canyon shadows were strikingly dynamic. Time was catching up to us though, and Jesse wanted to get to Nogales on the Mexican border by sunset. So, we passed Tucson with not so much as a howdy do.

The sun went down as we arrived in Nogales, but fortunately, Jesse had spent time here before and wasn't the least frazzled. We found a Denny's Restaurant, sort of, next to the border and consumed a decent evening supper. Following this, we found an unofficial campsite and constructed the four-cornered vinyl tent with bowed plastic arches. It was small, for 6 foot 3, but I adjusted with my head and feet pressing the tent out at each end.

The next day, we got Mexican car insurance for the bike, then filled up, and took off.

Crossing the border easily, it was apparent to me that Mexico of the early seventies was struggling, and border towns appeared to be struggling the worst. Still, all in all, it was quite apparent, Mexico was suffering. Fifteen miles south of the border was the main checkpoint at which we stopped to fill out our visas and vehicle permit. When this was completed, Jesse appeared more relaxed. Then at a stop he pulls off a handlebar and pulls out a long plastic bag. "What's that, Jessy?" I say naively.

"Mota," says he. "Really great weed. We can't take it back across the border though, so if we don't smoke at all, we'll have to bury it somewhere and come back for it on a later trip."

Onward south we flew through sunny, beautiful Mexico. Towns like Santa Ana and Hermosillo flew by. In a while just north of the city of Guaymas was the turnoff for San Carlos. Jesse had told me we were camping on the beach where the movies *Catch 22* and *Mash* were filmed, and some of the buildings and props were still standing. As we arrived at

We crossed the border in time and then decided to make a straight shot back to Ramah in New Mexico. This would be rugged, but money was running out. We just needed to get home.

Everything was fine until we got to Show Low. A Blizzard was starting to settle in and as anyone knows motorcycles and snow don't mix. We had no alternative in this situation, we had to continue. The wind and blowing snow weren't sticking to the road yet, so there were no stops. At St. John's though, we did stop out of necessity. A small convenience store was opened, and we used the facilities and with the very last few cents in my pocket I bought a half a pint of Old Crow. Jesse had a hit, and I killed the rest. I believe this might have saved us, and we continued. At Witch Well we turned east on Route 53. The temperature was dropping like a lead weight. Snow was starting to stick. When we got to Zuni, I told Jesse we had to stop. I couldn't feel my legs. We got to the main intersection of the Pueblo and found a pullover and stopped. I fell off the bike; I couldn't move my legs.

Jesse was worried, possibly frantic. His bike shield had sheltered him but not me. The elements had seeped into every crack and cranny of my clothing. Finally, aware the snow was getting more serious, we started banging and hitting my legs back to life. In ten minutes, I could drag my leg over the bike again, and we took off, though carefully. The snow was now really sticking. It was thirty miles to Ramah. We just made it in the heart of a blizzard, but we made it.

I love Mexico. My wife and I have traveled there by car, by train, by plane, and we have even cruised the mainland coast. But never again have I traveled there by motorcycle. If you consider yourself a real-world traveler, an adventurer of sorts or daredevil in disguise, may I suggest a trip on the back of a motorcycle in the middle of winter, plowing through sixty-mile per hour winds and blowing snow without barely stopping for twelve hours. You certainly won't forget it neither will your *cajónes*.

the site of the filming, the first thing I noticed was the runway of *Catch 22*. The track was still apparent, though time and sun were doing their designated duty.

The beach was beautiful, the western horizon over the sea of Cortez, breathtaking. Who could ask for anything more? I certainly couldn't. Having picked up beer and a few essentials at a Mexican quick stop, we parked, set up camp, and frolicked in the waves. The desert mountains to our east behind us included Goats Tits, the classic mountain, in front of the Mash Unit in the film's introduction. With the sun going down, we shared a doobie, had some dinner and beer, and passed out in inebriated bliss.

The next day was spent exploring Guaymas. This city is actually a shrimp center for the western mainland coast. But there is something else Guaymas is renowned for, sardines. There are sardines in oil, sardines in mustard, sardines in tomato. Hell, I bet if you looked long enough, you could find sardines in peanut butter. We bought plenty for the beach, weren't we poor starving teachers after all?

I collected shells, which a year later I carved as bear figures. I also almost drowned in an undertow that nearly took me. Later we met some Canadian hippies down the way, camping out of an old VW bus. I was thoroughly charmed and inspired by all I could see here and touch. I loved Mexico; I have ever since. I knew for certain this was a place of escape I would turn to many times in my future.

In a few days Jesse and I eventually counted our pesos and knew it was time to hit the road back home. We'd done it—had a few days of beach, sun, and fun, and exploring. We'd drunk Tequila and cervezas and smoked illegal weed. Hell, we'd had every type of sardine dish ever invented. What more was there?

The next morning, we set off back for the border. We had to cross before noon when the bike's insurance expired. As we returned, I caught glimpses of things I had missed coming down, including a huge cliffside painting of Our Lady of Guadalupe. The weather was still beautiful.

Mama Cat

If Mama cat had a breed it most likely was the color Gray. She had found a hole in the foundation of the old house Ron and I rented and was there when we moved in. She was obviously already well established in these permanent confines. There was no moving her and that was okay because Mama cat, it turned out, was a most amiable companion.

After the first couple of weeks we declared her name Mama Cat, because she was obviously pregnant. A fact that became more frequent in our enduring relationship with her.

Fortunately, she preferred to keep her little ones under the house, and they provided no inconvenience to our busy lifestyle. In fact, we'd seldom see the kittens unless Mama was moving them around.

In winter we brought Mama inside. She appreciated this and in return paid her rent as one of the most resourceful mousers God ever created.

For some reason Mama took a hankering to me and would bring me gifts of affection. In the early morning when I arose and went to the throne to perform my physical obligations, I would most frequently feel something wet and disgusting dropped on my bare feet. Looking down, there would be Mama Cat staring adoringly at me, and her personal tribute would be lying lifeless on my feet. Of course, I petted her and while praising her prowess and hunting skills, would proceed to flush the unfortunate victim to obscurity.

Now we never witnessed any of Mama Cat's boyfriends. We thought she got pregnant through divine intervention. But later that first winter when the temps dropped into the minus 20s and minus 30s, and Mama Cat was warm and toasty inside, I came upon, through an unpleasant encounter, what I could only conclude was her illusive amour.

In those freezing temperatures in Ramah, one needed to prepare their vehicle against the cold as best you could. Using an electric dipstick and an old electric blanket, covering the engine of my old truck was the best I could do. Even so, there was an unimaginable complication. During the night, the largest, meanest, most furious gray Tom I had ever seen moved into the engine block area and nestled down to sleep on the warm electric blanket. When morning came I would prepare to start the truck engine. Lifting the hood I was shocked to be confronted by this intruding vagrant and his refusal to move. I retrieved a piece of log from the woodpile, and the two of us engaged in a battle to end all battles.

Eventually my gray, furry adversary would relent and leave, and I could start the engine to warm it up. Problem was this went on all winter long. It was another "Groundhog's Day." Spring did eventually come, and an Armistice was finally declared between the great gray Tom and me. Peace returned to the house.

Well, at least the great mystery of Mama's romantic partner was finally revealed. No wonder there were only gray kitties.

OLD GAS HEATER

On the reservation central heating was a wood stove. Wood was in abundance at 7,000 to 8,000 feet altitude, but one still had to go collect, saw, chop and split it. This was an incredibly time-consuming reality in winter.

In our old rental house, there was a wood stove from the early 1950s. This stove was considered a modern marvel that worked abundantly well. Still, it ate wood like the monster it was. It only spoke two words, "Feed me, feed me." In insatiable hunger.

Yet, in the corner of the dining room stood an old gas heater. We had a gas stove and hot water heater but had been informed the small standing heater in the dining room didn't work and hadn't in ages. No one, past renters, or the landlord could ever remember it working.

After a particularly brutal winter of down to -30° below zero, I, in particular, was weary of feeding that beast of a wood stove. One day in frustration, I crawled down to the bottom of that dining room gas heater and found a pilot light control and tried adjusting it. I had the main gas line turned on as well. Bending closer I smelled no gas, oh well, so I left it on and drove to classes at school.

After a particularly busy day, I came home exhausted. As soon as I open the back door of the house, I was aware of just the least lingering odor of residual propane gas. Feeling optimistic, I found some kitchen matches, bent down close to the pilot adjuster, and struck a match. "Booom!" the heater lifted off the floor two feet then slammed down incredibly hard on the floor. Flames burst out of the stove, carbon and smoke blew everywhere. When the air finally cleared, the heater was sitting still producing the most coveted of all winter commodities, heat. The stove was working perfectly. All that time the poor thing was congested with dust and thick old carbon throughout its gas ports. Now she was running perfect as she was meant to.

It did take a couple of months for my eyebrows, sideburns, and hairline to grow back in, but it was all worth it. I was warm, warm, warm.

Cowboy Saturday Night

The night before I was to board the train at Raton for Las Vegas, it was Cowboy Saturday night, payday. I had been working at the ranch in Folsom, New Mexico. After working fifteen-hour shifts, seven days a week for three weeks, it was time to say adios. The school term for graduate school was about to begin on Monday.

My limited time working on the ranch had come to an end, and I would regret leaving this life though I do admit catching up with some Z's wouldn't kill me. My time on the ranch had opened my eyes to a real cowboy's life, not the TV one. There was so much more variety of work than I could ever imagine on a ranch, but since I left home early as a kid, lied to learn any job I ever got, I was well prepared for the jack-of-all-trades category that truly encompasses modern cowboy-hood.

Payday on the ranch was actually half a day off a month. That's right, you got paid at noon, and you were expected back to work the next morning. Do you think the livestock was going to feed itself?

So, Saturday afternoon the ranch foreman, Sunny, the rancher's daughter, and I took off for Clayton. This was a sixty-mile ride on old Folsom Highway 325 to Des Moines, where the road changes to Route 64/87. Then it runs straight through to Clayton. All of this is within the northeast corner of the state of New Mexico, which is composed of beautiful high plains ranch land. Sometimes it feels almost prehistoric with dormant volcanoes everywhere on the horizon. We caught sight of a lumbering black bear not far from the road at one point. We wondered, who dropped him off? Anyway, we took our time and enjoyed the drive.

This was the first time for the foreman and Sunny to be away from the ranch in thirty days.

Clayton was a true historic tale of cattle ranching success. The Good Night Loving Trail ran right through this area for bringing herds of cattle up from Texas, starting in the late 1860s. Later cattlemen and sheep herders would establish permanent livestock ranches aided by a new railroad link. The town of Clayton might be near a population of 3,000 at the present time. It is also the county seat of Union County which covers the entire northeast corner of New Mexico. It also meets the borders of Colorado, Oklahoma and Texas, the triple whammy.

We arrived late afternoon, shopped for the ranch, and stopped by the Hotel Ecklund for a draft beer. This establishment was an1892-saloon in its beginnings, but it would evolve into a hotel by 1898. When it was only a saloon, it was the rip-roaring center of cowboy life in Clayton back then. Between the bar, pool table, carrom tables, monte game tables, crap tables and poker, no one had to imagine very far where an old cowpoke's money went. Thank God he had only a day to lose it and get back to the ranch.

While sipping our beers one of us noticed a music promotion poster, which advertised Frank Larrabee and his band. Frank was an Albuquerque boy, but his music was reminiscent of "Dan Hicks and his Hot Licks," from LA. It was a kind of Texas rock swing. It was quite wonderful. The three of us stared at each other, and though we knew this would be a late-night drive back to the ranch, we also knew the opportunity couldn't be missed. We all agreed to stay for the show.

So, we stuck around Clayton's roving metropolis, and at seven thirty we made our way back to the Ecklund and had dinner not far from the stage and bar. The show started at eight. While eating steak I noticed two cowboys at the bar, one at each end, and they would intermittently shout some foul comment to other and then go back to their drinking. Even though it was annoying, I thought nothing of it.

After dinner there were a couple more drinks, and then we settled down to the show. The bar was filled up nicely. All the tables were attended, but no one was near the actual bar, not while those two riled up cowboys were positioned at opposite ends shouting at each other. Inconveniently concentrating on them I noticed one of these characters appeared to be older than the other. He was continually chastising the younger most angrily. Finally, when the younger had had enough, he would storm to the other and just before physical violence evidently would occur, he would back off and then a reverse pattern would happen with the older one.

In the meantime Frank Larrabee beat the band into a frenzy to entertain and to cover the noise of the two loudmouths at the bar. Why didn't the hotel management do something and why was the bartender looking at the newspaper? Was he looking at the want ads? This was all a mystery to me I had yet to solve.

The concert went on, it was stupendous, even with the undertone of violence at the bar ebbing and flowing. Would one of these men finally spring and kill the other? Was this a lifelong grudge that would finally come to its crescendo? Who would die? This cowboy opera played on all night, and Frank just played louder, but flawlessly, eyeing the pair to the left of him in their mortal combat stance.

About eleven o'clock the show was over. The band started breaking down, and the two cowboys had finally settled down—thanks to too much whiskey and beer. As we were preparing to leave, I watched the younger cowboy go over to the older, and I thought, ohh no, not now. Instead, he gently helped the older one to the door, slinging his arm over his shoulder. Then they slipped out and were gone into the night. What the hell happened?

The drive back to the ranch was a star-filled lovely night. The concert had been great; the steak dinner was perfect. Tomorrow, someone would take me to the train in Raton, and I would leave this life.

Something was bothering me though, something about the two rambunctious cowboys, so I thought I'd ask my compadres. "Who were the two annoying cowboy adversaries at the bar, and why did no one intercede?"

"Well," said the foreman thinking about it. "Here it goes. Those two are father and son and own of one of the biggest spreads in Union County. They have a lot of money and influence." The foreman then proceeded to inform me those two gentlemen were so impossibly difficult and irascible that the mother and her daughter-in-law had finally had enough of those two knuckleheads. One night they just got up and left with their suitcases and never returned.

So, the father and son were all they had left to each other and have been stuck in an unholy relationship of wills and regret ever since. Their ranch hands did their jobs, but they kept their distance. The conclusion to the foreman's story appeared to be that one afternoon a month the ranch hands took their break. Then the owner and his son came directly to the Ecklund and drank the rest of the day and night away—at opposite ends of the bar. They screamed and shouted their lonely frustrations at each other. Still, they were stuck with each other, father and son, and at the end of the night like it or not, all they had was each other.

I often think of those two and wonder at their circumstances living the lonely cowboy life. What drove them to this unfortunate situation of involuntary isolation? Was it the hard life of the cattle country? Was it the uncertainty of the round-up at the end of the season, or was it the contention that maybe rustling would reappear as the ranch's always potential nemesis, who knows? All I can imagine though, after one night witnessing them, was I hoped those women who were married to them had at least left the state, God bless them, because it appears they had finally discovered, life is just too damned short to tolerate absolute assholes.

The Great Escape to Albuquerque

Winter for the year 1975 was particularly brutal. It was my first in the village of Ramah. The Zuni Mountains would snag and clutch any storm clouds from any hope of escape. The closeness of 7,000 to 8,000 feet to the upper atmosphere draws and holds winter like a lover it is unwilling to relinquish. At least that's what it felt like in its seemingly never-ending endurance.

The school buses would bring the kids to school by eight each morning, and by ten with more new snow, the buses would return to take the students home again. This situation was a constant revolving door for what seemed like months. Would it ever end?

One Friday, I mentioned to three other teachers that I was going to make a run for it. Snowbound was not an alternative anymore. There had to be an escape from this monotony. The plan was simple, place 600 or 700 pounds of rocks into the bed of my truck, wear all the warm down jackets and vests we had, and steadily gain tracks in the truck to Bandera Crater, and then hopefully beyond to Albuquerque.

We met Saturday morning at seven, loaded heavy sandstone, which was already piled nearby, and exited Ramah in apprehension and high hopes. We had to give it our best shot. Slowly we gained miles towards the crater. At some point we became aware there was no demarcation giving us any semblance of where the road was any more. We were still on it but only with the memory of the landscape to guide us. We finally made it to Bandera Crater, the highest point on the Continental Divide.

There was a white-out blizzard waiting for us. Still we continued and somehow beyond, the sky was brightening up and we were descending the east face of the volcano. Like magic the sun peeked out, and the road was even visible. All of this occurred within no more than 1000 feet of the mountain pass above. When we reached the bottom of the volcano, the sun was in its full glory, and gorgeous blue skies were everywhere. Looking behind us it was pitch black, where the blizzard was still occurring. Only in New Mexico, I would conclude.

Finally we arrived in Grants to almost spring like temperatures, and we stripped off our encumbering down coats and vests. In another hour we landed in Albuquerque, and the temperature was 74°. I dropped the two teachers off at a friend's house, who occupied an apartment in a very nice new complex with a pool. We planned to meet the next afternoon at three and return home.

We remaining two found a room at the Motel 6, which was $6.00/night then. Of course, the TV and the "Magic Fingers" of the bed ran on quarters. You had to buy a half a roll of quarters from the front office to enjoy either of these, oh well.

After exploring the city that evening, we discovered "Red Dog Dan's," a ridiculous complex of buildings offering food, liquor, and dancing—quite outrageous. The exhaustion of the day's ordeal did finally catch up with us though, and any thoughts of staying up till two in the morning was obviously absurd. We returned to our motel room now thoroughly liquored up and dreamt of girls we were too tired to pursue. Still, there was nothing but gratitude for the diversion of the day.

On Sunday we found us a decent breakfast and in recharged spirits, we were now ready to shop. You must comprehend that the limitless opportunities of buying what you want as well as need had become quite alien to us in the isolated environment we were used to. It was a contradiction of our new reality.

Later everyone was ready at three in the afternoon, so we loaded up all our new purchases and took off, rocks and all. We shared experiences of the past evening and laughed at our newfound freedom. We'd had fun. When we arrived in Grants it felt nippy, so we put on vests. The sun was still shining, the sky was blue, and all seemed good on God's green earth.

Then we got to the east base of Bandera Crater. It was sunny where we were driving but at the top of the volcano it was black. How could nothing have changed? How could 1,000 feet away, the weather be the exact opposite of where we were at that moment?

Did you know the wettest place on the planet is ninety miles from the driest place? It is ninety miles from southern New Guinea to the northern tip of Australia, so I guess anything it is possible.

We pushed on steadily up the gradual ascending road. Soon the snow started. By the top of the volcano, we felt we had never even left. With down coats back on and jammed into the truck cab together, we soldiered on and slowly achieved the remaining 35 miles to Ramah. The only difference from whence we left was there was more snow.

Everyone got dropped off, and I proceeded back to my own abode. I can't explain the relief of arriving home at last. Somehow we had made it in that old, light blue '63 Ford pickup filled with rocks to Albuquerque. Maybe stubbornness is a virtue.

KTDB

There was a young radio intern from Antioch College named Eric. His assignment was English translation for the KTDB Ramah Navajo AM station. Eric was a young undergrad when I met him. He also had his own radio program and entertained us teachers through the long, lonely months on the reservation.

Now, not everyone appreciated Eric's record selections. Not everyone was totally onboard with Frank Zappa and the Mothers of Invention. Also, these Navajos were not the most loyal David Bowie fans. They were a picky group. At that time Johnny Cash's "A Boy Named Sue" for them was a number one hit. "The Ballad of Ben Gay" was also a regular play whenever Eric wasn't there. Let's face it, Country Western was THE reservations' most favored selections. Whatever happened to the "Zuni Sundowners" anyway?

When Eric's internment, I mean his internship, was finally completed, he had a few grievances that he felt he needed to shed before he made his adios. He had voiced some of these to Ron and me, but we never took him too seriously. After all, Eric was a sweetheart. Anyway, Eric said we should most certainly listen to his program on his last day as a KTDB disc jockey.

Listening to his program that day, there were no public announcements as usual—no DJ commentary, only music the entire day. The music included bluegrass renditions of pro- marijuana ballads. There was Steppenwolf's

"Don't Bogart That Joint, My Friend," Zappa and the boys with "Billy the Mountain and Tree," Janice, Stones, and everyone who was supporting drugs, not war. It felt like a mini-Woodstock on AM. Who could have asked for anything more?

Meanwhile, back at the station, Eric had barricaded himself within the DJ's studio. He had the door locked and jammed a chair under the doorknob, so no one could get to him. The Navajo radio manager glared and pounded uselessly on the studio door to no avail. Nothing would get him out. He had soundproofed himself within that space.

Much later at the end of his program and the day's siege, Eric surrendered to the authorities, the total being the manager and an assistant, and swore on his recognizances that he would never return to the Ramah Navajo radio station again in this lifetime.

The next morning, as Eric was leaving for California and a new college; Ron, Samson Martinez, and I stood in line and watched as Eric pulled out, forever into the sunset. We brave three saluted him in gratitude and heartfelt admiration and wished him a bon voyage. Wait, maybe that was the ending of a "Mash" episode.

Apache Laughing Tears

With World War II ending and victory achieved, many young Native American GIs returned home. These young soldiers had seen much and not just war; many had now traveled the globe. They knew the outside world was a mighty big place, and they now felt a part of it.

For some, going back to farm cornfields in Hopi and Zuni and other pueblos was never going to be enough. Sheep herding was competing with the Navajo code talker's new concept of the world's vastness. All these soldiers had shared in an inexplicable world event of unparalleled dimensions. They now needed more than their old life.

The very last WPA program (Works Program of America) approved by Congress, gifted many native soldiers with arts programs including silversmithing, fine art instructions, and also instruction in printing illustration. These programs filled a type of GI bill for Native Americans.

Charlie Loloma and Alan Houser were just two recipients of these programs and soon attained great fame thanks to its benefits.

For summer school of 1974, there was a planned field trip for the mid-session of school. It was planned that we would bus the kids to the Institute of American Indian Arts in Santa Fe .When there we would tour the school and meet the director and any summer staff still in residence.

Afterwards, we'd stay at the dorms for the night and then return the next morning, which would complete our planned trip. From Ramah, it would be a three-to-four-hour drive in a bouncy, old yellow school bus to Santa Fe. I don't believe school buses were ever designed for long distance travel. Oh well, as long as the kids didn't mind.

We arrived on a glorious July day with the sun shining. The school's campus was large and welcoming. At this time IAIA was a high school. In 1975 Rhode Island School of Design, would include a two-year college accredited program for young Indian artists. The Institute of American Indian Arts was only twelve years old at this point in time. The school would go on to be the wonder it is today through great initiative and hard work. Fritz Shoulder was just one of the previous instructors included in its teaching alumni.

Anyway, I shepherded my students into various studios and classrooms, talked about the different arts and crafts programs, and we eventually discovered ourselves in the sculpture department. A young student was carving stone in the corner of the building, and a middle-aged man was sweeping up the departments floor. As we approached I asked if this man was the janitor to which after hesitating, he said, "Why, yes."

I then asked him who was the head of the sculpture department.

He said, "Alan Houser."

I thanked him and we moved on with our little tour. Later we met the school director, and her last name was also Houser.

After inquiring, she informed us that yes she was the wife of Alan.

That night the kids did well within the dorms, and the next morning after a breakfast at Denny's, we toured Santa Fe and explored museum hill. At the time, only the Wheelwright and the Museum of International Folk Art were on location. Our adventure completed, we exited Santa Fe and made for Albuquerque. Arriving in Albuquerque we proceeded on I-40 to the 12th Street exit and stopped for lunch at the infamous Pedro's

Mexican Buffet (all you can eat). There's a Lowes hardware store there now. Anyway, at the time it was a monster of an operation with tables that had little flag poles with Mexican flags you would raise when you wanted seconds, thirds, fourths and to infinity and beyond. The kids loved it. When you consider mutton and fry bread was much of the family fare in those days, it was pretty good eats for them!

After a long drive we got the kids home safely and I collapsed at home in a pile of bones and flesh in a bed that night grateful all went well.

Years later, Alan Houser would achieve world status as one of the Southwest's foremost artists. No one could compare with his stylistic interpretations of Native American imagery. I had, by now, seen many articles on him and his work in numerous publications. I had also seen many pictures of him. One day in the 1990s while shopping in the old Allwood's hardware, I spied Alan in the stain/paint department. Of course we had both aged, but he was still quite recognizable, an older, noble Apache warrior/artist. Hesitantly, I approached him and said, "Hi Alan," and introduced myself and asked if he remembered that young no nothing art teacher from the Ramah Navajo school, who asked if he was the janitor?

Alan smiled, for an Apache this is quite a rare occasion, and then he said, "I sure do, how are you doing?"

Basketball

Somewhere along in the 1870s, a great feud destroyed the peace between the Navajos and the Zunis. Every few years or so, a band of tribe members would come together and raid the other tribe, and an act of murder would often ensue. No one is even aware anymore of how this feud even originated. The resulting vicious calamity would continue for all of one hundred years. A cavalry stockade was even built to create a dividing line between the two tribes. Still this regrettable situation endured the many years. Fortunately by the time I arrived as a teacher, the feud was just the vague residue of stories in the past.

In the early 1970s, Tony Hillerman would come and visit the Ramah Navajo School. He was still teaching creative writing at the University of New Mexico, but also he was branching out on a self-invented Navajo detective series still in its infancy. *Dance Hall of The Dead* was written, using the geography and much of the historical background of the local Zuni and Navajo. The only sour note Tony came upon in his research was the uncooperative attitude of this small, isolated community of Navajos segregated from the big res. Tony would finally catch on to this and eventually move to Window Rock for his research, where they appreciated him much more.

There weren't many sports in Ramah kids were able to play year-round except for basketball. Let's face it all you needed was a ball and a hoop. So indoors or out, this was the one sure thing sport.

Now, one time, Tony stopped to observe a scrimmage game amongst some of our Navajo students and declared, "They're terrible. What is wrong with the coach, can't he see it? These kids aren't even trying."

A Navajo teacher nearby overheard this and ambled over to explain, "Mr. Hillerman, this is a small reservation; most of these kids are related one way or another. As a result most will not betray their particular brother or cousin with intimidating behavior. That would hurt their feelings. They are just too close to shame."

We did have a fairly successful inter-school basketball team though, the Naabaahii "Warriors" and they were competitive. They traveled all over the county, playing local schools and always with hopes of returning with the glory of victory. Well, at least, we hoped, we were an awfully small school. Still we were, if anything, loyal to our warriors and followed them faithfully to the gates of success or failure.

Now, one major end of a season game was scheduled to be held in our old worn-out gym at our old school in the village of Ramah. This was a big game, the winner might go on to the state championships, and as you can probably guess, the opposing team was none other than Zuni High School.

This was, of course, an old familiar competition. We played regularly with the Zuni; they were after all our neighbors. So what if they had a nice new high school, with a nice new gym, and new equipment that sparkled with the freshness of its sheen. We had the warriors, the greatest Navajo team in Ramah, New Mexico, ha. So place your bets everyone if you dare.

This game was scheduled for seven o'clock in the evening and attendance was guaranteed to fill the indoor gyms bleachers. Of course, it was packed. Every shima, grand shima, fathers, cousins, uncles, aunts, friends and friends of friends were present and accounted for. This was the game of games, the end all competition as we knew it, we could not lose. We could also picture that shiny state trophy someday sitting in our glass awards' case, as soon as we built one, and people from far and wide stopping in our little hamlet to observe the magnificent achievement of our own basketball team. Wouldn't that be swell.

When game night finally arrived, the game commenced in a fury of lightning fast running and passing. Baskets were made on both sides in abundance; the light board scores were rapidly adding up. The teams were moving towards a most vicious struggle in the strain of competition, who would break? Who had the right stuff?

Soon though, it became apparent our players were smaller than the Zunis. Their stamina was not up to this much prolonged struggle. Well, hell, the Zunis even ate better. Eventually, the heartbreak of the situation began setting in, and the warriors were devastatingly defeated. The score was too embarrassing to even repeat after the game. How would we ever live this down?

With the game ended, we all slowly exited forlornly from the gym and made our way to the school parking lot. Old smoking cars and pickup trucks collected their passengers and sadly made their way home on the cold, starry night. It was all over. There was nothing more.

The Zunis hung around gloating in their victory and expanding the importance of this small-time league competition. They were full of themselves. Finally, they prepared to leave. Arriving in the parking lot, it was soon discovered the school bus had a flat tire. Hold on, was that two flat tires?

Maybe it was just my imagination, but I thought I'd heard distant war yelps of warriors long since past as I left the school parking lot. Were these memories, still alive and still beckoning the Zunis to watch one last war dance? Well, at least there weren't any scalps hanging from the school bus windows.

Cheese Please

The economy of the 1970s was a catastrophic disaster. The Vietnam War was ending scattering jobless GIs out over an empty employment landscape as far as you could see. Unions were being busted. Japanese cars were flooding the market. Steel was being imported. In most cases, jobs were just nonexistent period. Life was essentially a struggle everywhere. What to do, what to do.

Then one of the governments think tanks must have come up with this brilliant solution, cheese. Did you know, stored in caverns and excavated caves of Granite and Limestone in Missouri are phenomenal reserves of Velveeta cheese that could feed the entire planet for at least ten thousand years? Well the government did, and in their enlightened awareness of our struggling existence, knew for certain that Velveeta cheese was the answer to all our woes. Cheese would tip the scales of fortune, and we could now burst into a future of endless possibilities.

So Velveeta was shipped to all struggling communities across the nation, including to the chapter house of Mountain View for the Ramah Navajo. Trucks started arriving and cheese was distributed to all and any of the natives. Soon more trucks arrived with more Velveeta and then more trucks. Eventually we were totally unprepared for an epidemic of mass constipation that ensued in frightful aspect that no one had considered. Eventually so much cheese arrived we considered using it for currency. I remember attending the weekly meeting of the literary society (poker game), and an agreement on a dollar value was placed on each box of cheese. That night the game's grand winner, Marshall, had to go home and bring back a wheelbarrow to haul his winnings home.

The economic crisis wasn't over though, not by a long shot. Next came generic groceries. What the heck is that, Andy, you might be thinking, well, I'll tell you. The government think tanks devolved a concept of printing black and white labels for federally franchised lower-priced grocery items and subsidized them. These items appeared on shelves with names like "Corn" for a black and white labeled tin can of corn. The level of illuminating genius that conceived this entire project was breathtaking. Who would of thunk? The whole project was essentially beyond words to describe.

The trading posts, out on the main reservation, were dealing with a lot of these lower-end generic products. Hopefully this would aid to relieve the stressful economic burden that the Navajo Nation was experiencing. Let's face it, things were tough just about everywhere. Still, Navajos were most perplexed by these black and white labeled cans and were now dependent on the trader to translate the contents of each item. They'd only needed pictures before. Keep in mind many of these old Natives, back then, did not speak or read English, so the trader was their teacher, father, letter writer, and translator.

One day, an old boy named, Concho Begay, walked into the trading post near Coyote Canyon. He only made the trip once every month and was always weary of leaving his sheep too long. While he was in the trading post, he spied a short black and white paper roll and asked the trader what it was. The trader ambled over and eyeing the product said, "Why, Concho, that's just toilet paper. It just comes in that cheap paper cover now but is cheaper to boot. Why don't you try some and let me know what you think?"

Concho carried off some with his other groceries and headed back home. Time went by, the trader hadn't thought of the sheepherder in a while, and up walks in Concho one day. After catching up with local events, he'd been out of touch with, Concho suddenly says to the trader, "You know that generic toilet paper?" says Concho.

"Yes," says the trader.

"Well," says Concho, "I think you should call it John Wayne paper."

"Why's that?" says the trader.

"Well, because it doesn't take shit off an Indian." says Concho.

Slaughterhouse-Five

Why would anyone write about a movie as notorious as *Slaughterhouse-Five* in relationship to 1970s New Mexico? How would Kurt Vonnegut's 1969 book produced into a 1972 film about a time traveling WWII soldier, named Billy Pilgrim be relevant? Well let's find out.

March of 1975 was my birthday month. Having survived the last two years of graduate school, work, and then car accident injuries, I was ready for some sort of meaningful celebration. With the teaching contract under my belt, life finally felt a bit safer and secure. So, I planned a sheep barbecue and party. I would find and slaughter a sheep for the spit, make some potato salad, and purchase beer and soda for the festivities—simple and clear.

During my planning, my roommate Ron asked if I had a favorite movie. I asked, "Why?"

He told me that because of his position in the AV Department (audio visual) he could order a movie direct from Hollywood.

Thinking he was joking, I replied, "*Slaughterhouse-Five*," and forgot about it.

The intended date of my birthday party eventually came looming into the near future. Because I had invited a few teachers and neighbors, it was necessary to move forward with plans and purchase an actual sheep. No, I'd never purchased a lamb much less slaughtered one, nor put one on a spit and cooked it slowly for hours, but nothing ventured nothing gained, right?

Two students of mine had heard my query for a sheep. They wanted to assist me, through my great chasm of ignorance, and helped me find the perfect lamb. Two weeks later I would find out, I was a wanted man by the law, due to this sheep's transaction, but that's another story.

Somehow on the night of the celebration, everything had come together. The lamb was on the spit, flaming sizzling fat off as it was turned. Beer and soda were iced down in a tin cowboy bathtub, and Ron had appropriated the film, *Slaughterhouse-Five*. He proceeded to set up the projector with a sheet on the wall in the living room of the house for the film's presentation. We even had a little extra help in the personage of Ara, a friend of my brother's, who was visiting at the time. Everything was organized, prepared, and an unexpected jubilation of festivities was soundly in place. What could go wrong?

At sundown people started showing up. I was at the spit spinning slowly my prized sizzling spring sacrifice. I've been at it since midafternoon. It had never realized a sheep on a spit was such an enduring job, to get an even roast. Inattention to its rotation was not forgiven, the stationary lamb would burn and sear badly due to the high fat content of the flesh. So, in a sense, I would be imprisoned by the spit most of the evening.

Even so, I would go inside for quick observations to see that things were going okay and to bring in platters of grilled lamb. Later I would see Ron, now running the movie, give me a thumbs up with a funny glow on his face, huh?

The guests strolled or drove in, and I would go to greet them as I could. Suddenly though, from the corner of my eye, I observed an action so disturbing I nearly fell into the fire pit. This can't be real. Why? Sam, one of the school board members, and his wife, were climbing up the driveway to the house. I ran to intercept them and said, "Yat ta hay."

They said hello and asked where the grilled sheep was? After a little conversation I gathered them a couple of paper plates and carved some hot fresh servings off the cooking carcass. I then got them a couple of sodas, and I escaped into the house. Then I told Ron I was shocked at their attendance.

Ron smiled and said, "Oh, I invited them."

I said, "Why?"

His response alluded to the fact, "It's a party, man."

To my response, "It's my job, man, what were you thinking? I need this job."

Ron was from California; he simply wouldn't understand.

So now I'm watching this spit, surveying this celebration of my employment's termination, and catching glimpses of the movie while I could. Suddenly, I broke out into a cold sweat, how could I have forgotten. Ron really never prepared me for the decision of the movie selection. I just blurred it out, "*Slaughterhouse-Five.*" How could I have been so stupid? "Valerie Perrine." She was going to strut into the final reel in all her feminine glory and steal the ending, what was wrong with me? I slithered into the living room behind the projector and asked Ron to cancel the last reel and save my job, I knew he'd understand.

Ron had glitter on his face, what the hell, even in 1974 this was weird, also his eyes were acting funny. I asked him if he was, okay?

In all honesty, Ron replied he was just fine especially since he and Ara had just dropped some purple barrels of LSD and were now just peachy.

Okay, did I really need this job? Hell yes. Then I saw Sam and his wife were still in attendance and watching the movie carefully with those solemn Navajo faces. I was going to be dead. There was nothing I could do. Ron would not stop the film; he was tripping and obstinate. What a perfect combination.

Finally, near the end of the last reel Valerie appears as a gift to resolve

Billy's loneliness problem in the twelfth dimension. She appears in the lustrous glory of her whole being, come on, stark naked, and finds an affinity to Billy's time-traveling situation as she takes residence, happily, in the spacious dome on some distant planet in the universe, supplied by these dimensional beings.

Eventually the film ends, the loose film of the last reel is spinning, Ron is passed out, and Ara is staring at a spot on the wall in the open bathroom—just staring. I turn off the projector, turn on the dining room lights, and thank my guests for coming as they exit. It was one-thirty in the morning, the film had taken nearly five hours to show. Sam and his wife had stayed till the bitter end. I bid them goodbye, I figured for the last time since my employment would probably be terminated come Monday. Sam smiled though. That must mean his wife would have me fired, who knows? Happy birthday, Andy, you schmuck.

Ron was asleep, his face covered with glitter, passed out on the floor leaning on our bedroom door. Ara was still staring at that spot on the wall in the bathroom, and I'd had enough. I left them both where they were, turned off the rest of the lights, entered my bedroom, and as I closed the door, I found myself humming, "Happy Birthday to me."

SHALAKO

My first Shalako was early December of 1974. Ideally, a date close to the first of December is most desirable. This is the Zuni Solstice Celebration, ushering in a good harvest, many babies, and a general wish of good luck to all. It was a Chinese New Years of sorts, but much more beautiful in the Native significance—a celebration and feasting of this very special Pueblo on the western edge of the state of New Mexico.

The six Shalako figures travel down from the mountain top to celebrate in the Pueblo. The costumes of these messengers of God are magnificent and eye popping. The graciousness of the Zuni people and the general generosity of them has always humbled me. Maybe it's just Shalako, but this event definitely became my only respected religious holiday. So, I will describe my first Shalako and see if you can appreciate this most significant of Zuni feast days.

When I was first informed of Shalako, my impressions were somewhat vague to the significance of what I would be witnessing, so I played it by ear. The first instruction I received from veteran teachers was to drive with them to Zuni before sundown and witness the Shalakos marching over the grease hill down into the village.

Arriving around four-thirty in the afternoon and joining other teachers with a rush of the Native crowds, we walked to the specified site. Low and behold, at the top of the hill, large, white- birdlike heads followed by tall, white-conical bodies appeared with long, black hair, decorated with crowns of eagle feathers. A horn or a pair of horns was draped with strands and strands of turquoise beads. These were the Shalakos.

There were six Shalakos, and we in the crowd that followed them to each of the newly built houses, celebrating the blessing of the season. These houses were built by the chosen members of that year's Mudhead Society. These individuals were supported by the tribe for the entire year as they worked on six house construction projects for the celebration. These Mudheads would later be in costume, act as clowns, and assistants to the Shalakos throughout the night's celebration.

Having followed the Shalakos to these six newly built houses and marking their locations in our minds, we teachers then returned to our homes and spent the evening resting and eating. We were as excited as children on Christmas Eve.

At eleven-thirty in the evening we hauled into our cars and began the long drive back to the Pueblo. The temperature outside was plummeting, and by the time we parked on the side of Route 53 within the village, it had dropped to nearly zero. You can only imagine the number of sweaters and coats each individual one of us brought in preparation. I'm sure we doubled our body weight in wool alone.

Zuni was perfumed with the scent of pinon wood burning in every fireplace. It was intoxicating. In the cold, smoke clouded up like fog and gave a translucent mystical feel to our sojourn through the Pueblo. To me it was magical.

Arriving at our first house, we had to watch from outside the windows until a group of guests moved out to make room for us to enter and partake of the festivities. The Shalakos were magnificent. They stood eight feet tall, not including eagle feather tips, and have painted yellow and red border decorations at the base of their conical suit and midway also. They possess big black and white eyes and a straight long beak of two parts. Often during the ceremony, the beak goes clack. clack. down to a child who might be falling asleep in the audience. After that, trust me, the kids shaken, sit up, and pay wide-eyed attention from then on.

The Mudheads are the clowns and facilitators for the Shalakos. Their mud-painted bodies are barely covered in a breach cloth, and they dance in moccasins. A knobby-headdress mask covering, which is otherworldly and alien, completes the costume. On the headdress there are four-holed knobs and two-holed knobs for eyes. There is also one for a nose/mouth. They are expressionless, but their antics are most often hysterically comical. Many a Mudhead has raised its rear breechcloth to the frustration of the Shalako and has been chased around the performance floor with that long clacking beak to the enthusiastic laughter and delight of the audience and especially the little children. The joy just touches your heart.

During the festive ceremony if you can make your way to the kitchen through the crowded interior, there might still be some congealed leftover mutton and even some remaining Pueblo bread. This you will eat, knowing you will be braving the cold and the elements again. So, moving on, you will be in search of the next house if your memory can pick its way through the village now that the dark has set in. With the help of crowds meandering from house to house, you slowly start checking off the six houses.

The interior of these Shalako houses are an esthetic wonder and feast for the eyes. The wealth of all Zuni is displayed on these walls. For this one night the six residences are the palaces of the Pueblo. There are mounted-deer heads with mounds of turquoise beads, draping from the horns There are furs of fox and otter hanging beside concho belts and weavings of dogs, playing poker or pool. There are even weavings of JFK, MLK and RFK. There are even in places of honor—velvet paintings of Elvis. There is simply nothing or nowhere that I can compare this eclectic horde of treasured human accumulation to.

As the night crawled along, so did we. Though the wonders of the experience were indescribable, after a while the timely ordeal was becoming exhausting. Still, we soldiered on and soon dawn was beginning to gray on the horizon. When the sun creeped out of the morning fugue, suddenly, the Shalakos started departing the six houses. They marched west to the river with the crowd following, and as a final farewell performance, the Shalakos lined up. When they were ready, they raced each other into the dawn, and they were gone.

Returning to our cars we teachers drove home exhausted and awed. We felt blessed to have been part of one of the most beautiful and visually satisfying Native celebrations in this great state. It was times like these that beckoned our awareness to the gift of arriving in this unique place that was secreted away in a corner of the United States and called New Mexico.

Lebanon, New Mexico

Villa de Cubero is and was a small Route 66 trading post west of Grants about fifteen miles. This small concern of a few scattered buildings represents how struggling Lebanese families got their start in the early days of New Mexico Territorial existence. Names like Maloof, Budagher, Bellamah, Tabet, Solmon, and Francis were just a taste of the Arabic/Syrian ancestry, who migrated to New Mexico starting in the 1870s. These families would become traders and later shopkeepers mostly in the northern climes of the state. They would contribute much to the future of its prosperity.

One must consider the Lebanese, who these Christian Arabs were, and of their origins. It is not a long journey back in time to the Crusades and considering the convincing conversion technique of the Catholic Church at the time, that being, convert or swallow a sword, there were many Christianized Arabs on the coast of Palestine. These converts became good Catholics. Did they have a choice? As a group they thrived until the crusaders were kicked out and their Muslim brothers returned. Then the real fun began.

The Lebanese, who arrived in New Mexico, were escaping religious repression as a result in Syria. Somehow these survivors had discovered our fair state and flocked to its opening as a territory after the civil war via the new railway. The train permitted these new arrivals to transport trade goods efficiently to this brave new world. The opportunity this transport system offered was unprecedented for the times. And isn't timing everything?

No one was better placed for the commerce in this state as immigrants than the Lebanese. The similarities to their homeland, the trade in sheep and goat products, the hand wrought work of silver and other metals, not to mention the weavers who kept our state warm, all these industries were akin to their native home, now lost. New Mexico became these early settlers' salvation, and they worked well with the local Natives who loved to trade.

In the beginning, Lebanese traders would travel straight into the Pueblos and present their wares and build relations with the Indians few had ever accomplished before. Maybe it was their darker Arab skin, not so different from their own, or maybe it was the fact that five thousand years of sales evolved them into the successful middlemen they'd become to survive the stingy attributes of the desert. Whatever it was, these future citizens survived and that in itself was the miracle.

I have personally been in close association with many of these families, whether through direct friendship or business. I treasure them and the stories of their families' escape from Syria and their first footfalls off the train onto the Land of Enchantment.

In Zuni on the first Saturday of December, Shalako is held. This is the big celebration of winter solstice and preparations take all year to fulfill the holiday. There are six Shalako houses, and one Longhorn house and all the wealth of the Pueblo is adorned within these seven buildings. Turquoise jewelry and beads, fur pelts of fox and otter, pottery, weavings, treasures of all sorts crowd the wall for space. Yet the eye-catchers in every Shalako house are not any of these things—they are the woven tapestries made in Lebanon of cheap materials and fabrics. They are all nearly the same. The images on these tapestries hanging during the most significant of Zuni's holy festivals are the dogs playing poker.

It appears some Lebanese trader had a turn-of-the-century cigar box, a Zuni saw it, and traded the farm for it (figuratively speaking). The trader, as a result, through his contacts back in Lebanon, instructed distant family weavers to create dogs playing poker tapestries.

The original paintings of these images numbered sixteen and were a major hit in 1903 for the Brown and Bigelow Cigar Company. The Lebanese traders made gold from these weavings' images, literally. The Pueblos couldn't get enough of them, so as late as the 1970s, as I attended Shalako regularly, I had to wonder what the significance of the dogs playing poker symbolized to these Indians. After some contemplation my conclusion on the subject was that the Indians thought, with everything we Indians have lost to the white man, we'd rather be playing poker with dogs then play with them.

Chile Relleno

My first encounter with New Mexican food was in September of 1972, and it was incredible. Having spent three years in Baltimore earning a BFA at Maryland Institute College of Art, I had been acquainted with many world foods via the notorious Lexington Market. In addition to this, many Greek and Jewish Delis were also within my sphere of habitation. Of course, seafood was a constant. I could get a baseball size crab cake (all crab) on a saltine cracker with French's mustard for thirty-five cents. Oysters—don't get me started. I had even lived above the Greek fish market one horrendously hot summer at a rent of twenty dollars a month, and yes, that was a major mistake. The point is fresh fish, of course, was everywhere. Baltimore was a seaport. By the way, never rent a loft above a fish store in the broiling summer heat—it is a very, very bad idea.

When I was accepted into graduate school in New Mexico, it's regional food never occurred to me. I had traveled to Europe and dined from many individual national menus. There was nothing I felt I hadn't partaken of, until I came to New Mexico.

My first local New Mexico fare was in Old Town, Las Vegas. The restaurant was named La Cocina. Feeling like a mom-and-pop operation and everything mostly in Spanish on the menu, I braved the listings and settled on the combination plate. The aromas wafting from the kitchen were intoxicating. The smells were nothing I was remotely prepared for. Spicy carne adovada was blended with warm masa bathed in ingredients, the least of which had to be chili and queso(cheese). My anticipation was unusual, I had never felt an anxiousness, a lupine need to devour dinner before. What was wrong with me?

When the meal was finally served, it appeared to be simple fare, an entree, rice, beans, tortilla, and the entire price was a dollar twenty-five. I ate with enthusiasm, the perfume of the kitchen had done its job. Slowly though, I was aware of a fabulous spiciness creeping through my salivary glands. There was a heat, but not of temperature. This was all new to me.

Paying my check, I exited the restaurant and strolled back to my studio in a joyous contentment. My meal had been exceptional, and I had just partaken of one of the most important cultural experiences New Mexico had to offer—the food. Suddenly though, as I approached my studio door, a three-alarm fire bell went off in my consciousness. I quickly unlocked the door and shuffling across the floor, I found my chair and slowly, slowly lowered myself down. Then I sat very, very still and became aware that every pore of my body was perspiring. The fact that I couldn't breathe at all also terrifyingly dawned on me. Was I dying?

In perhaps about ten minutes, I was slowly escaping the anatomical shock to my delicate system. Thank God, I was alive, but now I also was in love. It was beyond question that my food had been the best meal of my life, and I couldn't wait to go back.

Pedro's Mexican restaurant in Gallup was the finest and most popular haunt of the 1970s. Yes, the owner's name was Pedro, and the food was New Mexican. This treasured spot was the reward at the end of the rainbow on payday for teachers. The long-isolated weeks on the reservation were finally interrupted by a rendezvous to Pedro's palace of green and red chile. The restaurant also included a small room to play pool on the only table I was aware of in Gallup. The bar itself produced a unique variation of the Golden Margarita which sang all the way down to our body's ecstasies. In short, Pedro's was the bomb.

We teachers cruised into town, to the bank, grocery shopping, and maybe buying an LP from the only record shop for 160 miles, but we would always complete our sojourn into town at Pedro's. It was our salvation.

By this time, I was well traveled in our New Mexico culinary state map. I had experienced the southern varietal version of our chile at La Posta in Mesilla. Chomping on their paper-thin tortillas, which were more

Mexican style compared to our thick northern ranchero ones, was also a floured extravagance. In different regions the salsas also differed from a northern fresh red to a brown, saucier Mexican blend. Our beautiful state offered variable food across all four directions, but always the core of our native sustenance was loyally New Mexican, red or green.

Pedro's food was indescribably fabulous. One of my favorite dishes was their chile rellenos. The kitchen would take two chiles filled with soft cheese, cut the ends, then overlap, and combine the two as one. They then battered, deep fried, and covered all with a chile recipe stolen from heaven. Truly the finest meal the human body could ever have consumed.

Many tourists journey to our fair New Mexico. They see our museums, observe our Moorish architecture, steal away into hidden alleys throughout Santa Fe and Taos, where artists and traditional craftsman still sculpt, paint, and carve, where weavers dye wool in colors of sunsets, and jewelers form wearable beauty of turquoise and silver. These many tourists probably soon imagined they now know everything there is about this treasured place at the bottom of the continental United States. But the truth is, if you don't know the food, you don't know New Mexico. Okay. Ole.

BEN HUR

Lew Wallace was territorial governor of New Mexico from 1878 to 1881. Before that he briefly served as a Major General in the Mexican army. Before that he survived the Civil War also at the rank of Major General. He eventually would complete his service to the nation as minister to the Ottoman Empire—quite a colorful career, all things considered. But the most notable accomplishment of Lew was that he wrote the incredibly famous novel, *Ben Hur*.

Ben Hur was considered, at its time, to be the most influential work in Christian literature of the 19th century. Nearly all present-day Americans, one time or another, have seen some version of the story on film. The most famous, of course, starred Charlton Heston.

What most Americans aren't aware of is—how and where the story was written. This is one of the greatest untold stories of the Old West.

Lew Wallace had participated in the Mexican American war, specifically, in New Mexico. Much later sometime after the civil war he was offered the governorship by Rutherford B Hayes. He accepted—optimistic this opportunity would become his writing retreat for a book that was originally inspired by his previous experience here. Lew was a good man with good intentions, but the previous governor was not. Samuel B. Axtell was tied to the Santa Fe Ring. Hell, he probably organized it. These no-good individuals wanted total commercial control over the beating economic heart of the New Mexico Territory.

Land grant documents were burned. Any contracts in the Spanish language were null and void. Every low-down dirty trick was employed by the Ring to take absolute control of the territory's government, and the populace's fate became their only concern. Lew Wallace was a thorn in their side and would have to be dealt with one way or another. This was the New Mexico that Governor Wallace was welcomed to in 1878.

Now let's spice this up with the addition of William Bonnie, alias, Billy the Kid. Early on Lew had promised Billy a pardon for the Lincoln County wars but later rescinded it. Political considerations had crushed the possibility. These two had met in Lincoln County, and it was then that Lew offered exoneration in exchange for Billy's court testimony of the bad guys. As time dragged on Billy finally wrote many letters to Governor Wallace begging for the pardon promised him. It never came. In frustration Billy threatened Lew's life and said he was coming for him.

All this drama was background to a writer who meanwhile was composing a story of Palestine and the Santa Fe Ring, sorry, I mean the Roman Empire, and the eventual persecution and enslavement of the Jews plus scenes of Jesus in the background working miracles.

Now, envision Governor Wallace hiding out in various small outlier villages, trying to avoid getting killed by the "Kid." It just so happened, also, Billy was very popular with the local Hispanic population. He was their Robin Hood. Being fully aware of this, Lew was constantly on the move. Finally on December 13th, 1880, he had had enough. Governor Wallace issued a warrant for Billy's arrest, which eventually led to Pat Garrett and Billy's last meeting in Fort Sumner in 1881.

At this time, Lew Wallace was also contending with Phoenicians, I mean Apache in the southern locales of the territory. Victorio, Chief of the Chimene band of Chiricahua Apaches, would eventually trap himself between the Mexican and American armies on the border, and this would finish him.

Lew Wallace completed *Ben Hur* in March of 1880. Eventually, it would become one of the most beloved tomes of the end of the 19th century. James Garfield, the U.S. President, took such pleasure in the reading that he offered Wallace the Consulate of Turkey. This new assignment would allow Lew to finally escape New Mexico. His final reference to the territory upon leaving was: Every calculation based on experience elsewhere fails in New Mexico.

So how was ancient Palestine that much different from the territory of New Mexico at the time? Both were lands coveted by empires, whether the Roman or Santa Fe Ring. Both were occupied by a secular pious people, who were defenseless to the oppression warranted on them. Maybe Lew Wallace unconsciously considered these juxtapositions, and finally incorporated them into a story that reflected current events of the time as well. No, Billy was no Ben Hur. Ben lived, but he was a character in this story who was not a good guy but also not a bad one entirely either. Without the struggle between this territorial governor and this two-bit outlaw beloved by most of the states, could *Ben Hur* truly have been written? Who knows.

Sheep

My first place of residence in Ramah was the last trailer at the most northern end of the Cowboy Stopover. My new roommate was a young Navajo professional whose first name was Marshall, and he ran a school Title Program at the time.

Many Navajos love names like Marshall and Sheriff and names of presidents are popular. I had a Truman and a Nixon in my classes. My trailer roommate, Marshall, was gay, and that was fine. But why was the art teacher assigned to his trailer? Ah questions, questions, never to be answered, but in obvious unspoken implications anyway.

Now what does any of this have to do with sheep? Absolutely nothing, I don't even know why I brought it up, but not long after I arrived in Ramah, Woody Allen produced a film named, "Everything You Wanted to Know About Sex but Were Afraid to Ask." In one of the major scenes in the movie, Gene Wilder played a successful Madison-Avenue doctor, who finds himself confronted by an Albanian sheepherder, who has brought his favorite sheep, Daisy, to be examined.

Wilder, as the doctor, is speechless that someone would audaciously bring his sheep into his practice. But the sheepherder is pleadingly insistent that Daisy is in dire need of professional observation. Gene looks deep into Daisy's eyes and, upon recovering, agrees to take her on as a patient. Well, let your imagination go wilder and after quite an escapade, the doctor's life is destroyed, and the angry sheepherder, upon rediscovering Daisy, absconds with her back to Albania.

The very last scene is shot of the homeless, divorced doctor lying in a filthy ditch guzzling a bottle of Woolite. I have never been able to pass a bottle on the cleaning aisle of any grocery store without cringing ever since.

Sheep, sheep, forever sheep, arriving on the Ramah reservation in 1974, sheep were everywhere. Sheep are known to erode the landscape with their insistence of, not only eating the grass but continuing to the roots. That is why they must be moved constantly or there is nothing to come back to in the future. At that time in history most commerce between the Navajos and trading post was founded on the business of sheep solely. Wool, hides, or meat, sheep were the kings of most trade transactions.

Navajo weavers needed the wool to also create some of the world's greatest woven treasures, never mind the fact that these weavers were lucky to get eleven cents an hour. The wool was from their flocks and with their dying and their imaginations, this was high art indeed.

It became apparent to me observing the local vista that sheep had contributed to often long stretches of barren landscape, especially during dry spells. On the way, driving to Gallup, the land appeared to have been chewed clean as far as the eye could see.

Something happened, within my first year in residence on the reservation, the US Congress removed trade barriers to New Zealand and Australia concerning sheep importations. Within months the nation's markets were flooded with cheap wool, and the Navajo market was simply crushed. This devastating situation may have contributed to the rise of more silversmithing as a direct result that sheepherding could not generate the needed dollars to sustain a family. Sheep were still prevalent but more for food consumption as meat than as wool for native weavers to turn into yarn for rugs. Sheep were now more of a cultural currency than an economic necessity.

The Zunis had sheep, as well I know, because I unknowingly became a wanted sheep rustler there, thanks to two of my Navajo students. Fortunately, I was never captured or indicted, but never will that ewe be forgotten either. I wonder what my two deceivers did with the twenty-five dollars they charged me for him. I still have nightmares of word getting back to the Zuni elders of my identity, and the Bow Society being sent directly to my whereabouts and promptly making an arrow pincushion of my petite derriere.

Think back when Navajo sheep herding was still king—sheep herders would move great flocks with the assistance of their dogs all over kingdom come. They'd be out camping all night and remaining vigilant of coyotes with their trusty Winchesters at their sides. Their dog's noses were ever alert to an unusual scent or two. It was most certainly a lonely life, no wife, no companions, just you and the sheep, sheep, sheep, alone with the sheep.

There is a story I was told of a ventriloquist traveling from New York to Las Vegas to perform. Since he had never traveled past the Mississippi River, he was inspired to detour through scenic areas he might never chance upon again. Following a questionable map the ventriloquist decided on a short cut across the Navajo reservation.

The temperature on the landscape was very hot, not the kind of drive for a stranger in this native region. Soon his car was seriously overheating, this was very concerning, what to do, what to do? He needed water.

On a rise, a native farm suddenly appeared. It was not much really, a hogan, a barn, a stable and some corrals. With no other alternative this hopeless explorer pulled into the main yard, and soon an older Navajo gentleman departed from his hogan and approached the strange man. "Howdy," says the stranger.

"Yat ta hay," said the other. Getting out of his steaming car the ventriloquists approached and explained his dilemma. The old Navajo, having enough English, listened patiently and then agreed to supply water for the unfortunate vehicle. Soon the car was running smoothly, and the driver was relieved and eternally grateful. What could he do for this Good Samaritan, this good man?

The ventriloquist hesitantly walked up to a horse, since all the barn animals had started congregating to witness this event, after all, there wasn't anything else happening that day. He asked the horse a question,

"How's this old man treat you, does he treat you good?"

Through the ventriloquist the horse replied, "Huurh. Oh yes, he feeds me oats and water and brushes me down, he's a good man."

The old Navajo stares in incredulity of shock, and the ventriloquist continues.

Then he asked the chickens, "How are you treated?"

"Buc, buc, buc, he treats us good, feeds us corn and feed, he's a good man," said the chickens.

The ventriloquist carries on throughout the barnyard. The old Navajo was way beyond a state of awe and wonder now.

Finally he approached the sheep, and the ventriloquist is interrupted suddenly by a demanding cough, turning he hears the old man say most emphatically, "Sheep don't talk."

Photographs

Cowboy Stopover

Trailer Park at Cowboy Stopover

Ramah Trading Post

East Side of Ramah, New Mexico

Andrew Shows in 1974 in Ramah, New Mexico

Kolowisi, a city of Albuquerque commission, was built by Anderw Shows in 1983. Kolowisi is the Zuni name for the plumed serpent. The arches are reminiscent of Mayan temples. This steel serpent is 70' feet long, part of a city block, and weighs approximately 12 tons. It is located on Lomas Boulevard near Old Town.

The Last Buffalo Soldier

In the 1970s there were a few notorious and well-known drinking holes (bars) surrounding Albuquerque. Some were legendary for the clientele; some for the entertainers who snuck into New Mexico to escape their fame's entrapment.

Placitas had the Thunderbird, and it thoroughly deserves acknowledgement as a premium long-time hippie dive. Bob Dylan, Joan Baez, and others were often entertainers at this famous haunt. The group, America, supposedly wrote "Another Tequila Sunrise" here as well. A fire would eventually end the Thunderbird's notoriety though.

The Golden Inn, located within the area of Golden on the eastern side of the Sandia Mountains east of Albuquerque, was a favorite of Richie Havens. He performed there often along with the likes of Asleep at the Wheel. You never knew who would sneak in to perform there. Later, when the Golden became a biker bar, a fire put an end to this establishment also.

New Mexico, back then, was a safe place for the famous. I had an Army veteran buddy, Wayne, who told me he had just finished a six-week gig as a bodyguard for Sting when he stayed here incognito to dry out and rehab in a private facility. Wayne would take Sting up into the Jemez Mountains to climb and hike the surrounding area. There are many such stories connected to this period, which will never rise to the surface. Maybe that is for the best. Still, they were another part of our history like it or not.

As a Navajo reservation teacher, getting to Albuquerque was a fortunate once every month trip at best. So, exploring famous drinking spots was an adventure in itself, and I concentrated on discovering their locations and unique libations.

One night, via someone's suggestion, I discovered Rosa's Cantina in Algodones, way north of Albuquerque. This was a small, narrow, packed to overflowing operation, and I almost left my first time when a black Indian approached me and through drunk speak, an unusual language, only familiar to those who frequent the fruits of libation, he convinced me to stay and give the bar a chance.

After a couple of drinks, I bought another round or two. I discovered my new friend's name was Dominic, and he was a Jemez Indian. He informed me he was also the last of the lineage of Buffalo soldiers alive on the Pueblo.

Buffalo soldiers fought with the cavalry after the Civil War. They received this special name from the Indians for their nappy hair which resembled that of the Buffalo. Most of these soldiers were ex-slaves from the South, who in the post-civil war period joined the cavalry and served in much needed territories to fight Indians and protect settlers traversing the Southwest. Never mind the fact that they were often protecting the same people who had been their previous owners. These same people, who refused to sign the oath of allegiance to the union, instead moved West, and formed what would be later known as the Bible Belt across Texas and all the way to southern California. Black soldiers did their job and got these good-for-nothings out of the South and somehow on through Indian territories safely.

I feel obligated to mention a repugnant neglected fact of our American history that has always irritated me. Why is there no transparency to remind us of the fact that our American Revolutionary Army, the Army which gave us our freedom from English tyranny, was in fact 15% Black. Would we even be a country today had we not had their assistance? I don't think so.

Anywho, back to my friend Dominic—Dom was a wonderfully affable character. I was thoroughly charmed by his honesty and heart. He started telling me stories of his ancestors, members of the Buffalo Clan in Jemez. His great, great grandfather had been an Army trooper, who chased

Victorio in the Apache Wars from 1878 to 1881. Many of the Army scouts and guides at this time were from the Jemez Pueblo. The Apache really didn't have many friends amongst the Pueblos. When on maneuvers Dominick's great, great grandfather befriended one of the Jemez scouts, as the campaign ended and Victoria was eliminated, he was invited to the Jemez Pueblo after his muster, completing his term of duty.

This ancestral grandfather of Dominic's was revered at the Pueblo almost as soon as he stepped foot in it. His buffalo hair and skin color were an immediate sensation and stardom followed him throughout the Pueblo. With the Apache gone everyone was relieved and hungry for a hero. It appears, with their united coaxing, he decided to stay. That was ninety years ago now, according to Dominic. He was now the very last one of the Buffalo soldier lineages in Jemez Pueblo.

I was gob smacked; I knew nothing of this history. Why would I, America was all White, wasn't it? What a joke. I had to climb into a local Algodones dive to be schooled on the real history of these United States of America.

Dominic and I made a date to meet in another month, same time, same place. All the time I was back at work, I was constantly reminiscing about our conversations. I had been touched by a truth unbeknownst by most anyone I knew.

In a month I was free to journey back to Albuquerque. That Friday I arrived at Rosa's on our agreed scheduled time and found no Dominic. So, I waited. For a while I put it down as Indian time. But after an hour and a half, I was concerned. Somehow, I caught Rosa's eye. She had seen me before with Dominic and came over and said, "*Como esta?*"

I replied, "*Muy bien y usted?*"

And she asked me why I looked so worried.

I mentioned I was to meet my friend Dominic here, and he hadn't shown.

Rosa asked, "You mean Black Dominic of Jemez?"

I said, "Yeah."

Rosa clouded over, she changed from bar owner to caring *madre* in seconds. Then she told me, "Dominic died a month ago hitchhiking back to the Pueblo. He was hit and left on the road dead." Rosa said, "I am so sorry. Did you know him well?"

I stared at her; I didn't know what to say. Finally, finally as the mist cleared from my eyes, I responded, "I only knew him that one night, I can't believe it."

She patted me on the shoulder and said she was sorry again and returned to the bar.

This is how life is, you never know who will present you with the gift of their heart and mind and share truths that will infinitely change you. I had such a short time with my Buffalo soldier, but he gave me a lifetime to think about everything he shared with me in one night in Rosa's Cantina. Happy trails brother, I'll see you again real soon.

Sunday Beer

Sundays in Ramah in the summertime were dead quiet. Mormons went to temple, some Navajos dealt with hangovers, and the locusts buzzed, buzzed, buzzed. Those of us teachers, too poor to leave the village, listened to old albums and contemplated our belly buttons. Well not quite, but you get the gist of it. We were stuck and the only possible solution in the end was cold beer.

There were only two places to get beer on Sunday—Witch well or Tinaja. Now Witch Well was just past Zuni and the Arizona State line, where Route 53 ends. The bar and carry-out window were spartan affairs, but the beer was cold. There was only one problem though—Witch Well was forty-five miles away. Tinaja, on the other hand, was ten miles away and had plenty of beer on Sunday. But there was no carry-out. The Blue laws of New Mexico were a pain back in the 1970s. If you wanted to drink some cold beer at home from Tinaja and take it easy on a hot summer afternoon, there was only one solution I could formulate.

I went to my closet and found an old light jacket. Wearing my combat boots loosely tied, I proceeded on to Tinaja to procure the afternoon's liquid refreshment. Once I entered the bar I ordered two beers, like I was ordering for two people. Thanks to the joint being the only drinking hole we had access to, there was always a busy, Sunday crowd. In fifteen minutes I ordered two more beers. Now I had both of my jeans pockets, holding a cold beer and one in my jacket pocket. In another fifteen minutes I ordered another two beers. Then, I opened my boot laces enough to accept a beer in each boot. Now I had a six pack in total and could go home. I'd only sipped the first beer a small amount—six cold beers, well mostly, but they were all opened.

Slowly, doggedly, I sashayed towards the front door victorious. When suddenly out of the blue, I heard, "Hey, Shows, want a beer?"

The Navajo buddy, who addressed me, owed me some money, a friendly loan, which I might never see repaid. Considering this, I felt a cold beer was better than no payment at all, so I said, "Sure, I'll have a beer."

I slowly sloshed over for my prize, becoming too aware of my bootlaces that were rebelling against me, an offensive jolting. Still, a free beer on Sunday was like winning the lottery. My buddy patted me hard on the back after presenting me with my prize. My whole person tensed up as liquid splashed within my garments. Ah, the smell of spilt beer was starting to permeate my entire being. I needed to jettison this joint but slowly, slowly. I chugged my new beer and quickly, and very, very slowly I made it to the door and carefully slid outside. I'd made it, six beers and a chaser on the way out, wow. Then I got into the truck. Uh, how was I going to get all six beers home safely, I had no carrier?

One by one, I retrieved the bottles and leaned them against the truck's seat. Then, I took the jacket and jammed it up close around the bottles and trusted this would hold them. Leaving the parking lot, I slowly cruised back to Ramah. Everything was going smooth as silk. Ah. Sunday beer at home on a hot afternoon, who could ask for anything more? I glided into Ramah and made it to my drive. But then disaster hit, I entered the driveway, this passageway wasn't really a driveway, but it was more a pair of matching arroyos. Traversing them was like fording two competing roller coasters. By the end of the driveway, I was able to save two beers half-full. So my expedition for Sunday beer had not been in vain, I had brought home the equivalent of one full, lukewarm bottle of beer. "Ah. Victory was sweet," said the scarecrow. Or was it, "If I only had a brain."

Navajo Divorce

Many would find it hard to believe that a Dionysian, nomadic society like the Navajo is in fact matriarchal. Women drive the tribe. They are the sustainers of the tribe's future. They are the collective consciousness of this society.

Before The Long Walk, long before that, it was the women who demanded their lazy warrior husbands get off their rears and go steal some sheep or corn or cattle or whatever and, "Don't come home empty handed." Living in a hogan alone with a bunch of screaming kids was hard enough. Being without food was impossible. So getting the oldest male child, I mean husband, to go out and get a job, I mean invade some poor Pueblo or tiny Hispanic hamlet, was much better than having him take up space in their tiny Native domicile.

Being nomadic, Navajos had nothing, so theft was life, without it—death. There was much competition in this precarious occupation. Apaches, Utes, Comanches, all were striving to survive. Besides, was it stealing if you considered your victim an enemy invading your homeland? What would you do? Where are the lawyers when you need them?

So Navajo women shouted and shamed their men into action and got results, until Kit Carson. Kit was commissioned by the United States Army to round up the Navajos. In the middle of the Civil War, the Navajos just went too far. They were stealing to the point where the government gave Carson carte blanche to gather every red-skinned Navajo into one place and then proceeded to march them on foot to Fort Sumner on the other side of the New Mexico Territory.

Kit was successful, and the Navajos were led, struggling through savage weather. Many died along the way, but finally they arrived at Fort Sumner. Their ordeal was not over though; the government then tried to make farmers of these nomadic people, but the land near the fort was too poor and swampy. Then, disease stole another portion of their population.

Finally, it was the Navajo women, who approached the commanding officer. With crying, pleading, and begging, they asked for permission to return to their homes in the West. It was only the women the Army trusted, not the men. Once these women swore to never allow raids by their people ever again, the commanding officer agreed, and the Navajo people, "The Dine," were freed to return home.

The fortitude of these women continues to this day even through their struggle with domestic necessities. Good old-fashioned Navajo divorce was short and sweet. If a wife had finally run out of gas and decided her good-for-nothing husband had gone too far, it was her decision that ended the marriage. All she had to do was place her husband's saddle outside the hogan's only door and that was that.

You might say, heck, that's too easy. No man's going to tolerate that kind of subtle abusive reaction. Now I just laid out the history of this society as concerns to women. Their backbone, their perseverance, and their struggle to keep family and home together through all kinds of calamity speak volumes of the strength of their matriarchal status. So, if I was a Navajo man, knowing all these facts and being aware of the Winchester also inside the hogan, I'd feel lucky I got a saddle.

Forty Below Zero

Applying to New Mexico Highlands University in January of 1972, the school catalog informed me the average temperature of the area of Las Vegas, New Mexico, was 85° year-round. Due to this wonderful revelation of the gentle climes of northern New Mexico, I rejected my acceptance of graduate school to Missoula, Montana. I also shed myself of any winter wardrobe since they would be unnecessary in these new inviting fair horizons. Ah paradise, here I come.

Two weeks into September, my first scholastic quarter, the first winter blizzard hit. I had no winter clothes. It appears the word average is a single most misleading word, and one must be aware of its malicious intent. Yes 85°, was average, between 110 and the low average of say -10. I have never trusted an average ever since

Flashing forward to January of 1975, I was at home in our Mormon rental planning and preparing to leave for school. For some reason the house was much colder than usual, but I needed to get my car warmed up to leave early. At this time I was driving the red Volkswagen bug. Stepping outside I noticed how everything was frozen still. Checking the old, rusted thermometer on the porch landing of the house, I discovered, wait that can't be right. Was that right? There's no way, really? The red line in the skinny glass tube of the thermometer read -40°.

Taking my car key, I tried to unlock the door of the VW but it just wasn't happening. There was ice sealing and filling the keyhole. Going into the kitchen I lit a gas burner on the stove and with a pair of pliers held the key to the flame. I heated the key to almost red. With the hot key held with the pliers, I was able to defrost and unlock the Volkswagen door. I had to work the door a while to get the ice to release it from its frame but eventually victory was achieved. Now I was in the driver's seat and prepared to enter the key into the ignition. No go, the key had cooled. Returning to the kitchen I started the key heating process all over again. Soon I was back in the driver's seat, holding a red-hot key with the pliers and placing it into the ignition Finally success, but no success. Yes, I was able to turn the key in the ignition, but all I heard was the slightest whisper from the battery under the back seat say, "Would you start at -40°? I don't think so." There you have it; this is the land of manana; better luck tomorrow.

Only two vehicles started in the whole community that day, our wannabe Chief Chavez's International truck and Mr. Lewis's, who owns the trading post truck, a Ford and brand new.

People say to me, "Oh, that's hokum, you're too near to Mexico for those kinds of temperatures."

Well, see, here's the thing. Ramah lies within the lower Rocky Mountains at nearly seven thousand feet, so even though we are south and next to sunny Mexico, we are also high in Continental Divide country, welcoming any stray blizzard Colorado has tired of. Being that the cold loves our narrow finger canyons, January offers quite an array of ice parades.

I realize this is all a bit much, and who needs to go on about the weather. But the lesson learned and shared with you is in fact, if you know a young graduate student traveling to a faraway destination for college, please inform them to be attentive to any mention of the word "average" in that school's promotional catalog. Just a thought, okay?

Ramah Rodeo

In the movie *When the Legends Die*, Frederick Forrest, who will go on to perform in *Midnight Express*, plays a Ute Indian kid, who under the tutelage of an old drunken former rodeo rider, becomes a major star on the bull riding rodeo circuit.

Richard Widmark's performance was excellent. The storyline follows the Ute kid's early struggle trying to survive BIA dorm life and forced assimilation and resounded a core truth resonating on 1970s reservation life.

Although these social Native issues were apparent to us teachers, our students, who were watching this movie, were more engrossed in the action of bull riding. Our Navajo boys all dreamed of becoming bull riding stars. That was the big brass ring for them.

We showed this film in the new school in early 1977, and of course, it was a hit with the kids. Probably the only movies any of them ever saw was through these school assemblies. It wasn't much, but it was what we had.

Bull riding is a vicious, insanely dangerous, suicidal exercise in the elimination of fear through pure near-death expectation. There is something missing in some male brain's frontal lobes where common sense is supposed to inhabit, and they feel the need to fill that hole with the terror, horror, and fascination of a 1,500-pound bull, looking through the eyes of hell, looking to eliminate their existence.

In later years my wife, Turza, and I would travel to Crete to the Knossos Palace of King Midas. The Minoan frescoes of acrobats, performing for the Royal Court in gyrations over bulls of obvious massive distinction, fascinated us. There were stylized images of women and men performing in sync with extremely-long horned beast of mythical proportions—quite beautiful really. This romantic image of ancient 4,000-year-old frescoes is obliterated in my mind's eye though, when recalling past rodeo realities of living in the American West.

Our bulls were bred to kill, let's not kid ourselves. The real kick riders got was surviving and being able to ride again for a few seconds more than their opponents. No mention or warning would deter their obsession with the bull. Being a cripple or having early onset arthritis meant nothing to these young bucks. Those few seconds of riding a death machine was life for them.

The Ramah rodeo grounds are north of the village on the way to the lake. The annual rodeo draws all the locals, and what was once a pleasant, hardworking community of farmers and ranchers, becomes for a weekend, a shit kickers' paradise. Navajos, Mormons, Mexicans, and Zunis compete to see who among them possesses less sense than the rest.

Wild Bronx and bulls are impatiently prepared to do battle with these numb skulls and may the best man or beast win. The spectacle of the rodeo is spectacular for what you can see and if you can see through the dust. Of course, sometimes you don't want to see either, dust or not.

There's a rodeo dance Saturday night, and only Mormon kids appear to be in attendance. Maybe a few Navajos stand by the doors but not many. The last dance I recall was at our old school gym in the village, though they've torn it down long since then.

In the 1970s, there were still unspoken race lines in Ramah. Lines brought on, not just by color, but by historic abuses and misunderstandings. All I know, in the end, is people are people, and they all have a bone to pick. So if there is just one absolute in this western world, it is from the flaming eyes and on the back of a raging bull, that all men are created equal.

Buses and Telephones

In the early 1970s there were no interstate highways yet in New Mexico. This was the land of Route 66 and the Camino Real. New Mexico was more a small country than a state at the time. Small rural roads were our expressways.

The population for the entire state of New Mexico, at the present time, is around 2,300,000 people, and this within the fifth largest land mass of any state in the union. Was it no wonder why Native Americans struggled with distance to get their crafts to market. Traveling in a state so vast resulted in either a pile up in the bed of a pickup truck with the wind blowing and every sort of weather or season, or the only other alternative was waiting for that ancient edifice of road travel, the Greyhound bus.

Route 66 followed the path traversing all the Pueblos, small towns west of Albuquerque, north to Las Vegas, and beyond. From Santa Fe to Las Vegas, that by-way was also known as the Old Pecos Trail. From Rodeo Road in Santa Fe, you then travelled through the Pueblos on the Camino Real south. All of this comprised and was included within the artery known as old Route 66. When it came to this by way of the old TV show of the 1960s, "Route 66," Marty Milburn and George Maharis didn't have a clue of it's true significance.

When I saw Native women in the 1970s with blankets spread on the concrete in front of the train station in Albuquerque or in front of old La Placita in Old Town, or even in front of the Palace of the Governors on the Plaza in Santa Fe, shaking down pigeons from the east, I was sorely aware of the struggle it took for these women to get those beads and silver creations there in the first place. The Greyhound bus was the transport of

New Mexico's cultural treasures, that is if you were close enough and lucky enough to catch it, and if the driver was awake.

Navajos never had this transportation luxury, which made them easier targets for the trading post. Transportation was a premium on the rez. Rides were not free. If you were Navajo and wanted a ride, you held a dollar bill up in a raised hand and that was your best chance ticket of getting a ride. Navajo drivers had to be careful though, because Zunis often pretended to be Navajos to get a ride. Navajos were so isolated on their huge sprawling reservation that many simply never ventured far. Most of their own land itself was unknown to them.

Just getting to Gallup from the main reservation was like a trip to New York City, a world of endless wonder and trade and alcohol. Not many Navajos benefited from a Greyhound bus. When you saw a group of them cruising through Gallup, it was in the bed of a pickup truck all jammed together to keep warm. That was the Navajo transit system chartered for party central.

Telephones. Telephones were mostly accessible along Route 66. The cities, of course, had abundant service, but once you got into the rural areas the telephone became a dear and valued tool not easily shared. This was understandable with a public telephone system stretched to the limits with the cost of trying to connect a state with only a population equivalent to Queens in New York. They did the best they could at the time, running wire all over to the distant New Mexico homes. The only cell phones at that time were on Star Trek, and they weren't taking orders.

In 1974, at the old Ramah Navajo School, there was one telephone in the office—one. I know there were phones at the trading post and the post office and other places, but we teachers had no access to telephone booths or any other telephone facility other than the one phone in the school's office.

Now the real trick was getting to that phone without any trouble. So here was the questionable equation—how did one access a phone which was school property for school business only and was guarded by a watchman at night? The solution was, first you needed a key to the school, second you needed to get by the guard. The conclusion was we teachers shared a key to the school when we needed to make a phone call. It turned out, the guard left at midnight anyway, so when the cats away the mice can finally call home.

I am certain the school administration knew of our little deceit, but on the other hand, they knew firsthand our predicament. Communication was a most dire necessity, and the mail back then was run by snail express.

Now you obviously are thinking, Andy, what good was it for teachers to call anywhere at midnight? Who would be awake to get the call? Even with time changes, it still was an incredible imposition for the receiver. Well, kiddos, back then nearly everyone in these old United States owned an answering machine. So, teachers could leave messages and other contact information on a recorded tape, voila.

There was another benefit to these up-and-coming marvels of telephone recording history. Later models allowed you to change the recorder's cassette tape with a new faux celebrity answering tape. Your phone could take a message in an imitation of Jimmy Durante's voice or Carry Grant's. Any number of celebrity sanctioned recordings were available. But guess what the number one taped celebrity imitation was in all the land? It was Richard Nixon. "Hello, this is tricky Dick, Janet's not here right now, but if you will leave your name and number and a short message, I promise, I won't erase the tapes."

BAR-D RANCH

The second field trip of the summer of '74 was to Colorado. For the school this was quite an ambitious journey for a big old reservation school bus, but the kids had earned a break, so come on, it's summer school. I could tell the kids were excited, no not really; I hadn't learned enough Navajo facial expressions to formulate the equation of excitement. But even so, I was excited. I'd never been to Colorado. This was a first for me.

The drive took us through Gallup, then up to Farmington, and on to Durango. Our driver was Herbert Henio, and there was no steadier hand at the wheel of a school bus. Our destination was in fact Durango, Colorado. We would stay that night at the Fort Lewis College dorms. The journey was smooth overall, and eventually, we arrived at the dorms around three-thirty in the afternoon. We rested for a couple of hours and eventually got organized and made our way to the Bar-D Chuck Wagon, north of Durango.

What was it about the Navajos in the 1970s that made anything cowboy, the greatest thing on earth? Nearly every one of the boys at that time wore a cowboy hat, and if he collected enough pinon nuts in the fall, he might even have a Resistol straw hat for the summer. But why the boys wanted to be cowboys became a simple deduction to me—the rodeo. The rodeo was that quintessential image of Navajo masculinity, and most of these boys had dreams of bull riding into history, that's if they didn't get stomped to death first.

The Bar-D Ranch Chuck Wagon started in 1969. It is in a gorgeous mountain valley with an incredible western setting. The ranch is still in operation to this day fifty-five years later, and the menu is still the same—steak, cowboy ranch beans, chunky applesauce, and biscuits. Dessert is home-baked spice cake. But it was the floor show, and the cowboy music show that drew me back to the 1950s as a kid. It was just like the Roy Rogers and Gene Autry extravaganzas I remembered.

These "New Riders of the Purple Sage" of the Bar-D did not disappoint. This cowboy band delighted and humored and soloed their hearts out and like it or not, the kids enjoyed every single moment of it. We climbed into the bus afterward and made our way back to the dorms to our beddy bye. Well, not all went beddy bye. Durango had a nightlife quite the opposite from the Bar-D. This was where the university crowd hung out, and there was Blues and Rock and libations galore. This university town was struggling, but so what, at that time in the seventies many Colorado small town colleges were struggling.

The next day we traveled north to Silverton and then to Ouray, a steep and arduous peak-filled ascension that scared the bejesus out of us all, but boy the beautiful views. We later returned the way we came. The day was sunny and magnificent. Many of us dozed from altitude dissension or to tried to forget how hard a school bus seat was to the human posterior.

Eventually, we stopped in Farmington at the KFC. The only franchise, which I had run into near the Navajo Nation, was this Kentucky Fried Chicken. I would also become aware that KFC was so popular with the Navajos that the Farmington store alone on a Saturday night had a consistent line out their parking lot down the main avenue, through the town, and on to the Colorado State Line. Nothing could deter these Navajos from the greatest of the white man's creations, KFC.

So, the kids got small boxes of chicken with biscuits and cleaned the bones till the meat and the gristle were vacant from them. I was thoroughly impressed. Later, we got them home, delivered them to their hogans or houses, and then we few teachers ended up at the school in the night.

I walked home from there, and tired though I was as I strolled along, I wondered, what kind of world do I live in where some Indians want to be Cowboys, and some Cowboys want to be Indians?. A very cool one indeed, I thought.

Camel Calvary

In the late 1950s, there was an extremely popular TV western series named "Have Gun Will Travel." The shows starring character was named Paladin, played by Richard Boone. There were 225 program episodes, but only one has never escaped me.

In that episode the setting was in New Mexico Territory, and Paladin travels to a ranch because he received a very intriguing letter, requesting his professional assistance. The assignment was to investigate a so-called Red Devil that had been disrupting cattle herds and scourging the countryside, driving terror into the hearts of the surrounding populace.

Paladin surveyed the surrounding territory and finally located one isolated small ranch, whose owners had currently been plagued by the beast. With the rancher's assistance Paladin prepares that night to await the terrifying desert specter. Later in the night there are frantic disruptions from the barn and corrals, and Paladin arises from his hidey hole and comes face to face with the monster. He fires his gun, empties the barrel, and all is suddenly quiet. As the sun rises, the beast is observed for what it is, a very old U.S. Army camel with an ancient tattered uniformed skeleton of an officer still tied in place to its back with a few Apache arrows sticking out to boot. This episode was based on real history, now, of course, long forgotten.

El Morro National Monument, southwest of Grants, New Mexico, possesses carved sandstone graffiti, marking a bivouac camp for the United States Army's camel cavalry. Throughout the 1850s up to the Civil War, the army used camels for surveying sorties from Texas across New Mexico and all the way to the Colorado River. Our own Route 66 is part of these early surveying expeditions, but there were many others. It appears the camels were more suited to the drought stricken Southwest that even the heartiest of mules, which were at the time the backbone of military transport. Mules would die of thirst; camels continued. I believe, the first camels were a gift from Morocco in gratitude for service the Marines performed because of the Battle of Tripoli in the early 19th century.

Many have forgotten how much our New Mexico culture is accented by Moroccan culture. What we consider New Mexico colonial architecture is, in fact, Moroccan as are our traditional tile works (blue and white). Camels in the 19th century should not have been that surprising in the Southwest. Were it not for the Civil War's interruption in the region, many believe camels would have been with us to this day.

There is a predominance of Paleolithic-fossil camel skeletons throughout New Mexico. It is obvious they thrived on the predominant Creosote plant, covering the extreme desert sections of our state just as the calvary's camels did later. In the dawn of our state's prehistory, camels were kings.

All these things passed through my mind when I first observed that El Morro camel cavalry graffiti. I struggled to wonder why the army did not take to these four-hooved wonders of the desert. Their reliability, constancy and capacity to haul up to six to seven hundred pounds of supplies at a time was unheard of. In the end, I believe it was a question of conversation that terminated this program. I'm sure lonely soldiers with no recourse for discourse with each other's repetitive stories finally turn to their camels. As everybody knows camels spit if they are sick of hearing the same story again and again.

Patty Hearst and Richard Nixon

The Ramah Post Office was the beating heart of communications for our village and the reservation. Since our community was so small, we were alphabetically filed and our address was: full name and then in care of postmaster, Ramah, New Mexico 87321. Mr. Lewis, our postmaster, would hold our mail until we stopped in, and then he handed it off to us. That was all that was to it. The post office was also our social gathering place as far as social gatherings occurred in Ramah. One must know there were no telephones in Ramah for teachers at the time.

If correspondence wasn't in a letter to you, then obviously no one cared about you, and you'd better start writing to let the world know you still existed. Mr. Lewis was a fatherly, helpful, diligent and attentive postmaster, and we greatly appreciated him. He was part of the greater Mormon community and as a result he knew everyone. As post offices go this was your typical western interpretation. President Nixon's portrait was centered on the wall above return receipts, money order request, and all other postal paraphernalia. Tricky Dick would stare down on you with that kind of an expression that insults a smile. What did Pat see in him anyway?

Now the other wall, alas, was the FBI's most wanted. Now that was most interesting. You always checked that board just in case some relative you'd not heard of in a long time showed up with a price on their head. No wonder my mom didn't talk about Uncle Ray anymore. Oh, well.

this was from the Office of the Army in Washington DC. It was embossed in a beautiful, graphic type set. Later that day my two students showed up, and we proceeded to open this written opportunity for the future of two of our Native Navajo's finest.

The letter read, Dear Mr. Shows, though we appreciate your two student's interest in the United States Army, we must relay our regrets. The army is only able to enlist U.S. citizens and since you live outside the United States, this is not possible. Thank these young men for their interest, and we wish them a bright future. I am yours, Master Sergeant etcetera.

I looked up in disbelief at two stunned young faces and had to laugh. I told them this Sergeant is so stupid, he thinks we live in Mexico. Are you guys really set on the Army? What about the Navy?

Now one day, a cataclysmic event of epic proportions occurred. Mr. Lewis nailed above the FBI's most wanted board a poster of the most notorious of all our current national criminals. An individual terrorist so dangerous John Dillinger would wet his pants. Yes, I'm talking about none other than Patty Hearst. A criminal, who single handedly, caused so many trusts fund Republicans' children's sleepless nights. You could almost hear them scream, "Oh God, she's out there. The country would never be safe if she is on the lamb. Patty is coming for us."

Well, as you can imagine, we all coveted that poster. Her image exuded the obvious criminal intelligence it took to mastermind the dastardly deeds the Weathermen were crippling our country with. We had to have that poster, but was it worth going to federal prison for the theft of government property? What to do, what to do. Many sleepless nights were attributed to Patty's poster, who didn't want this poster hanging over their bed. Everyone loves a bad girl.

Now, I am not a brave man, I believe there is even some Rhode Island Red in my genealogy chart, but I had to have this poster of this bad girl on my wall. I planned; I covered all the angles, and I decided I would have Mr. Lewis look for a fictitious package and steal this beauty from his wall. Then I'd lean it under the counter, and when he discovered no package for me, I would thank him and walk out with Patty.

The day finally came; I followed the plan to a tee. Later, at the house my roommate, Ron, asked what the picture was I was carrying into the living room. Upon seeing it, he shouted, "Richard Nixon." I explained that within the time I had formulated the perfect plan, someone else had pinched Patty. Anyway in frustration while Mr. Lewis was busy, I grabbed Nixon as a consolation prize and split. We grudgingly accepted this as a booby prize and in homage of our dear president, placed him on the bathroom wall as a deterrent for mice unbelievably. It worked.

I never did federal time, thank God. I never saw the inside of a penitentiary, but I might have for the girl of my dreams, Patty Hearst. Well, maybe in the next life.

TAZHII

In 1970, I worked as a substitute teacher for Baltimore inner-city middle school in Highlandtown. The school's student population was comprised of one-third poor Catholic Polish kids, one-third Black ghetto kids, and one-third Jewish kids obviously bussed in. The social dynamics were quite extraordinary to say the least. Still, it was Baltimore.

At this time, I was nineteen years old and a beginning sophomore at Maryland institute College of Art. So how did I get this job? The daughter of a man I worked with at another job was a teacher at this school and mentioned how desperate this particular area was to the Board of Education. She suggested I try and apply, so that's what I did. With all the brass that I could muster I entered the school, continued to the office, inquired as to an application for substitute teacher. Then I filled it out, and in only moments the principle appeared and gave me an interview on the spot.

Everything to her was satisfactory. No birth date was required. I was asked if I was advancing a further degree program, and I replied absolutely. Only later did I realize that they had taken me for a graduate student. Thank God, I was tall and pretended to be mature. All in all, this was a tough school, really tough. Each time I filled in substitute teaching the question I asked myself was always the same, am I going to make it through the day? Somehow, I did, and in time a total of a year and a half's experience was under my belt. I had also earned that inner-city moniker students bestowed upon unsuspecting victims such as I, that "jive turkey." What's in a name anyway, huh?

In May of 1974, the Ramah Navajo School hired me to teach summer school and later a full-time position as art teacher. My colorful background though was still an appendage of my past. I was unconsciously trapped with Baltimore inner-city street slang and accidentally referred to some of my students as "jive turkeys."

I had no knowledge that in the creation stories of the Navajo the turkey was a sacred animal. He was the last animal to rise from the pool of life, and his tail feathers are clipped in white to prove it. I was not aware of any of this lore, but the result was positive to the point that even the smallest children from the school bus windows would shout Tazhii (turkey) at me every time they passed by for years to come. I had my own Navajo name, and everyone knew it, Tazhii. Oh well, maybe I was a "jive turkey" after all.

THE IOWA TEST

The GRE, Graduate Record Exam, was a prerequisite to enter graduate school in any field of study, but there were a few universities who passed on the requirement and substituted their own facsimile or version of a graduate entry exam. Highlands University preferred this recourse. Their's was simply an English proficiency exam.

The November after my arrival at the university, this required testing was to take place. I have taken many exams throughout the years but still, this one made me antsy. Oh well, I thought, buckle up and get over yourself. One Saturday the date of the exam arrived, and I made my way to a particular college hall that had been designated for the occasion. It never really occurred to me, who would be attending this sort of event. After all, most graduate students had already taken the actual GRE before applying to the school. Since I was twenty-one when I received my BFA, I hadn't the opportunity to even schedule the said examination, much less take it.

So, the audience attending this event was more, one could say, in an association with that scene in "Animal House," where the two plebes are searching for a fraternity and are placed into a small group of foreign students wearing turbans and fezzes, etcetera. Later when I saw the movie I felt a direct kinship through these global brothers I had taken the English proficiency exam with. Still, it was awkward to say the least. What the Hell's this tall white guy doing here, is he a spy?

This impression was my take on the situation. I wanted to respond, "No guys, I'm from the East Coast, and here that is a foreign country."

Any who, the exam proceeded. It was all essay of course; I believe five hundred words. The subject choices were varied enough to enable us to compose smoothly.

Of course I finished early, it was my native tongue after all. Then, well, I wanted to stay and assist some of my new brothers. Bad idea. I was motioned to leave the premises, still in my heart I wished them all luck and departed.

I never forgot that exam, and while teaching I often reflected on the whole testing process itself. Was it fair if a test was focused on a specific socioeconomic group only and was not inclusive of fringe or outlier groups like say Native Americans? I was soon to find this out when I was assigned to administer the Iowa Test to our own Navajo students. I was leery of this national grammar school exam and broke a number one rule of the test kit—I read over the test questions.

Soon, I became aware why these kids had scored so low in previous years. There were questions about city buses and using transfers for instance. This test's focus group was oriented to American cities and suburbs. My kids had never used a telephone much less seen one, and the only buses they knew about were yellow and said school on the side. This test was directed to fail them, even if unintentionally.

Gathering the three other teachers assigned to participate in presenting the test, I forced them to see the problem and we resolved a solution. The test had, of course, a specific time sequence. So, before we began the stopwatch, we went over some of the particulars unknown to the students and explained as best we could—what these otherworldly objects and situations were. Then, we would start the test's timer.

Those particular Iowa Test scores at that time had the most rewarding results of any in the history of the school. The principal and the school board were happy and impressed. Our kids were indeed very bright. The moral of this story is simple, give every kid a chance, they certainly deserve it.

Rafael's Silver Cloud

The Cloud is located on the frontage road north of Algodones set back from the interstate and specializes in a clientele of Hispanics, Indians, and Rednecks. Yes, Raphael might have had a Rolls Royce Silver Cloud at one time or another.

Once traveling from Santa Fe to Albuquerque, I had the unfortunate pleasure of breaking down in my mother-in-law's Ford Galaxy across the interstate from the Silver Cloud in 1979. The car's radiator hose was blowing clouds of steam and preparing to play taps. I pulled over, opened the hood, saw the premonition of disaster, and walked across four lanes of traffic. Crossing the parking lot, I entered the establishment, not knowing what to expect. I had never frequented Raphael's before, though I'd heard rumors. I mean, what's a reputation without rumors?

I knew Tom Waits had recorded here once, right? Anyway, upon entering, I approached the bartender, told him my situation, and requested an empty beer can. Receiving one graciously, I thanked him and continued on my way back. Finding some bailing wire on the side of the road, I took my Swiss Army Knife, cut the can, removed the top and bottom, wrapped it around the now cooled hose at the bruised location, then I wired it tight and prayed to hell it would get me back home. It did.

There are naysayers who claim Tom Waits never played at Raphael's, say the performance was a studio fabrication. All I know is the album was recorded with the dedicated dereliction of spirit of Rafael's Silver Cloud Lounge of the 1970s. No one can ever take that away from us, right?

"Nighthawks at the Diner" was supposedly the live recording at Raphael's, but maybe only in spirit. Still the album makes it pretty hard not to miss the entertaining hilarity of such belly whoppers as "Making the Scene with a Magazine," taken from the cut, "Taking Myself Out for a Date." Tom is also mesmerizing in his rendition of the ghost truck driver who gives a hitchhiker a silver dime for a cup of coffee, a totally unforgettable and timeless number.

Tom stands alone with his gravelly voice style in his non sanctimonious revelry between life and death. I wonder if he was maybe a Koshare in his past life. "Nighthawks" takes us through a luscious menu of Tom's sick beautiful mind and serves us an entire succulent delicious pathos. Really, who could ask for more.

Rafael's Silver Cloud Lounge isn't open anymore. It has been closed a long, long time. This was one of the last of our drinking dinosaurs and a piece of history that will be sorely missed. But, but if you are interested in purchasing an old lounge where Tom Waits might have recorded an album, this address could be for sale, 604 Frontage Road, Algodones, New Mexico. Good luck to you and let me know when the reopening is.

Mongolian Spot

The Black Rock Hospital is located on the far eastern side of the Zuni Reservation, and as a result, it is easily accessible to Navajos in need, though it is a thirty-to-forty-mile drive. This was an Indian Health Services, IHS, facility at the time I was an employee of the Ramah Navajo. If we needed emergency medical help, this was the place. All doctors and nurses were government health employees. Most were paying off their medical degrees with this term of public service. God bless them, they were all that we had, and, as a result, they were our heroes.

I remember one of our teachers, who cut off her thumb with a paper cutter while being distracted by troublesome students. This teacher fortunately was a smart cookie. She grabbed the thumb, threw it in her mouth, and drove one handed to Block Rock Hospital. She didn't even ask for driving assistance, just took off. She, of course, had her hand wrapped in a towel, but she got to the Black Rock Emergency, and they stitched her up, put her in a cast, prescribed pain pills, and sent her home. She's still good as new today, though hitchhiking is now out of the question.

Those doctors and nurses, public servants really, were part of a regiment of necessary frontline medical services, otherwise nonexistent to reservation life. They performed miracles every day, saving lives of Zunis and Navajos alike.

There was one peculiar situation though that inadvertently occurred and created an ongoing problem at the baby delivery department. It appears more than a few times, Zuni and Navajo babies had been accidentally switched at birth. Quite a plausible reality due to the fact these tiny native babies all basically look alike at birth.

There had been any number of stories of Navajo babies being brought up on the Zuni Pueblo as endeared daughters and sons. And yet by puberty physical attributes of the dominant genetics of which tribe they are from was too late to deny. Well, what are you going to do?

There was one sure identifier that separates Pueblo babies from pure Navajos. All Athabaskans at birth possessed the Mongolian spot, a yellowish spot at the base of the baby's spine. This spot is a mark of many legends including Buddha's blessing. The most realistic interpretation of its uniqueness though, is a direct genetic link to China long before the great migration down the Bering Strait. This was the only ace in the hole for babies that were mixed up, due to shift or paperwork changes. Those who learned this identifier saved the hospital and families future endless grief.

This discolored, yellow spot on an upset screaming baby, crying her heart out, entering this new world of trials and tribulations beyond anyone's expectations, had one certainty in her life no others without the spot possessed. In a sense, she was biologically made in China.

Hopi Basket

When I first arrived at Ramah to work at the summer school, everyone associated with the school lived at the trailer park at the Cowboy Stop Over (Stoop Over). Tom Cummings, my ole buddy, lived in one of the units. At the time Tom's trailer was like all the others—it was a trailer, had a trailer-like interior, and the only thing that could improve it, was possibly a fire. But Tom had one possession on his wall of his temporary domicile that made it special, and that was a very large, beautifully decorated shallow basket. At the time I was not knowledgeable of its tribal makers. After a couple of Heinekens, I asked Tom of its origin and his appropriation of it. On this questioning Tom hesitated, kind of choked, and with a smile finally spilled the beans.

"In 1967 I had an invitation to attend the snake dances at Hopi," Tom said. "I was a guest of dear Hopi friends that I was familiar with through an educational grant I had written. Snake dances had been recently closed to outsiders, but special friends were still made an exception." Tom delayed and opened another beer.

I said, "And?"

He took a swig from the cold bottle and continued, "The dances were stunning, there was no other way to describe them, and the rattlesnakes in the dancers' mouths were most definitely alive and writhing. Now Hopi had a special relationship with the rattlesnake and a bond of sorts, but we in the audience were still most certainly expecting a snake strike at any time."

Tom took another slow swallow of Heineken, and I said, "Yes?"

"Well," said Tom, "everything was going swell with all of us on the Hopi rooftops, pleasantly watching the festivities. Then a group of Koshares suddenly showed up behind me and grabbed me."

"Yes, yes?" I said.

"They dragged and partly carried me down to the plaza near the dancers, but not interrupting them, and proceeded to prod and pull at my clothes," he said.

Now Tom was a Kennedy-era, Harvard grad, the good guys, but he only wore suits and ties—white shirts and black shoes. I believe he was trying to compensate for his poor, Irish South Boston upbringing. The point is, these Hopi clowns, according to his story, had him surrounded, and they meant to have their fun and used Tom as a prop for a comic performance to the crowd. The audience, of course, found the situation hysterical since they weren't the victims themselves. Now the Koshares, clowns, were striped in black and white with their hair done up and pseudo-horns like ears of corn. They have white faces with large blacked-out eyes and a mouth with a huge, crude red area surrounding it. What clothing they wore, if they wore anything besides a breechcloth, was a caricature of white society. Maybe one would have a policeman's shirt and badge, and maybe another would favor a fireman with helmet and a piece of fire hose. They were all inventive symbolic poses and hilariously represented. "Tom, what did they do?" I asked.

"Well," Tom said. "They grabbed me tight and removed my tie and suit jacket, and one of them dressed in them and started to prance and make pontificating gestures, while walking in large circles to the laughter-consumed audience. The clowns were imitating office professionals, stamping approvals, shaking their heads 'no' to requests, basically reflecting their opinion of white society as opposed to Native life on the mesas. The problem was you never knew how far Koshares will go in their fun-filled abuse of their victim."

All this was so new to me; I had never been to Hopi. I had no idea what was going on? What were they doing to him? Now in reflection I was terrified.

Tom continued, "The clowns bumped me in faux-accidental ploys, and finally I fell into the dust. Now I was really scared. They circled me even closer now, and then they all grabbed me and lifted me up. The fattest one reached from his back and presented me with one of the most beautiful Hopi baskets I had ever seen. With this the crowd went nuts, and the Koshares bowed to their enthusiastic appreciation. Later I was in a daze. I was a hero of sorts for not being overreactive and responding to the expected horror of being a comic victim. Only it wasn't comic to me, and I was the victim."

With this Tom explained how the enactments were all made in fun. Afterwards the personal relief and the gifted reward made it all worthwhile, right? The appreciative crowd, hitting him on the back and telling him he was a good sport, didn't hurt either. Tom, thank God, was a good sport.

I have never owned a Hopi basket. Firstly, there are very few in existence, and those that do exist are prized, coveted collector's pieces. I haven't seen one of these baskets for sale in years, and nothing at all as large as the great basket Tom acquired.

I have been to Hopi Bean Dances, but snake dances are off-limits to white-eyed outsiders. I often wonder how I would have reacted to Tom's predicament. Would I fake it, play along, be the brunt of the Koshares' antics, or would I simply dart from the Hopi housetops to the mesa floor and run for my life to hopefully escape the terrors of snakes and clowns? Who can say? Who can say?

Western Pesto

The very first line in the manual for western survival for a teacher is food. The period between paychecks reels eternal and so stretching resources to that final night's dinner is all but imperative. As a result, it is a certainty that that last night's menu will offer one and only one alternative—western pesto.

All you need to know, first, is there is usually nothing left in the pantry by this time and as a result the ingredients are easy to identify. There will be the package of semolina spaghetti on the shelf all by its lonesome. Then, of course, a container of McCormick's dry basil leaves will be keeping a bottle of olive oil company. Did we forget the garlic salt?

The first step is simple, boil a sufficient amount of water for the semolina. While this is readying, a separate dry pan is heating up, and in this pan you will dump the pinon nuts you collected from your students during the fall's pinon harvest, which they have stuffed into their pockets and brought to class. If you did not confiscate these nuts at the beginning of class, then by end of each class, the floor would sound like snap, crackle, and pop all day long.

When these nuts have been heated enough, they will spring from their shells. If you then place them underwater, the shells will float to the top, leaving the nut meat at the bottom of the pan. By this time, you can also place the dry noodles in the boiling water. This done, you can finally move on to the real roundup of ingredients. In a frying pan you will pour your olive oil and slowly warm. In the warming oil you will generously add dry basil leaves, garlic salt, and if there is a dry garlic clove lying around, that even the cat won't have, you will chop that up and include it too.

Now as the *Piesta de Resistance*, you will throw in the pinion pine nuts. As the frying pan mix starts really heating up and browning, you drain the semolina. At the exact final sizzling moment, you drop the entire colander of noodles into the pan. Pop, bang, sizzle, sizzle. Soon with all the ingredients are calming in the pan as you stir and stir to the memorable aroma of heavenly Italian bistros so far away in San Francisco. The only final salute to this gourmet's dream realized is, of course, Parmesan Cheese from Kraft.

Why, you are saying, why would you write about food? There were so many more important issues facing the world in the 1970s than a Last Supper. Tell you what, you wait fourteen days to get paid, watch your larder of sustenance disappear before your very eyes, and then you can address me with this issue. When your tummy finally has had enough and asks you, "Hey stupid, the tanks empty, what's up?" You'll be glad some starving teacher gave you the recipe for survival. If you don't have pinion nuts, just take off the western part of the name and simply call it pesto.

The Weavers

Within the art department in the Ramah Navajo School, Betty Henio was upstairs in her weaving studio; my classroom was on the main floor. Betty's classroom was actually a balcony projecting halfway over the art room. Her studio was a quiet, inviting respite from regular school academics for students to sit and absorb the fundamentals of traditional Navajo weaving. Downstairs there was a noisy, sometimes funny art teacher, who had only three rules for his students. Have fun, do your work, and never curse in Navajo or English when the principal was visiting. These two juxtaposed classrooms within one, composed the total artistic, cultural experience of the arts in the Ramah Navajo School.

Weaving was the artistic artform anchor of the Navajo people. This artistic, cultural binder had established an economic benefit to the Navajo long before silversmithing existed. Even basket weaving could not compete with the output of the blanket weavers. The primary function of the wedding basket was to create a ceremonial, corn pollen blessing for bridal couples, and these baskets have too much significance for mass production.

It was the women, Dine' weavers, who brought the hope of dollars or trade at the trading post with their one-of-a-kind woolen creations. These women would create a commercial culture that would draw collectors from all over the world. It was these women who originally put Navajos on the map of the public's consciousness. Their hard work and initiative would rebuild the tribe.

When anyone is thinking of the Southwest in terms of Native Americans, often the first classic image of their cultural contributions would occur as that of a Navajo blanket. The geometric or figurative designs, embedded within a framed border, are identifiable anywhere on this planet as Southwestern and Navajo.

In the 1970s a Navajo Weaver earned an average of eleven cents an hour, eleven cents an hour. Their isolation and lack of mobility limited any transactions outside the reservation. The sole outlet for their weaving was the trading post, which often paid for individual charges through the store with these magnificent woolen creations in trade. From there the rugs would be sent on to larger commercial traders for public consumption.

In Gallup, being a poor teacher, I frequently combed through the Gallup Samplers at the larger commercial trading posts. Gallup Samplers were basically saddle blankets in the 1970s and were priced at $25.00 each. Because they were all individual works of art, some weaver artists were so incredibly talented, I felt humbled beyond words just browsing through these creations.

Navajo sheep produced the majority of the wool employed in the weaving process. The wool was dyed with native colors from roots, berries, leaves, and any other family secrets, handed down through the generations. The trading post though, has offered supplemental colored yarns throughout the last 150 years, primarily from the Pennsylvania Dutch and Mennonites. The cardboard wrappers, this wool was shipped in, often had painted illustrations from their farms, and these images had also traveled on through each Navajo women's interpretations of another world other than their own. Yet they made it their own through their arts' unique showcase.

Sheepherding over the barren landscapes of the Four Corners was the first economic step to survival for regional Navajo families. The wool, meat, and byproducts clothed and fed them and gave them life. The weavers brought the real dollars though to trade for frying pans, enamel dishes, clothes, boots, saddles, and in short anything the family needed. The weavers brought the tribe prosperity first and even contributed to buying back Native lands the US government had earlier claimed.

Money from silversmithing contributed greatly to the family by the end of the 19th century and forward, due principally to the railroad bringing adventure tourists out West. But it was the weavers who sustained the family until that opportunity arose and continued to this day to create the essence of their cultural experience through their art.

Often at the end of the school day after Betty had left, I'd sneak upstairs to see the progress her students were making. This semester they were working on traditional tight red sashes. They were anywhere from three inches to four inches in width, six to seven feet in length, and varied in colors of red, green, white, blue, and black. They were tight woven and displayed traditional designs, often interrupted with someone's name incorporated. The ends of these sashes were twisted and knotted as long fringe. These were Native costume devices, worn from weddings to healing ceremonies and even in traditional dances. They were precious to the individuals they were made for, and no two were ever alike.

I often visualized a Navajo woman kneeling at her loom, set up under a jacal in the open air of the Monument Valley landscape, and I watch as she, within this background of sand and sage, incorporates the magic of color into a new woven masterpiece, while her baby plays with colored yarn cuttings on the blanket on which they sit.

I was jealous of Betty. Sure I taught art, but Betty taught art, history, culture, and Native survival. She covered it all, and with grace and humility she tolerated a loud, and sometimes funny clown who called himself an art teacher.

"THE MAN WHO FELL TO EARTH"

In 1977, I met Turza, my future wife, at the Albuquerque Crafts Guild, a small cooperative I had been selling at while teaching at the Pine Hill School on the Ramah Navajo Reservation. Turza had been teaching at Zia Pueblo previously for Headstart. Since we both cared much about our past Native employments, we would eventually have much in common in comparing notes of our reservation experiences.

Turza was a University of New Mexico (UNM) girl. She had finished her art education degree there but elected to eventually become an artist instead. With all her talent and discipline, I understood why. While at UNM Turza, of course, had many college friends; some I even met later. One was Eloy Phil Casados, when he was returning to his Tierra Madre, New Mexico. Phil had a break between movie shots and was homesick, and yes, you guessed it, Eloy was an actor.

To his credit, Eloy had starred in many films we were all familiar with. To name just a few of them—*White Men Can't Jump*, *Born in East LA*, *Bridesmaids*, *Red Dawn*, and many others you have certainly been entertained by one time or another. Phil was truly a gifted actor.

What drew me to Eloy, though, the most was in his heart of hearts, he was still a New Mexico homeboy. I miss Eloy. He was much more Turza's friend than mine, but what time we did spend together, Eloy shared some wonderful stories/anecdotes of characters and actors he encountered in Hollywood and at film sites. Phil has unfortunately passed away since we saw him last in Pasadena, California. But his smile and gracious nature, which set him apart from Tinseltown's herd, still stays with me every time I think of him.

Phil had an especially funny story about David Bowie that I'll never forget. "The Man Who Fell to Earth" was filmed in 1975 on locations throughout New Mexico. Albuquerque, White Sands, Artesia, Fenton Lake, and even the red cliffs of Jemez were staged sites. The original script was from an old 1963 English sci-fi about an arriving alien who tries to calculate the possibility of transporting water back to his drought-ridden planet. The production was sketchy. There were many interruptions in the filming's schedule, and the Hell's Angels were even camped at the White Sands desert location during one important specific film shot. Eventually, the film was completed, and Bowie continued with his cocaine-addled life of the stars. He hadn't been happy in New Mexico.

Eloy Phil Casados, years later, was attending a gala party in Hollywood and bumped into Bowie. They got to talking about the biz and mutual friends, and somehow the subject of Phil's native New Mexico came up. By this time, it was rumored Bowie had never been satisfied with his work there, and it appeared he blamed it all on our dear state. Eloy confronted David and asked him why he felt such disparagement towards our fair state of New Mexico. We are, after all, a sensitive people. It must be the chili.

Bowie thought about this, hesitated, then looked Eloy straight in the eye and said, "Eloy 'I don't know what you've heard. I can tell you one thing for a fact, ask me about anything you like, but when it comes to the 1970s, I don't remember a thing. I don't have a clue what occurred then." And that settled that as far as he was concerned.

I often think of this story and remember those crazy years of surviving a war and preparing for a new threshold into a future unbeknownst to us all. I remember Eloy, and I honestly conclude they should have left Bowie out in White Sands with the Hell's Angels. Knowing the train wreck of a lifestyle David pursued, Bowie most likely would have later been observed riding tight-backed behind an Angel off into a drug-induced sunset of his dreams, screaming, "Adios, Hollywood, this bitch is out of here."

Yee Naaldooshii, Skinwalker

We had a new student, her name was Laurie, and she was from the main reservation. She was the girlfriend of Bradley, one of my favorite students, even though he was part of the famous Zuni sheep debacle. Laurie was a senior finishing her last year here at Pine Hill School. Eventually, she became more of a friend than a student, thanks to Bradley, and shared stories of the main reservation I would never have heard otherwise.

What was most interesting about Laurie, though, was why she was here in Ramah Navajo land. In her own words, with Bradley sitting next to her, Laurie told me of her family being invaded by a skin-walker, a Navajo witch. It was a gradual assault with late night appearances in smelly hides that cowered their dogs into whimpering and howling. Later, intermittent evening disruptions seeded terror into their hogan. Finally, violence evolved in the act of cutting the hamstrings of Laurie's beloved horse. This was when her family decided on her safety, being more practical in a place like Ramah Navajo, near her boyfriend and his family, who could look after and protect her.

Though my knowledge of skin-walkers comes from early 1970s reservation life, it was there that I learned men and women dressed in animal skins at night and assaulted their victims with threats and fear. Later, I was particularly taken by an insight of Douglas Preston's book, *Talking to The Ground*. Preston hits on the general points of greed and envy being the foundation source for this extreme of Navajo witchcrafts. Death is a binding initiation right in fulfilling this unforgivable contract with evil. To be a skin-walker you must cause the death of someone close to you, maybe not by your hand, but obviously by desire or intent. All of this is eventually inspired by some form of jealousy, or hate, or retribution.

Douglas later resolves in a conversation with Selene, his fiancée's daughter, a simplistic insight I have taken completely to heart with its truth—that the human drive for greed is essentially founded in some form of evil or fear. Not that any of us would ever admit it, but why do we have to have more than we need? Why do we envy those who work hard and achieve? Is it in the impotency we feel that we need to blame on others' successes. These are not his questions; they are mine, and I find that the term evil is often a total surrender to the failure in one's own hopes and aspirations. It is a need to strike out at the world in general with obvious expected results. In short, there is a little skin-walker in all of us, though it is how we prevent the witch from getting out that makes us who we are.

Now that Laurie was with us, her parents were left alone. Laurie was a competitive barrel racer with an exceptional horse and there, finally, was the cause and effect of the curse—jealousy.

She was with us now and safe, and we all cared for her. A year later I would attend her and Bradley's traditional wedding. It was beautiful. Laurie was radiant and happy, and the memory of the witching was apparently fading into the sands of the desert's forgiving memories. Fear is not a product of nature, life is, fear is the incomprehensible reaction to the unknown in a response for survival.

Bradley and Laurie and my future family remained friends for years after my teaching career. Later Bradley was in the Army during Desert Storm. He and his crew were a utility unit, designated to rebuild power lines and restore electricity to Kuwait. That is not what the unit did though, they were reassigned to collect the bodies of the fallen as the Iraqis retreated. This was a major taboo for the Navajo. Bradley paid for a costly medicine healer's cleansing ceremony when he returned to erase the evil stench of death on his soul.

I have always admired these two kids, friends, maybe the episode of the skin-walker was unfortunate and despicable, but it brought two of my favorite people together and again proved the amazing resiliency of my favorite people—the Navajo.

The Christmas Festival

At the Ramah Navajo School in the fall of 1975, all was peaceful, and students were fortunately following the flow of our teacherly ministrations and gratefully there was contentment in the school's halls. In short, we needed some shaking up before the spiders nested in our brains, so I suggested a Christmas festival in the gym for the end of the term. I knew no one in their right mind would take the advice of the crazy, art teacher, wrong.

Everyone including the principal and even the school secretary were enthusiastic and receptive to the whole concept. Great. Now I was the festival chairman. Why do people take me seriously anyway? Anywhoo, everyone got involved. Home economics volunteered with Christmas decorations and streamers. The coaches suggested a basketball toss for student activity games. Others thought of friendly, fun activities such as a cakewalk, pie throwing contest, senior ho, ho, ho Santa contest, and other contributions included a bake sale that would truly pull this seasonal celebration into line.

The art department, meaning me, would contribute an extra-large Christmas pinata, for the smaller children of the school. This would be the final climax of the evening. The Christmas festival took on a life of its own. Everyone was involved, contributing, and excitedly anticipating the blessed event.

I believe the cakewalk and bake sale were preliminary imagined olfactory advertisers to us bachelor teachers. Who would resist sweets at

Christmas time. Seasonal preparations occupied our every minute outside the classroom. I remember another teacher and I traveled to Gallup, trying to collect donations for hard rock candy for the pinata. The generosity of those local store owners was so heartfelt and supportive towards the small school 65 miles away, it truly touched us. Thanks to them we ended up purchasing 120 pounds of hard candy, and all I had to do now was build the pinata large enough and strong enough to contain it all.

This took some design consideration, but eventually I contrived an armature that would support the chicken-wire endoskeleton. The class and I used papier mâché on the exterior of our Christmas horse, which was with wet paper treated with wallpaper paste. After a week of drying, we painted it bright red with green Appaloosa spots. We dubbed it, funky horse, oh well.

Traveling to Albuquerque, I rented ten Santa suits for the school festival from Disco Display on Central Avenue. These suits would adorn our male school board members and a few other of our Native dignitaries. The older gentleman would compete in the ho, ho, ho contest which was gauged to discover the most realistic Navajo Santa laugh. This was the most ridiculous endeavor submitted by an annoying art teacher out of touch with reality. But what are you gonna do?

Finally, the big day came. The gym was strewn with crepe paper, Christmas ornaments, and decorations were everywhere. The entire school staff had done themselves proud—way beyond anyone's expectations. The gym was an explosion of green and red and silver and gold. We had much to be proud of.

The basketball toss was set up on the west hoop side of the court, and the pinata was to be hung on the east side. Some parachute cord was discovered to support the 135-pound, creative monstrosity from the art department. Funky horse hung like the sword of Damocles over all, who trailed under it.

The stage to the east of the court was where the Navajo rock band was set up. They had volunteered to supply musical distractions for the event.

This was also where all ten Santas were set up by a microphone to convey their ho, ho, ho-full utterances.

The cakewalk, of course, was doing a brisk business. Prices were ten to twenty-five cents a turn, depending on the culinary donation. We walked around numbered papered steps, taped down on the floor in a circle, and when the music of an old record was stopped, we stopped on the numbered spot we stood upon. At this point a number was drawn from a jar, and whoever resided on that number won the cake or pie or brownies. Well, you get the idea.

The pie toss was, I believe, a dollar, and the victim volunteers were teachers. One I'm sure was Maureen, the home economics teacher. She took the hit like a champ, though the clean-up was enduring. But she was a professional.

The bake sale was cleaned out of stock nearly as fast as they could set the treats on the table. Parents and kids were hauling in and experiencing this event with much humor and curiosity. This was a first for them. What was all this Santa stuff about anyway?

The entire festival schedule flowed flawlessly. Soon the Santas marched up to the microphone one by one. They then projected their rendition of ho, ho, ho. The band would hit the drum and do a rift between each Santa. Our big winner was of course, Sam, of the school board. With his sense of humor, he was a shoe-in anyway. Everyone, of course, applauded and cheered at the results.

The final event was the small children's pinata. This was for preschoolers and first graders. These students surrounded the pinatas staging area, and one child was chosen to assault the funky horse with the long pole. The band played some kind of prelude, and our chosen one struck the pinata hard. It did not break the first time, but it did knock on a door in my shallow mind's awareness.

Let me see, 125 pounds of hard rock candy falling on one 40-pound native child divided by the inability of a good, intentioned art teacher's common sense carried by the fact that reality isn't forgiving, equals? I sprang to action at lightning speed, I had to. As the next strike to the pinata hit, I heard the paper give way, grabbed up the child, and sidestepped 125-pound rainbow of water falling hard candy. The sound of the candy cascade echoed throughout the gym. Every kid, not just the tiny kiddos, scrambled to the floor to grab as much of this immense bounty of sugar as they could. There was no stopping them. The kid that I luckily had reached in time, was safe and wrestled out of my arms to attack the treats.

That was the end of the evening. The festival had been a blast. My principal was very pleased, and everyone appeared to glow from a really good time. It was the seasonal medicine we all needed as we leaned towards the cold of a winter coming.

There are still nights at home now though, where every so often I wake up in a cold sweat, shaking and mumbling. My wife knows what it is, she's heard it a hundred times before, my PTSD. It is the nightmare that chases me still through those school hallways. In the dream I don't make it in time to prevent the glaring red-eyed pinata. Its evil intent is prepared for my expected lunge and interrupts the clock by half a second. The new results are horrifying to behold. The Navajo Police see this drastic catastrophe, approach me promptly, and throw the cuffs on me. They inform me of my rights in Navajo and drag me to their squad car. Realizing this offense is so heinous for the local lockup, the police drive me to Gallup to the big house for arrest and confinement. When we arrive, I am taken to the desk sergeant and then I am fingerprinted. Later, when the judge asks the charges held against me, it is always, always, always the same. You are being charged with the use of a pinata as a deadly weapon.

Ammo Boxes

It is a well-known fact that many of the older residences of Ramah, built by the Mormons, were constructed from World War II and Korean War ammo boxes. The buildings, of course, are dated after those two conflicts. Fort Wingate either gave away or sold these boxes so cheaply, that they became building gold for struggling young families.

There were plenty of rough timber sawmills on and off operation, but free access to the lumber, offered post war by the government, couldn't be beat. It must be noted—plywood was also not an available solution either at this time. New Mexico was poor, so any structure you could nail together, and later paper, and wire, and then stucco, was as top of the line as almost any home in the state could be.

In 1976, my then future wife moved in with Ron and me since housing was so dear and inaccessible. Before the wedding, I worked on shaping up the guest room as a surprise for our bridal suite. I carved out the cracks in the plaster from the ceiling to the floor. Some cracks I also taped over because of their depth. I even plastered all the cracks around the window no matter how small. Next, I prime coated the room with the first coat of paint. The cracks were nearly unrecognizable afterward. After the second coat of paint, they were nearly invisible, and the room was perfect. I repaired a faulty light switch, a few other minor annoyances, and the room was ready for occupancy.

The wedding was in Santa Fe at the Catholic Cathedral's Conquistadora Chapel, and the couple's photo shoot was at the Santa Fe bowling alley, which is now the location of Meow Wolf. In the 1970s it was the hottest ticket in town. Later, after the insanity of this giant step in nuptials had sunk in, we made our way three hours back to Ramah.

Returning home I proudly displayed the bridal accommodations I had prepared. Excited, exhausted and not sober at all, we fell into our nest of wedded bliss. We had done it; we were hitched. Soon sleep sent us off to dreamlands of rest and repose, lost to the world.

Something was shaking me. Was something wrong? I didn't understand. Coming out of my deeply, restful stupor, I was finally aware that the room itself was shaking. Together, my new wife and I were experiencing a rare Ramah earthquake. Hell, I didn't know New Mexico was ever subject to them, but then thinking about it, I realized this was the western side of the state and only one state away from California. The quake was actually short, but the surprise of it felt like an hour.

The next morning, we awoke to a beautiful day with birds chirping and the sun shining.

I opened my eyes and surveyed the bedroom. Every single crack I had patched was wide open again, every repair I had managed to rehabilitate was now yawning awake as if to say, good morning, miss us. The only difference was now with the fresh paint everything was much more blatantly obvious. I was mortified and newly married.

Alas, the marriage did not evolve into the mutual understanding and unconditional affection which is referenced and insinuated by romantic novels. Within six months we called it quits. At the end of the school year, we went our separate ways.

I never experienced before or after, another earthquake in Ramah ever again. What are the chances of coming home after the wedding vows and the ceremony are completed and settling down to the one night that an earthquake occurs? What are the odds? It does unnerve one, doesn't it?

There was no earthquake on my second wedding, and my wife and I are still together almost fifty years.

BLOOD SAUSAGE

In the spring of 1975, we teachers were invited to a day of a major cultural event—the making of blood sausage. Now if you are squeamish of live sacrifice, bloodletting, and disembowelment, that's too bad. If I had to stand and watch it, you can at least sit and read about it. This sausage was historically a principle component of the Navajo diet, especially in winter.

Katie Henio was our sheep's executor. She was also our traditional master of ceremonies at this event and thanks to one of our student translators, her granddaughter, we were able to follow every bloody detail.

One must keep in mind this demonstration of Navajo food processing most likely preserved the sustenance of this tribe throughout the last three hundred years. Sheep fulfilled the blessing of nourishment to a nomadic people competing with so many others for survival. Blood sausage was an ingenious utilization of the least of the animals' flesh food sources. It realized a maximum benefit through the sheep's raw blood alone. In addition, this sausage would stay throughout the cold season and get many a family through hard times.

Katie said a little prayer, and with one quick stroke of her incredibly sharp knife, she cut the throat of a sheep. She had done this before. The sheep's head was placed over a large enamel bowl and every drop of blood was collected to the last.

The carcass was then tied at the hind legs with a rope, and the body was raised with the assistance of a large branch of a pinion tree to an even level with Katie and her knife. This being done, Katie now starts with her knife from the genitals to make an incision clear down through the abdominal cavity to the chest cavity. With this cut the warm organs started tumbling out and were captured in a very large bucket. Katie now sorted through these internal organs searching for the large intestines, which she takes and cuts and squeezes out the internal bodily residue. With this completed she sticks the lengthy organ into a bucket of clear water to clean and soak.

By this time she asked if anyone wanted to take a lunch break. Funny, there were no takers, so Katie continued with the demonstration.

It must be noted; at this point, Cooper and Orlando, Ramah Navajo High School students were filming VHS this entire demonstration. They were getting wonderful close-ups of everything, including the disembowelment. The brothers were a major asset to our film department, I mean audio visual department. Also, at home they were still trying to organize a Native rock band.

Now the true culinary suspense was about to begin. Katie took the huge bowl of raw sheep's blood to a table, and she proceeded to add generous heapings of ground corn or maza to it. Then stopping, she walked outside and collected wild sage from the bushes. Bringing this sage collection back inside, she added it to the mix. Roughly and slowly Katie integrated these three ingredients into a developing large amount of sausage filler. Now, after wiping off her hands, she went to the bucket with the large intestine soaking. Here she gently grabbed the large intestine and making a clean cut, she rinsed and raised two large sections of the organ. Now we were in business. Taking the intestines to the bowl on the table, Katie started stuffing the intestine with sausage mix. You'd be surprised how far that intestinal tissue can stretch. With a knot tied at one end, these sausages were becoming the size of large salamis. When the desired length was reached, another cut was made, and another knot became the finishing touch, voila.

With her demonstration complete, Katie, a traditional Navajo by all accounts, decided it was time for a history lesson or sermon; I could never tell the difference; and she explained the origins of the gift of traditional sheepherding. Staring at us White Eyes, directly, in an intimidating way, which is strange coming from a Navajo, Katie decided it was time to straighten out our preconceptions of how the great spirit provided the Dine, with the first sheep.

Now we backward-leaning white teachers just assumed the Navajo warriors stole the sheep along with slaves, corn, various crops, horses, turkeys and anything else they could get their hands on just to get their wives to stop badgering them when they got home. "No," said Katie, "The great spirit gave sheep to us." All this was in Navajo, so it sounded really great. She continued for quite a while longer to straighten us know-nothings out, and finally, being no spring chicken herself, she indicated that the daylong seminar was over, woosh.

I must confess that to this day I have never had a slice of blood sausage. They just don't sell it at Trader Joe's, and I'm not saying I wouldn't try it if I could, I'm also not saying I would. No one in this lifetime though, can deny I know how to make it. You see, Cooper and Orlando bootlegged some copies of the VHS recordings. So, you guessed it, if you have an old VHS player still working, I know where we can get you a copy; and in four- and one-half hours of viewing you too can have the secret recipe of the Navajo blood sausage—Ciao.

Hopi Bean Dances

An opportunity arrived at my doorstep one night in the persons of two dear friends, Bob and Kasha. They were passing through in February on a Friday evening and asked if I would be interested in attending the Bean Dances in Hopi with them. I thought about it, remembering my friend's Tom Cummings' experience, and decided, why not? Tom was still with us, and what's the worst that could happen? With my friend's bedded down for the night, after we had finalized details, we planned to leave the next morning.

As many know, Hopi is locked smack dab in the middle of the Navajo reservation near the Four Corners. No wonder they are so leery of outsiders; they probably always feel under siege. The Hopi Pueblo is primarily located on three high mesas with magnificent views of the desert horizons. The fortress-like safety of the mesa top Pueblos feels ancient and otherworldly beyond words. The buildings are all stone and adobe structures with flat dirt roofs supported by vegas. Everything is brown and beige in color and appears to have just freshly grown out of the earth itself.

My friend Bob told me I had an admirer in Hopi, and his name was Delbridge. He was a hunched back of the Bear Clan and possessed one of my bear bolos. He loved the bolo and wanted to meet me. It seems, not only was Delbridge of the Hopi Bear Clan, but he was also a famous Kachina carver. When I found out Bob had given Delbridge the bolo I had carved, I looked forward to meeting this representative of the bears of Hopi.

We arrived at lunch at the Hopi Welcome Center, a motel/cafe combination, and we checked in and then had lunch. Delbridge soon met us and filled us in on the ongoing schedule of events for the bean dances. I liked Delbridge immediately; he had spunk and courage considering his handicap and was enthusiasm incarnate. With his instructions we proceeded to the plaza after lunch and searched for the famous pottery makers, whose wares were the most expensive of any tribe. This was due to their subtle beauty and rarity. Hopi pots, for me, are the Tiffany of this art form in all the Pueblos.

Eventually, we discovered small pots, displayed on a towel outside a woman's mesa rowhouse. After knocking on her door, we engaged with her in a little bargaining. I had enough money to make two small purchases, which I still have to this day.

At exactly the moment we completed our purchases and standing satisfied with ourselves, there was a disturbance to our left. Oh, God. There was a kiva ten feet away, and we were never even aware of it. The only giveaway was the top of a ladder poking out. Suddenly, outpoured Kachinas of every kind, preparing for the festival. Of course, one of them was a Bee Kachina, and he buzzed straight for me.

This Kachina displayed two yucca whips, which he started walloping me with. Hell, what did I do? I didn't know your hive was here. I just bought some pots, probably from your mother. He wasn't having any of it. He whipped me till I moved a further respectable distance from the kiva. The pain of the whips was more humiliation than anything. Even so, I felt officially initiated into the dumb, white guy society of Hopi, if there was one.

Later, we had dinner and rested in our motel room until a loud knock came to the door. It was Delbridge and a small crowd of young men. Then they all asked for cocktails. Now I know booze is forbidden in Hopi, and yet here was a line of dressed dancers with Delbridge expecting happy hour. In surprise, I watched Bob pull out a bottle of whiskey from his suitcase, and with the plastic cups provided by the motel and some cold cans of Sprite from the outside vending machine, he started pouring drinks for the boys. It was quite a sight in all their regalia of colors of the rainbow. Bob and Delbridge, of course, had this planned in advance, and I'm sure this got us into the kiva an hour later. We were the only white eyes seated amongst only Hopi women. This was odd, huh.

The air inside the kiva was stifling. Keep in mind it was a cold February night. With a wood stove cranking in the corner of the kiva and a horde of bodies surrounding the central dance floor, the temperature was unbearable. Too bad, that is the price of the ticket to attend this soiree.

The dancers started appearing at midnight, climbing down the central ladder onto the dance floor below, the area amongst the audience. All was pitch black and the only light was from kerosene lanterns surrounding the dance floor. There were three sets of dances, and there were lengthy pauses in between. The concept of time evaporates before your very eyes in this claustrophobic situation. It was the last set of dances though, that threw me into the twilight zone.

Down came a line of women dressed in raincoats, house coats, galoshes, umbrellas, and very bad hair, shouting out shrill things in Hopi to the women in the audience. There was chuckling at first and then downright laughter as the women dancers circled the ladder and shouted out statements of preponderance as alien to me as Mars.

A Hopi woman next to me, pitying my hopelessness, explained, "Those ain't women, they're our husbands, and they've been saving our gossip all year for this dance."

I couldn't help myself, I burst out laughing. Fortunately, it was swallowed up by the women's own blatant revelry.

Finally, the kiva dances ended, and we all exited into an early dawn on the mesa. We were hot from the kiva's engagement, but the air temperature was freezing. This now was the tricky part of our adventure; we had to hide 'til full sunup. Everyone else was behind doors with their cozy warm stoves and adobe abodes. We needed seclusion quick because the Kachinas were coming.

These Kachinas were here to visit the children of the Pueblo at their doors. If you were good, a Kachina carving, or some other gift would be left at your door. If you were bad, there was a hard loud knock on your door, and you would have to open it and face the music. Trust me, I've seen those Kachinas, and being good would be on my dance card. With luck hiding behind corners, we kept moving every time we eyed a Kachina. Soon the sun rose fully, and now people started arriving in the plaza. They climbed to the rooftops to get the best view of the upcoming dances.

With the sun warming our bodies, we were hungry but content. At this point we had been awake twenty-four hours, so you had to expect a little giddiness was also setting in. At the entrance of the plaza, rows of dancers started marching in of every variety of color in the rainbow. The phenomenal contrast of these dancers against a gloomy, dirt-painted landscape was incomprehensibly beautiful. The image is, to this day, still burned into my memory like a brand I would never forget.

But of course, this wouldn't be my last enduring memory of this Hopi event, oh no. While I was standing on the roof observing the ceremony, the same Bee Kachina that had already whipped me the day before, showed up beneath us, and made threatening gestures towards me again. Now what had I done? He continued his threats until a Hopi woman out of pity told me, he doesn't like you having your hat on. Now I'd been wearing my black Stetson since I got here, and most people were wearing hats. It was cold, but this busy bee needed mine off in a sign of respect, so I removed my hat. But no, he had to make sure I learned my lesson by climbing up and whipping me a few more times for luck. Maybe I should have bought more pots from his mother, who knows.

As early afternoon set in, we were done. Everyone could now expect a good bean planting and harvest. A fresh new world was now set to rights. Slowly, we trudged back to our car to make the long drive back home. We would take turns driving and sleeping as well.

I wondered about that Bee Kachina. How did he keep finding me and what was his beef anyway? Then I thought about my ole buddy Tom

Cummings, he had contacts in Hopi. Maybe I should have given him that twenty bucks I owed him before I left. Huh, what do you think?

Japan and Sweden Go West

With the opening of the new school in the fall of 1975, there was much interest in this new educational institution. At this time, the school was one of two independently established contract Indigenous schools in the United States. We were the model of a new endeavor to release Native Americans from the iconic grasp of the Bureau of Indian affairs. There would be checks and balances to align with educational standards, but the day-to-day operations and supervision of our school would be that of Ramah Navajo.

There was interest in this newfound movement of unusual educational opportunity that attracted the attention of other countries, who were contending with their Native minorities that were slipping through the cracks of opportunity. Two of these representatives who visited our school of foreign inquiry were from the nations of Japan and Sweden. They had traveled to observe us.

I knew these two educational professionals, representing their country's interest, because Ron and I had the sole guest room available to them. Both of these individuals were women, and both spoke nearly flawless English. These women were impressive educators who were obviously wholeheartedly concerned with the difficulties their minority populations were suffering.

The dilemma for our Swedish representative, who visited first, concerned the Laplanders of northern Scandinavia. The Swedes struggled to introduce educational opportunities to these nomadic reindeer herders. Navajos also were a nomadic people, and our new Scandinavian friend was exploring the options of Native education, supported but not controlled by a nation's government. After staying a few days and garnishing as much data as she could find appropriate, our Swedish visitor wished us well and returned east to the Northland of Europe.

Some months later, the second touring visitor arrived. She was sent by a delegation of Indigenous Island educational factions, who were Japanese citizens but ethnically were island minorities closer to Polynesian descent than Oriental. These Japanese island people were not in the same circumstance as the truly nomadic Lapps. Their difficulties were simply race oriented by a narrow-minded Japanese majority.

Ron and I liked this woman. It was apparent she was going to help these outcasts of Japan one way or another. She was driven by a great heart. This was an admirable individual of any nation.

I had prepared evening meals for both ladies as best I could with the limited grocery options the Village of Ramah possessed. Each representative had the small guest bedroom with the double bed and Spartan facilities. This was the reservation of the 1970s after all.

The only fly in the ointment was with our guest from Japan. She would rise awake from her room looking exhausted and troubled. This prompted concern from us and inquiries as to her sleep, but she never complained and said everything was just fine.

Two weeks later after her departure, I went into the guest bedroom and stared in horror. Our courteous guest had stripped the bed of its sheets and left them at the foot of the bed for washing. It was then that I realized the mattress was missing. You see, all our mattresses came from surplus trailer stock, and they were not much more than three inches deep. Sometime between Sweden and Japan, I had removed the mattress from the guest room and placed it on top of my own bed's three-inch mattress to have a pretend mattress of six inches. Never did it occur to me for a single moment that the guest room possessed a bed of box springs only. I was mortified. That gracious Japanese woman never once made a comment of her discomfiture. She simply accepted it.

No matter how you describe the term grace, that wonderful lady proved to me, that again, like the Tin Man, I was still in need of a brain.

Outlaw Country

A section of land is a square mile. Sections are designated on county and sometimes even state maps. When sections are divided up between BLM, railroad, private, state, federal, Indian land, and other interest this confusing mass is called a checkerboard.

Checkerboards are impossible to police due to jurisdiction. What property is enforceable under the law and where, what is Indian land, what is private, and what is government? Sheriffs wash their hands of these territories that is if there is a sheriff anywhere around. As a result, this is the perfect formula for the sheltering of illegal activities if not for outlaws themselves to hide out in.

Rumors of Billy the Kid, living out his life as the alias John Miller and even Clyde Barrow, before the infamous Bonnie and Clyde, supposedly found sanctuary between and with the Navajos and Zuni. The checkerboard which divides the Ramah Navajo from the Zuni Reservation is covered with every inconceivable outside interest, squared off in a sectioned maze of confusion that no law man in his right mind would ever contend with.

There was once an army stockade bordering the two reservations, trying to avert what would become a hundred-year-old blood feud between the Zuni and Navajo, but eventually, the US government had enough and pulled the army out of this endless quagmire. So self-policing became the norm until the BIA helped institute local tribal police. At least the reservations had some enforcement.

From 1920 to 1933 prohibition was the law under the eighteenth amendment. This law made checkerboards prime real estate for moonshine production. Not far from where the old stockade was dividing Zuni from the Navajo, was a large hogan and some very unsavory characters ran a successful still. It produced, some say, the finest white lightning this side of the state. The location of this site was named Candy Kitchen. Candy kitchen, you're thinking, really? I kid you not, it appears these unsavory characters were quite clever as well in the deception of their prime industry. When the government revenuers showed up in the village of Ramah, the locals would send a kid on horseback through a back road to Candy Kitchen called Five Gates. Sure enough, the kid would have to stop and clear five gates to get to his destination. Once warned, the hogans' occupants had enough time, thanks to the revenuers having to use the main reservation road, to remove the still to a large hidey hole, they then replaced it with a stove, heated up with wood, and prepared a batch of their also well-known pinon candy. It was the best anyone ever had. The government men would show up as expected, and after a casual preliminary search of a rumor of an illegal still in the vicinity, would then sit down to sampling the latest new candy product straight from the oven.

The candy makers would of course have some of their product bagged up for the officers' families to compensate them for their fruitless venture doing the government's work. After all they were just doing their jobs. For the next twenty years, this still probably continued to operate since Indians couldn't legally drink until 1953. There were no more candies produced, but the area's name stuck—Candy Kitchen.

Later the state would institute a voluntary, petitioned sheriff for communities desiring some law even if it had to come from their direct intercession. If they elected one of their own neighbors and paid him a dollar per term, that individual could act as their sheriff with a tin badge to boot.

One such volunteer sheriff in Candy Kitchen was a man by the name of, and I kid you not, Rusty Crooks. Now Rusty did a damn good job, but I wonder if his last name kept the bad guys away, figuring he was legal competition. There's just no telling the criminal mind.

This area now is still and will probably always be this notorious checkerboard, and I am certain outlaws of some sort are still hiding out there. All in all, things have quieted down, and the population is reflective of a large minority of America in that they are annoying and blame the government for everything, you know, just normal.

THE ROUGH RIDERS

In the 1970s there was an epidemic that spread like wildfire across the Navajo reservation and, to be honest, probably throughout all reservations in New Mexico and the remaining US. The severity of this malady had no foundation in modern medicine much less a history. No doctor, scientist, therapist, or any other professional had explanations that would illuminate or even insinuate some reasoning for this traumatic viral experience 1970s Indians were succumbing to.

There were no ifs, ands, or buts about it, the American pickup truck had enslaved Native minds. This was one that monkey truck junkies were quite willing to live with. How many souls did Ford or Chevrolet trade for those four-wheel drive wonders, we'll never know.

Anyway, one such victim was a new elementary school teacher at the Ramah Navajo School named Verylis. She had newly arrived and was a pleasant looking, hard worker that we all liked. Verylis was funny and a team player all around. She was from somewhere near Coyote Canyon on the main reservation and found working with us suited her to a tee. I don't think she wanted to be too near to her relatives. Obviously, Verylis was a free spirit and needed to spread her wings.

Everything seemed to be going fine with her until her birthday—a Friday in early October. Like the rest of us she picked up her paycheck since it was payday and took off for Gallup with some friends. On Monday morning Verylis was different though; she was more confident even cocky and assertive than before. What had happened?

At the end of the day, we all suddenly knew what happened as Verylis pulled up to a group of us teachers, driving a brand new, shiny gold-tone, four-wheel drive Chevy pickup truck. Maybe it was me, but I swear, looking at it I heard trumpets. It must have been the astonishment of a similarity to the chariot of Apollo that Chevrolet was interdimensionally inspired by. In short, the truck was really pretty if you know what I mean.

It was apparent though that Verylis had bought more than a truck. There was something else, I just couldn't put my finger on it.

Nada was an office assistant at the Pine Hill School of the Ramah Navajo. She must have been nineteen or twenty years old, and she and Verylis became friends. Well, I think she was a friend and not just because of a hot gold-tinted Chevy pickup that she couldn't take her eyes off, but what do I know. Anyway, this duo became a team, and on the weekends they drove that gold beauty all over the main Navajo reservation.

Were they visiting friends, were they collecting pinon, no one knows? All we knew was come Monday morning these two young ladies would show up for work looking like they hadn't slept in days. These two girls were beat-up weary. In a few days though they were good as new, and everything was back to normal. Their cheery dispositions returned, but when Friday returned, like a shooting star, they were quickly gone from sight again. This routine, you wouldn't believe, continued for a full year. No one could intercede, no advice was ever invited, and it was obvious Verylis and Nada were Chevy pickup 'Riders of the Purple Sage"—the western roads owned their souls.

Eventually, as time passed the shiny gold on the truck's body took on a flat brassy look like a very old hooker, who would never get those youthful hair color highlights back again. A few minor dings and dirt also added to this poor Chevy's beast-driven looks. Time and wear and tear were eating away at the pickup dream, and Verylis and Nada were showing it also. On and on they went like dust devils with no direction or intent, just spinning through existence.

By the end of a year from the original purchase date, Verylis and Nada had reeled up 100,000 miles on a speedometer ready to spring from the dash. The gold paint, having been sand blasted through storms on the reservation, was nothing close to that original gold color—now burnt tan was more like it. The girls had gained weight, their eyes were puffy, and their once youthful exuberance was now a vague memory in the past. These girls were tired beyond words. The only thing that could save them was getting any kind of trade-in on a 100,000-mile abused truck. I don't know what happened at the dealership in Gallup. I don't want to know, but on Monday morning Verylis showed up in a used baby blue Nova.

Okay, it's not a truck, but sometimes in life Mr. Right isn't always Mr. Right, and after a year of a golden romance showing him off to all your friends, driving him, having fun with his flashy promises, you become aware of that nagging voice in the back of your head that says this isn't going to last. You now need to think about a dependable regular car. Something that will always be there for you. It may not be flashy, but it will always be there. You need to think about a Nova.

Surprise Party At Pedro's

The greatest thing to occur every two weeks for a Pine Hill schoolteacher was, of course, payday. Friday, at the end of class, you jumped in your car and ran down to Mr. Lewis's at the trading post in Ramah. Here you paid any charges you'd accrued within the last couple of weeks, and then Mr. Lewis would cash your check and pay you the balance. Next, you'd hop back in your car and drive off to Gallup. Your first stop in town was Pedro's, absolutely, where chile rellenos and margaritas and cold cervezas awaited you. It took fourteen days to get here, but here you were.

One Friday night several teachers had agreed to meet at our favorite place at six o'clock. We'd had an especially tough week, moving into the new school, getting organized, and running classes as well. We really needed a break at Pedro's; we needed to celebrate.

Arriving at Pedro's early I proceeded to engage Pedro, himself, into helping get some tables reserved for us. While doing so I found another table already organized of teachers from Zuni. Shyly, I introduced myself and revealed that our own group of teachers would be joining me soon. Then I asked—would they like to join us as one very long table.

They smiled, hesitated, then said, "Yes, why not." So that is what we did.

Other Ramah Navajo teachers started staggering in within minutes. There was an immediate joyous celebration as the relief and tension of the week was shed in the shadow of exhaustion. We all certainly knew; teaching was hard work.

As margaritas were ordered and dinners were expected, we bantered with our somewhat reserved table partners from Zuni. We did learn many things about teaching at Zuni that was contrary to our own school system. First off, Zuni teachers were paid once a month, which was tough. Secondly, at this time, they were still tied to the BIA and used an Albuquerque Public Schools' schedule. All this meant nothing if Zuni, like a lot of Pueblos, also scheduled their own holidays and festivals, which could also change year to year. Scheduling disruptions were the norm there, and these teachers just had to deal with it. Zuni teachers, it turns out, did not get paid as well as we did either. This was another discrepancy in our tribal organizations.

Then the Zuni teachers also complained of nepotism, interfering with promotions in the school system itself. This is when I reminded them the foundation of the word nepotism was seated in tribalism, and why was that a surprise? We then shared more comparisons in employment systems. During this time my intuition played on the fact these teachers were either afraid of us or jealous. I couldn't tell which, but there was a gulf they were not willing to cross in newfound friendship.

What finally occurred to me was these Zuni teachers knew we worked for the Navajos, and they, through some kind of socialized osmosis, were associating us as this counter tribal culture. In essence, to them we were Navajos.

Now the truth was we were all of us a mix of whities from all over the nation. No two of us came from the same state. We were as diverse in backgrounds and education as you could be. But for some reason there was a divide that couldn't be reckoned with.

Suddenly it occurred to me, Zuni was an Apollonian culture, an anthropological term meaning city dweller or Pueblo. Navajos were Dionysian, nomadic hunter gatherers. Though many things have changed, these two cultural distinctions still played a precedent in their definitive societies. They were opposites, and that was who they were.

We teachers of the Ramah Navajo enjoyed great freedom. We were not restricted to the dictates of a Pueblo in their isolation and confinement. We were free agents like the Navajo. It was only natural we would assimilate to our employer's culture while we worked under the roof of their hogan. They were now our people.

Now I understood the Zuni teacher's hesitancy. They were Zunis not by blood but by association and tribal routine. They had assimilated as survival to the ways of their host. They were Zuni teachers.

After the dinner the party broke up, and we all went our separate ways to gas fill ups and grocery shopping. I pondered on the drive home. Were there really two kinds of societies distinctly—ranchers and farmers opposed to city people? Dionysian versus Apollonian? Were these two sides of human nature necessary to bond our society as one? Maybe it is the friction between these two sociological opposites that makes human life so interesting.

Devil's Highway

Route 666 was created in 1926 and was decommissioned in 2003. Just as the original Route 666, Route 491 traveled from south in Gallup and continued north to Cortez, Colorado. The varied names the old timers gave to Route 666 included highway to hell, Satan's highway, beast highway, and, of course, the simplified was Devil's Highway. All have no bearings on the regions it passed through—the rugged desert and sheep country, I believe everyone just loved the hellish connotation of the number 666. It was pretty hard to avoid the signs. Why even Damien of "The Omen" had 666 tattooed in his scalp. He was most definitely a fan.

Is it no wonder legends grew from this highway's inception in 1926. The ghost of the girl in the white dress, who would wander onto the road and then disappears before their very eyes if drivers stopped to assist her. This is just one of many such stories. The witnessing of Navajo Skin Walkers has been also claimed by lonely drivers late at night. This actually feels more plausible since getting a ride anywhere on the reservation is hard enough. I couldn't blame a Skin Walker for trying.

Who, anyway, had the audacity to create a 666-highway road sign designation in 1926. Was it a wannabe comedian or some redneck engineer who had a beef with the Indians? Let's be honest, this highway was positioned to cut right through Navajo reservation land and on through to the Utes in Colorado.

On this route there were stops like Yah Ta Hay, Twin Lakes, Tohatchi, Buffalo springs, and Naschitti—all the way north to Shiprock and beyond. All the locations were cursed with the Devil's Highway, cutting through their communities. No wonder the Nazarenes loved this country, and Gallup was the end of the line for them to proselytize—the cherry on the top.

The original name of this land route, before the highway department's 666 number fiasco, was The Navajo Trail. Another oddity to add to the puzzle was the fact that nationwide even number signs were always intended to be east-west not north-south. This bears significant noting. I don't care what the highway department says. In 2003, 666 was finally changed to 491. It only took seventy-seven years to take the devil's horns off Gallup and Navajo country finally.

On old 666 there were quite a few Friday nights after a great meal at Pedro's that friends would join me for a sojourn up to Tohatchi Hot Springs north of Gallup. Of course, there would be hot springs on the Devil's Highway. What would you expect, a popsicle factory?

The springs were not deep, but they were relaxing. After a few drinks, a full tummy, and forgetting a hard couple of weeks of teaching, it was just what the doctor ordered. Afterward, the drive home would be quiet except for occasionally the Devil's advocates appearing—sometimes in the hundreds, red-eyed sheep got loose on the highway and awaited you. One had to be especially alert of this evil in manifest. Then to boot you could fall asleep waiting for them to clear off the road. In the end, we would continue along and arrive home having escaped the Devil one more time.

Highways statistics average the number of deaths on old historic Route 666 to have been much, much lower then than later with this conversion to Route 491, surprising? Was it the connotation of the repetitive 666 signs reminding you whose highway you were on that possibly inspired your alertness to the consequences of falling asleep at the wheel? Was it the suspicion of those furry white agents of the Devil wandering on to the road around the next corner preparing the surprise of your life? Maybe it was another drunk Skin Walker trying to bum a ride, who can say.

I know the Devil is a busy manager of hell, but come on, when the highway department dedicates a significant byway to you, you're going to proudly take notice. So, when that numeric sign designation changed to Route 491 from 666, why should you give a damn anymore? Hell, I wouldn't waste my time, would you, talk about an insult.

BEETHOVEN'S FIFTH

The Milky Way at 7,000 feet elevation in New Mexico is a phenomenal sight to behold. Winter is its time, and the chilled crispness of late evening only enhances the experience. The waves of endless stars humble and beguiles the human soul in its symphony of galactic innuendos, never endingly beautiful. It is quite an uplifting inspiration and certainly meant to be shared.

So on evenings like this, especially after a snowstorm, I would trudge through the snow and place a single chair in the little field west of our house, and then I'd return and turn up the stereo as high as I wanted after placing Mueller or Bach or Mozart on the record player. Following this, I would grab a bottle of B&B and the snifter and march back to my chair encased in the snow in the starlight field.

Socrates, my dog, would be out on the porch. He would sit by his steepled old doghouse I built with painted stars and moons of old scrap wood I'd scrounged from the neighborhood. He loved these rare evenings, where we'd share our abundant appreciation of the classics. But he was not a Beethoven man himself. I never ever could understand that, oh well.

The Brandy-liquor would make the frigid ordeal nearly unnoticeable. Only my cold, revealing breath gave the moment away. No problem, the music would warm my soul; my body would catch up.

The stars seemed to play a symphony of their own within their own sparkling infinity. How many were there? Billions? Trillions? God zillions? Who cared? I'm just glad they didn't mind me and my dog's meager attendance. Their performance far exceeded any cosmic concept of their devastating beauty that our little minds could ever appreciate, and yet they allowed our participation anyway. God, the stars were great.

As the stereo played on, I heard a distant click from the house and anticipated with bated breath the first chords of Beethoven's 5th. I knew what this meant, I was ready for it, this was always the evening's prime entertainment. No one other than I in the whole of the modern world had ever witnessed the enthralling and devastatingly, tragic rendition of da da da dah as howled by Socrates the great. What did he ever have against Beethoven anyway? He would howl and howl and howl and howl until I lifted myself up from my snow throne. Slowly, inebriated, amused and flabbergasted, I would march to the house, tramped to the stereo, and end his persecuted ordeal. What did Beethoven ever do to you? I guess I'll never know. Maybe somewhere in the past long ago a critic of a young Austrian composer didn't appreciate the brilliance of music's future genius and wrote an opinion too critical for his unique, aesthetic sensibilities.

Was Socrates this critic from another era, now endowed with all the charms of a canine?

Who knows, life is too bizarre to discount any and all possibilities. All I know is that any dog who chose this particular composer among the hundreds throughout history, must have some kind of bone to pick.

BANDITOS

Bang. Bang. Pause, Bang. Bang. Bang. Frantically waking from a deep sleep I sat up. Bang. Bang Bang. Somehow in a daze I sprang from my bed and dressed in my birthday suit, realized what I'd heard wasn't gunshots. Suddenly I became aware the kitchen door was the object of my distress. Someone was there banging at one o'clock in the morning, and with dreadful apprehension I approached and addressed the door, "Yes?"

"Andy, it's Leo Montoyo, Louie's brother from Santa Rosa. How are you, can you let us in?"

Now awakening to the fact that I was naked, I said, "Give me a sec." Running to the bedroom I pulled on my lime green and pink kaftan and went and opened the kitchen door off the driveway. There stood Leo, now tall with black shoulder length hair, and with him was a skinny blonde and a shorter slender Hispanic fellow holding a closed pillowcase.

I invited them in, and my roommate Ron had also awoken, so I introduced him to Leo. Leo made intros to his two companions. Then Ron asked out of curiosity, "What's in the pillowcase?"

Leon's friend Sal said, "Take a look." He opened the bag and at the bottom was a sidewinder, which now nearly catapulted from the bag when it saw the opening.

Leo's older brother was Louie Montoyo. He was an undergraduate when I was a graduate student at New Mexico Highlands University. I had fit the stereotype of the rich blonde Anglo to Louie when he first met me. I had also traveled to Europe and obviously was not worth his time. But we were ensconced in the ceramics and sculpture departments, and there would be no way for him to avoid me.

As time passed Louie became aware that I'd only enough tuition money (saved from painting houses in Baltimore) to get through two quarters of the four quarters it would take me to achieve my Master of Arts. He also soon discovered I was illegally sleeping on the floor in my uncle's old 1938 army sleeping bag in my university designated studio under the student union building. So no, I was no rich kid.

Eventually Louie and his girlfriend, Sombra, and I made peace, and we became fast friends. Racial tension was still in the air following the previous years of La Raza demonstrations, but Great Society was dying, and the movements flames were now smoldering.

Somehow Sombra became aware I was on food stamps like everyone else, and our camaraderie in poverty bonded us further than anything else. She proposed we pool our stamps, and with their purchase power we could buy more. As a result Sombra kept a huge pot of Pinto beans on a low flame all the waking hours of the day. With flour tortillas this was the fuel that sustained us throughout the school year. Occasionally, if there was a sale on chicken wings or necks we would add them as a side. Thanks to Louie and Sombra and an unexpected graduate assistantship in art history, I was able to complete my MA.

Now the snake was not out of the bag and Ron calmed down and responded amiably to these Santa Rosa friends of mine. Leo said through the Montoyo grapevine he had discovered I was living in Ramah teaching and decided a visit was due. Well this sounded like a fine idea, but somehow it felt like there were suspicious details lagging behind this explanation. Anyway, it was two o'clock now, so after setting up sleeping arrangements for our guests, I crawled back into bed before the next day's classes.

After bidding my friends goodbye the next morning, it was off to school. Worrying about trusting them with the house or possessions was really ludicrous, what did two hungry teachers have to steal anyway? The day flew by, classes went well, students appeared happy.

Arriving home I found our guests relaxing and recovered from their late-night sojourn. I prepared all of us a great platter of basil pesto and we sat down to eat. Leo caught me up on the Montoyo clan and eventually, brazenly revealed that he and Sal had broken through the skylight of a coin shop in Albuquerque and relieved the store of some of its excess silver specie. Afterward, in a flash of brilliance, Leo had decided to visit his older brother's friend, Andy, living on the western side of the state until things cooled off in Albuquerque.

Now I am not a perfect person, but I had never harbored criminals before. This was all new to me, how does one act in regard? So after careful consideration of the situation, I responded, "Really?"

Now during the day with the house to themselves, my friends nosed around and discovered a couple of new painted, carved wooden panels I had stacked to take to my new consignment gallery in Santa Fe. Leo and his girlfriend had somehow become attached to "Kiowa Mother and Papoose," a round panel with a 36" diameter. I thanked them for their appreciation, but they then asked the price.

"Two hundred dollars," I said and figured that would end the subject, but no such luck.

Leo stepped outside to their car and returned with an extra-large coffee can with some heft. He said, "Open it."

I removed the lid of the can, and it was packed solid with silver coins, half dollars, quarters and dimes. Doing the math in my head of ten pounds of silver at three dollars an ounce, I appraised the value of the can to be within five hundred dollars. What could I say? "Are You sure?"

Leo gave me a big old hug and said, "Now I have a great work of art by Andy Shows."

I was touched, keeping in mind it would be far better for an art teacher who also taught silversmithing to eventually melt this evidence on a distant reservation than being caught with it back in Albuquerque.

After packing the art into the back of their car and exchanging salutations and goodbyes, Leo and his crew drove off into the sunset. I've never seen him again in this lifetime.

That silver served me quite well. I learned to tufa cast with it and was able to create a line of work which I sold to a museum gift shop in Albuquerque. All my future silver casting endeavors were thanks to Leo's generosity.

In the fall of 1972, Louie and Sombra took me to Santa Rosa to meet friends and family. Later, we dropped Sombra off to her family's house, and Louie, driving his old Chevy Bel Air, which ran on the grace of God almighty, took me to his family's abode. I met his father and mother, neither spoke English. I used what pigeon Spanish I had picked up in Vegas, and both of them gave me hugs. His brothers and sisters were all over the house. They all welcomed me, and I was part of the family at once. That night, Louie and Sombra took me to visit their friends at a small farm. It was communal, and a meal was soon served from a fresh picked harvest. The food was benissimo. Afterward, these fine young local farmers picked up guitars and proceeded to play music brilliantly into the night.

Later back at Louie's house, I slept on the couch. Early the next morning I was awoken by his mother. She was in the kitchen sitting at their small table sorting Pinto beans. When she saw me standing, she got up and poured me a cup of coffee. I sat at the table with her, just her and me, and watched as she sorted very dark beans from the other normal pintos. Legend has it those dark beans contain the seeds of evil, and one must always eliminate them to preserve the family's well-being. Louie said it was hogwash and superstition but sitting there in the quiet of the old adobe in Santa Rosa I realized, no Louie, it's just love.

ELK WHO LOVED A COW

One fine spring morning I prepared to depart Ramah to collect an order of clay and supplies for the University of New Mexico ceramics class I taught for extension college. The clay was in Albuquerque as almost everything else was back then in this great state of New Mexico. If you couldn't find it there, it wasn't to be had. Albuquerque was the last line of supply of almost anything.

The day was already beautiful and the drive most pleasant. Just east of Grants on the new section of I-40 there were cattle grazing in basalt, crowned meadows, edging the Interstate. Tranquil and peaceful was this idyllic vision of spring, you could almost feel love in the air and life fruitful in expectation.

The cows were blissfully munching away on fresh grass thriving on warm sun and snow runoff from Mount Taylor. Even the elk appeared content. Elk? Is that an elk? I pulled over to make sure my eyes were not deceiving me. Sure enough, a young bachelor elk was standing side by side with the cutest little female Heffer you ever did see. Her markings were lovely; I'm sure she had those deep, bottomless brown eyes bulls dream about. But not this type of bull. Though he was obviously determined to declare his love to her, our brown eyed princess wanted no part of it, skedaddle.

Was it his immaturity, was it his lack of a colorful heritage, or maybe his deep woods cologne was a bit much? Who knows, women. I pitied my backwoods friend and wished him, rots of ruck *compadre*. I drove off with miles to go.

Returning late afternoon, I'd been lucky to accomplish every one of my errands and was completely packed with supplies, bought with the ever-promising school purchase orders. The light was lowering to sunset, and our magic golden horizon was beginning to engulf our world. It was all quite magnificent.

Suddenly, becoming aware I was in the vicinity where I had eyed the lovelorn elk this morning, I saw him. No kidding, he was still there, so I had to pull over. His brown-eyed beauty was also still there, munching away while he, love starved, was apparently wasting away.

Oh. The agony and ecstasy of love, is there no cure? I had nothing but pity for my four- hooved brother. Was there no solution to love's anguish? Was she really the one anyway? We all know this was going nowhere. Cupid can be a real prick sometimes, so get real. She's a cow. You'll forget about her by morning; besides, you're much too horney.

Interscholastic Activities

Introducing private seasonal parties were an absolute necessity for the survival of the morale of our teachers. The first party, Halloween, was at our house, but there were no expectations. It was Halloween, so come on, and it was a blast. The wood stove was cranked up. There were meager decorations I cooked up from the art department. Everyone, I mean every one of the teachers and friends, flocked to this quick rigged attempt to celebrate. We were hungry for adult fun.

The secret to a successful conflagration of human bodies in anticipation of a good time is, of course, dance music. Once the beat resonates from the stereo's yearning speakers, the body has no choice but to respond. As far as music we, of course, had the Stones, Fleetwood Mac, Heart, and every other offering presented and coveted by these pleasure-hungry teachers. We would dance all night.

Food and drink and weed were always contributed to the function. Breaks would be taken from dancing for a little sustenance and libation and maybe a step outside onto the driveway to smoke a joint. We could then appreciate the stars and cool off from our enduring ecstasy. Some would call this blowing off steam, at the time in the turbulent seventies, we just called it celebrating being alive.

Other parties that followed were always coordinated with holidays and spring and summer breaks. These get-togethers were all we had. There were no relatives to sweep down into the reservation and show us a good time.

We were too far from anyone or any venues of entertainment to celebrate back then. So these opportunities to share personal time and let down our hair truly saved us and built a core of friendship that contributed to our survival. We inadvertently became a tight group as a result, and this also cemented mutual appreciation and camaraderie in group projects at school. We worked and played together.

Eventually the parties moved to the mud castle, a wonderfully huge adobe home, being built by Pam and Eddie. Pam was already one of us, being the other art teacher now. Her house, still in construction, became the heart of our beating seasonal releases. The acoustics from the echoing dirt, brick walls only added to the frenzy of the music's dance beat. Fleetwood Mac drove our feet to unsustainable speed and drove our shoes to flames. They were good times, and boy we needed it.

I remember one of Pam's early parties. As I said there was much about the house still in construction, but at that point it was fully functional and party central as a result. There was one event that occurred after a long, long dry spell of teaching. We were desperately in need of release. Morale demanded quenching. So enthusiasm was at a peak and teachers in tearful gratitude partied 'til the cows came home, or some facsimile of that quote.

Now I was in the most need of joyful aspect. Being released from the day-to-day pressure of classwork and school politics, I was ready to party. Somehow the idea of dry martinis crawled into my lizard mind, and I couldn't shake it, nor did I want to. So shaking up an abundant supply to get me through a thirstful night, I proceeded to join the celebration.

The Rolling Stones were hitting us hard, they had no mercy, we were their adoring slaves. The martinis were doing their job, there was no slacking off. Our frenetic oblivion rolled on and on to everyone's delight. This for us at the time was truly heaven.

Soon I found myself spent; I needed recovery time. I grabbed another martini and marched through the kitchen. Opening the patio door I stepped out to cool off and take a break under the moonlit canopy of the night.

When I came to, in a daze of dust, I became aware I was uncomfortably sprawled on and within a very rough pile of broken cinder blocks and cement breakage. I should be dead. The fall was about twelve feet. It was now obvious to me the balcony had not been completed. Slowly I crawled out and up from this brick-crumbling bodily disaster. After a momentary evaluation I realized that I was not only alive, but that nothing was broken or bleeding. Hallelujah. The martinis had saved me.

After careful consideration the conclusion was to rejoin the party, slip in quietly, and disappear into the revelry of our bacchanalia. Which is what I did. I walked around to the front door of the house and slipped in. Eventually though Pam and Eddie discovered me and took me to the side. They were the only ones who had witnessed my attempt at flight. They, together, stated the obvious, "You know there is no balcony."

To which I responded, "Oh?"

THE OLD MAN AND THE SEA

In grammar school *The Old man and the Sea* was one of my required books to read. It was one of the few I enjoyed very much as a child. The story of an old Cuban fisherman battling a giant Marlin, what's not to like?

Hemingway had heard the story, by word of mouth, fifteen years before he wrote it. Supposedly, he had already started writing it, and Hollywood caught wind and wanted to reserve the rights of the story for a film, starring an actor named Spencer Tracy. The only problem was the book of his was mostly talk, and Hemingway had yet to type a word. Hollywood, as to verbal agreement, expected Ernest to arrive soon with a finished manuscript, and Hemingway at this point didn't have it.

The Old Man of the Sea was Ernest's last work of fiction. He won a Pulitzer Prize for it, and the next year it was the only book mentioned when he received the Nobel Prize. Who would have guessed a book about Cuba, the ocean, an old man and a fish was manifested in the western desert highlands of New Mexico, out of a village trading post called Villa de Cubero.

Hemingway was frantic driving cross country in 1951. He had a deadline, and at this point no one close to him, public or private, knew the book, he had been bragging about, had not actually been written yet. The old Route 66 had been newly paved, thanks to the war, so it became the cardinal east/west artery of the country. Ernest was driving this way to Los Angeles under the pressure of other's expectations and all the while trying to formulate a solution.

Stopping on Route 66 at a small, quaint respite known as Cubero for gas, I'm sure he was obviously stretching and surveying his surroundings and discovered the trading post had rooms for rent and most importantly—a Western Union. A light must have gone on in his noggin because he marched in, rented a room, sent the telegram to Hollywood, informing them he had car problems and getting the parts could take some time.

He had his Hail Mary. Ernest brought his typewriter, paper, and three cases of French Bordeaux into the room and closed the door. As time went by all the locals knew was that the man in the room never came out, he smoked incessantly, and typed day and night. He was most definitely a strange one.

No one paid any more attention to the stranger, and eventually, after what seemed weeks the man came out. He smelled bad, but he at least was leaving, thank God. He settled with the trading post. Then he telegraphed Hollywood and stated he had finally received the auto parts, and the mechanic was able to complete the repairs. He was on his way.

There was a sign on the old motel in Cubero that used to state the fact of Hemingway's patronage there and the book he wrote within—*The Old Man and the Sea*. I believe it was on room number 5. I-40 now bypasses old Route 66. No one explores those old haunts of the bygone days on the old cross-country artery anymore. All I know is if I had three cases of French Bordeaux and I'm in the middle of nowhere, I'd find a friendly place to hide away in like Cubero and why not write a book.

Ranchos de Chimayo

Tom Cummings had a wild hair for northern adventure, so he approached me and another teacher and inquired if we were receptive to a Saturday sojourn to the region north of Santa Fe, specifically Chimayo. I'd heard of Chimayo, having lived east of there in Las Vegas, New Mexico. So ever the explorer, this hit my curiosity's sweet spot. Oh boy. Yes, of course, I'll go. Then Saturday morning came, and I was sick as a dog—stomach flu. I don't get sick very often, and yet here I was.

Tom pulled up to the house in his infamous old black Oldsmobile. This car was so old there was a BC stamped after its year of creation. Even so, she was the love of Tom's life, and we strode carefully to appreciate her in Tom's presence. Seeing me, Tom observed my situation and said, "Well, you can lie in bed all day in agony or ride with us and see New Mexico's northern mysteries in agony."

Obviously I chose the latter, so I dressed, grabbed a blanket and aspirin, and climbed into the welcoming springs of the Oldsmobile's' back seat. Humph, comfy, surprise.

A dinosaur this old gives a heavy and solid ride. I immediately went to sleep. Nearing Albuquerque, I was in my fevered state, catching Tom lecturing my fellow teacher on the history of the Civil War in New Mexico. Tom stated in 1862, the Army of the Confederacy invaded New Mexico Territory in an attempt for a run at the gold mines in Colorado. This army consisted primarily of regiments of Texas rifles and their unified command fell under a General Sibley, if he was sober that is. They traipsed north up the Rio Grande and watched as Union Forces, all Native reserves, retreated from south Albuquerque to Santa Fe and then settled in a defense at Apache Pass and then finally Glorieta Pass north of Pecos.

At the Battle of Glorieta, a Union Contingent was sent to bypass the Confederate Army and to find any surviving military stores in Albuquerque. Through a hidden pass behind enemy lines, this Union Complement accidentally stumbled upon the supply train of the Confederate Troops. So overconfident were they, the Confederates had only posted two guards for the entire field supply.

The jig was up, the Union Troops absconded with the supply train, and at the end of a victorious battle, the Confederates returned to no shot, no powder and no beans. They were finished and slowly faded down the Camino Real and slithered back to Texas.

This victory for the Union, in a faraway territory called New Mexico, literally saved these United States. If the Confederacy had reached the gold fields in the north, they would have had the resources to pay England for munitions much less for mercenary support to finish off the Union.

Tom continued elaborating on especially Albuquerque's place in the confederacy's territorial siege. Old Town was the base camp for the invaders, but they skedaddled quickly after their defeat. Confederate paper currency was found years afterwards in stacks; all were worthless printed specie notes. There were stories of Hispanic kids finding stashes of these bills and playing their version of poker or faro with them.

Another story that stuck in my mind was of a Hispanic spinster pair of sisters who were teachers and much beloved by the local community and family. They had inherited a small lot on San Felipe Street in Old Town proper and desired, with the help of family, to build a small house to live out their years since they had no husbands. Many volunteered and while digging the foundations, they discovered, stacked side by side like logs, iron cannon left in the wake of the Confederate retreat. At this point in time, Albuquerque had no museum and had no historical receptacle of any source, nothing. The result was the cannon were left, and the foundation footings were placed around them. They are there to this day, long forgotten.

Tom had driven through northern sections of my state that I had never been aware of. This was the old, deeply religious Penitente country, hidden on the high road to Taos. Chimayo was the beginning of this trek. It was extraordinarily beautiful, a beauty deep with unexplainable emotive power. The *Santuario* was certainly a contributor, but the land itself held you spellbound. Ranchos de Chimayo was in an apple orchard with the smell of the fruit in its final stages of maturation. Everything was scented pleasantly of aging apples.

I crawled out of the Oldsmobile's back seat, still an embarrassment to humanity, and staggered to the restaurant's entrance. Oh my God. The aroma of this fare of *del norte* hit me like a shot of B12. This food would give me back my life and help me shed my unhealthful woes, let me at it.

We sat in the simplicity of the old ranch environment. A kiva fireplace infused us with its welcoming heat, and in pleasant expectation we placed our orders which included the world's best *carne adovada*. We couldn't ask for anything more.

While waiting in anticipation for the greatest meal of my life, I became annoyingly aware of the boisterousness of our immediate neighbors. They were drunk. Not just drunk, loud, rude, inconsiderate ego shams. I was patient, no I wasn't. I don't know how to be patient. After about ten minutes of this abuse, I finally started coughing loud. The next tables offenders were two roly poly fellows, past middle age, and having an enormously good time. In the following seconds I waited, finally they turned and stared me down, "Problem?"

One of them was Burl Ives and the other had a Russian accent, but I did not recognize him. I waved, hello, and minded my own business. They were gone soon, and our meal arrived to fulfill all our expectations.

Riding home in the back seat, I finally felt healed and refreshed. I owed Tom a heap. Years later I still think of that wonderful journey. I remember Tom's lecture and his anecdotes on New Mexico's Civil War history. I'm aware of the unknown cognizance of historians, who have never considered the consequences had the union not been successful at Glorieta. I also think to myself, if Texas ever again gets some uppity idea to invade my fair state of New Mexico, I know where to get my hands on some cannon and we'll see how those lone stars like that.

Zuni Witches

Ramah Navajo School had special education. The teachers for this program were probably the most respected to the otherwise regularly formatted staff. Their day-to-day courage to tackle unforeseen situations with difficult and unfortunate students put the rest of us standard curriculum educators to shame if truth be known. They were our unsung heroes, and I doubt any of them even knew it.

Our social services struggled with parents of let's say, needful kids. These parents would hide their children from the staff in old locked hogans and sheds hidden from view. Even though it was explained that funding was in place to care for these children, they would deny having any disturbed children and shoo the social workers away.

Late at night some parents would sneak off the reservation and drive to Zuni, where they would meet with the witch who would work some hokey ceremony, hum a prayer or two, then chant, pretend to pull a piece of bone from the skull of the child. With a cure proclaimed an exorbitant fee would be charged, and you were on your way. Recovery was forthcoming for certain.

This wasn't an absolute situation, only a very few families carried on this tradition of using witches in Zuni. It was more a habit from the past when there were no doctors, no social services, no native healers, and those simply were too expensive for any poor Navajo sheep herder to afford. The witches filled a marketplace position, and their competitors hated them.

According to oral tradition of the Zunis, a couple of witches came up from the underworld and brought two gifts to the people—corn to feed them and death to keep overpopulation from being a problem. This belief goes back far into the earliest of times.

When life on the Pueblo was hard and droughts, plague, hunger, floods and any sort of natural calamity occurred, witches were rounded up. Let's just say their future fates were not pleasant, and that is if they had a future at all. But if life was prosperous for the people, the business of charms, potions, curses, etcetera was blooming, and you might have to take a number and wait.

Navajos from Ramah had been using witches in Zuni most likely for hundreds of years. The fact that Catholic priests and soldiers often attempted to eradicate witches from the Pueblo made them that much more desirable to the Navajos.

Back at the Ramah Navajo High School, I team taught a class with my ex-sister-in-law Lana. She had conceived of a class called books, in which the students would write and illustrate their own creative publications. I had agreed to team teach this class with her, even though I had doubts of a future for the project. I felt the kids just weren't ready. My God, speaking English was still a new concept.

We went forward, and by the end of the second week, I knew we were losing half the class. Something had to be done. Scratching my head for ideas one day, when disorder was becoming the rule, I informed the students if they behaved, I would tell them a story the last five minutes of class. It worked, and I was stuck. Somehow the stories came to me, and with them we finished the semester.

Well of course, the favorite stories were of Zuni witches. Their most favorite story in this vein was of Jimmy Begay and the magic Chevy pickup. Here's how it goes: Jimmy Begay was a hard-working, young sheepherder on the reservation. Through his own good luck and industry, he owned an old blue Chevy pickup truck, but what many didn't know was that this truck was magic. It was special, very special because this truck had feelings and loved Jimmy like a brother.

It was their secret bond and theirs alone. Now Jimmy did have another special friend also, a little blue bird, who Jimmy had once saved from a hawk when the blue bird had collided into a sandstone cliff. Jimmy had rushed and rescued her, and the rest is history. These three were secret friends, and their sworn loyalty to each other was their bond.

Jimmy also had a girlfriend. Her name was Nada, and she was the most beautiful Navajo girl on the reservation. She was also the kindest. She would help anyone, and as a result she was loved by one and all. Jimmy knew he was lucky beyond wishes to have Nada. He was blessed. They would drive in the magic Chevy pickup everywhere, checking the sheep, visiting friends, and watching sunsets. Eventually they agreed to get married, and life couldn't be sweeter.

Then one day Nada disappeared, vanished. Jimmy checked her hogan, but she was not there. He checked with her friends, not there. He went to the chapter house, thinking maybe she was helping someone, but she wasn't there either. She was gone.

Jimmy was sad beyond belief and so were his friends—the magic Chevy pickup and little blue bird. No one knew what to do. Finally, blue bird volunteered to fly as high as she could and try to see if she could locate Nada. She flew everywhere watching and watching as time flew by. Exhausted from her travails one day, she flew near the outskirts of the Zuni Pueblo and saw a long white yarn flag flying from the window of a very old mud and stone building. Blue bird, out of curiosity, flew down and discovered, low and behold, Nada crying behind a heavy, pinon posted window. The yarn had come from her hair, and it was the only thing she could think of to save herself.

Blue bird shrilled and tweeted, and Nada saw her. Nada somehow found all the attention of the little bird unusual, almost magical. For some reason through her tears, she revealed the story of how a witch had stopped at a trading post on old Route 53 and seeing how beautiful Nada was offered her a free ride to her hogan. Nada jumped in the witch's truck. Suddenly the witch blew magic dust into her face, and that was the last thing she remembered. She was now the witch's prisoner, and the witch was slowly stealing Nada's beauty day by day.

The blue bird flew back to Jimmy. Now blue bird language is a little tweety, but Jimmy somehow got the gist of it. With that information the two friends roared away in the magic Chevy pickup, barreling down the highway with tires in flames.

Nearing the old house, the witch was standing outside and seeing them she shouted powerful spells and chants to stop their swift progress. Unfortunately for her, pickups don't stop easily. They drove right over the witch and smashed into the front door. Getting out of the pickup, they stood staring straight at Nada. She cried, oh hell, they all cried, and after a while they hauled into the pickup truck, which hadn't a scratch on it. Remember it was magic, and they drove away from the sunset since this Navajo reservation is east of Zuni.

Now that the witch was dead, Nada's beauty returned except now she glowed even more than ever. Jimmy finally introduced his friends—the blue bird and the magic Chevy pickup. They would eventually act as godparents to the many children on the way. Nada married Jimmy, and they were very, very, very happy. The end.

If you are a new teacher or an old teacher, and you have to formulate a new innovative class plan for some unique creative writing proposal on the reservation, please, please consider all the consequences of overzealous expectations or you could end up storytelling for the rest of the semester. If not, you could always drive to Zuni and ask a witch's advice.

Coronado

El Morro National Monument was the site of the encampment of the army of Francisco Vasquez de Coronado after their failed conflict with the Zunis at Hawikuh. El Morro offered a desperately needed respite with water and a natural topography to shelter and regroup. With an army of an estimated three thousand plus cattle and camp followers, this was the first alien invasion of America by force. There were only, supposedly four hundred to seven hundred Spanish soldiers involved, the remaining troops were a mix a veteran Aztec and Indigenous tribes from Mexico. They were searching for the legendary seven cities of gold revealed to them by a Friar, Marcos de Niza.

Before Coronado arrived in the year 1539, a black Moor, named Esteban, was escorting Friar Niza, and he was familiar with Hawikuh. He also had astronomical knowledge of eclipses, so he escaped the friars charge and hurried ahead to the Zuni Pueblo. There he presented himself in a doublet of bright blue velvet with attached silver hawk bells, ringing annoyingly through the air. It appears he had this opportunity planned all along. Esteban was a fast study and learned quickly the nuances of Indigenous languages, utilizing this talent to his fullest advantage.

Esteban arrived in Hawikuh on an intended day and informed the Zuni priest that he was a great sorcerer and threatened to block out the sun if he didn't acquire his heart's desires. No one in the Pueblo believed him, because no one could stop the sun. Esteban proceeded to chant magical spells, probably in his native Moroccan. As minutes rolled by, sure enough, the moon started covering the sun, and the following result was a descending darkness that covered the village and all the land.

Suddenly becoming aware of the formability of this Black Sorcerer, who with a few magic words and a flick of his wrist could make the sun disappear, the priests howled in fear and summoned the Bow Clan to put a stop to this abomination of the normal course of nature. The native archers filled Esteban's body with about fifty to a hundred arrows, and lo and behold, in a few more minutes the sun returned, and all was well.

Two years later, when Francisco appeared, the Zunis, remembering Esteban, did not set out the welcome wagon. After an apparently horrific defense of severe consequences, Coronado's army barely escaped to El Morro, and there they licked their wounds but survived.

When I visited El Morro the first time, I was aware of this story. From the monument's peaks I could envision this mercenary army of old searching for golden riches and finding only golden corn tacos with questionable garnishes. I imagined old Francisco sending his Captain Alvarez to explore further east. After some time, he returned and lead Coronado's invading force to the Rio Grande.

I also remembered that they stopped and conquered the Sky City People, Acoma, through some treachery of unspeakable deceit. Coronado then placed one of his Catholic priests to oversee the Christianization of the savages of the Pueblo. As Coronado departed, it is said his soldiers, while marching away, heard the screams of that priest as he proved incapable of flight from the cliffs of Acoma. It appeared to the Acoma—the priest's God did not favor him after all, so why should they? Anyway, I'm sure Francisco conveniently heard nothing and quickened the pace of the armies march east.

While exploring the vista atop El Morro, I became all too keenly aware of our historic hubris as a species. Who did we think we were peddling moral superiority by force? All I know is if you come into some one's neighborhood and proceed to sell them a wolf in sheep's clothing and promise the sun and the moon as a bonus, you deserve a butt-full of arrows.

Viva La Fiesta

It was Labor Day weekend in 1976, and that meant two other teachers and I were traveling to Santa Fe for Fiesta. Fiesta is a yearly event held in honor of our history and culture, and all that makes being a New Mexican a celebration.

Zozobra, who we call old man gloom, is burned each year to erase the woes of the past year and to free our spirits to soar toward new hopeful futures. At least that's the idea some wonderful, crazy artists came up with over a hundred years ago, but still, it sounds good to me.

Leaving after school at three o'clock Friday, we three raced towards Santa Fe with hearts and minds filled with bountiful expectations. Truthfully, none of us had ever participated in the event, but now finally attending, we realized who would want to miss the state's only yearly event to let down your hair and have a good time, not us.

The three of us had been stuck on a small reservation on the western side of the state. The population there was so small that while driving through the village of Ramah, passing Indian packed pickup trucks, passing through Mountain View, and finally arriving at the school, you had just about accounted for three-quarters of the local population in thirty-five minutes. We loved our work, but hell, there was another world out there. Was a weekend away asking too much?

Arriving in Santa Fe, everyone's spirits were running high. We were at party central. Zozobra was burning, and the revelry and release of everyone's spirits was in the air.

The origin of Santa Fe's Fiesta was historically founded on the 1693 colonist's reentry into the Spanish territorial capital thirteen years after the 1680 revolt, which had forced them out—a move, at the time, was justified by the injustices experienced by the Indigenous population. The returning colonists, led by Don Diego De Vargas, had placed La Conquistadora on an altar once De Vargas retook the city and enshrined her within the Palace Chapel on the plaza. This was the key historic significance of our state's annual blowout.

There was music blaring on the plaza. People were dancing and carousing throughout, bumping into each other, and then swearing in Spanish, English and even some French. We teachers were entranced; no place in the continental United States had this kind of cultural bacchanalia.

We partied in the streets until exhaustion and hunger drove us back to my truck. Driving south on Cerrillos Road, we made our way to the Denny's. This was the only eats on the south side of Santa Fe. After a meal of what you could expect, sleep came crashing down. I found a dirt road alongside the Yucca Drive-In Movie. After crushing down some weeds, we laid out our sleeping bags. The bugs weren't too bad, and we were off to dreamland under the stars.

The next morning was cold, frigid to the bone. People forget Santa Fe is right smack dab next to the Rocky Mountains. We loaded up and made it back to Denny's to a fine breakfast of again whatever they were serving. The plaza was a wreck, people were passed out in bushes, Tequila bottles were lying everywhere, in short, it was an optimistic start to the new day.

Later, we viewed street performers of all sorts—including a medicine show, an actual medicine show, with a Yankee top-hatted, tails-suited showman doctor, expounding the curatives of a small medicinal bottle of obvious black tea. His monologue was superb, and the hilarity of his performance had us in stitches. It's sad that I never heard of him again after that performance.

The day rolled by in expected and unexpected revelry. There had even been three stabbings that we were not aware of until later. Soon we concluded that we were smashed. Then I came up with an idea of driving up the mountain canyon road and finding an easier place to camp. Everyone agreed, and we did just that. The stars were even closer there, and you had to be careful not to bump into them. Not far off the side of the road, I finally found a pullover and the perfect set up for us. We settled down, mumbled a few drunken comments, and passed out.

But no, no, no, no, no, this was not the end of our night, not by a long shot. Our nocturnal ordeal was only just beginning. Down below us and on the opposite side of the road, some bikers came and set up camp. They started a campfire and stumbled around, raving in some manic-drug ecstasy. Not long after their arrival came the real biker horde that had followed from way behind. They were blitzed, fried, psychopathic, utterly insane drug induced vicious excuses of the human race, and yet they were our neighbors.

I didn't sleep well that night, I don't know why. Was it the fact I was across the street from father rapers, mother stabbers, and brother killers or had the previous day's activities overtaxed my delicate disposition. All I knew is the three of us were buried so deep into our sleeping bags, finding our way out the next morning would take a while.

Quietly, and I do mean quietly, we tiptoed through our camp and tossed everything into the back of the truck and coasting quietly down the road. Eventually, we started the engine, took off, and we never looked back.

Maybe you're thinking ultimate cowardice or some sissified description of these three runaway teachers feels appropriate about now. Go ahead, take your best shot, see if I care. I'm alive.

We didn't even stop at Denny's on the way out. We were just fine. We were getting ourselves back home to our little reservation, where the deer and the antelope play. We'd had quite enough of the outside world. Well, at least that is until next year.

Viva Fiesta. If your life is getting too blah and a tall shot of adrenaline is your cup of tequila, please come and join us on the plaza next year. Just remember one thing, if you can't take the heat, don't eat the chili. Viva Fiesta.

SILVERSMITHING

When interviewed by the Ramah Navajo school board, one of the understandings was an agreement that I would not only teach art, but I would also demonstrate making art. This included all crafts within our limited curriculum. I fulfilled this agreement and beyond including silversmithing.

Silversmithing for the Navajos originated in our area. "Slender Maker of Silver" was from this region. Early, before access to silver coins, Navajos worked with Mexican blacksmiths in Grants, forging scrap steel and eventually brass into fancy horse bridles and early jewelry. They traded these to the Utes, who in turn traded mountain lion, buffalo, and even bear hides. Silver was another story though. There were bells formed from quarters, domed in the forge in smithing early on. But it wasn't until the Navajos returned from Fort Sumner and the railroad came through, was there any way to develop the necessary skills for jewelry creation. The railroad, bringing strange folks from back east, brought silver coins to trade for native goods. This made for the purchasing of tools and supplied the precious metal for the creation of fine silver jewelry. The rest is history, but the birthplace of Navajo silversmithing was right where I was standing.

Now I won't lie to you, I had no knowledge of this history at the time. Hell, I didn't even know how to silversmith. The closest I came was a lost wax ring my friend Louie instructed me through when I was in graduate school at Highlands University. What mattered was that the school board believed I knew silversmithing. Yes, *cahones*. Preparing the silversmithing department wasn't possible until we were transferred into the new school anyway, so I had a year to gather as much information and advice as I could grasp.

The end results were not so bleak, if I must say so myself. My art department had a generous budget to purchase all the necessary equipment and supplies even including a small lapidary. It was coming together. I was pleased with myself. Now all I had to do was learn how to use all this stuff. I had two weeks before classes started, that should be enough time to learn the fundamentals of a hundred-year-old art form, right? Oh God, what was I thinking.

So lessons began. Teaching someone with a head thick enough to get themselves into a mess like this was certainly going to be challenged enough. Much less it being myself. Obviously, the fundamental concept of soldering needed to be first. That comprised an interesting two days alone. I would wonder why with torch and solder in hand, silver dripping liberally, I so often smelled pork burning. Then I'd observe my pants on fire and there were pieces of silver solder sizzling gently into my legs. Fortunately, this situation inspired me to learn quickly and to purchase more Neosporin, but I did learn. Casting silver in tufa was a whole other world of traditional jewelry creation, and I succeeded in mastering it and loving it. I even created shortcuts of my own, using clay to continue to test the image depth carved into the stone.

Lapidary would follow later with water spraying me, soaked, and wet for the entirety of the second week. I did finally understand the machine adjustments and walked away almost dry one day. When classes started, we had a jewelry department—two benches, two acetylene tanks, one lapidary, and an instructor covered with bandages and a funny smell of excessive Neosporin use. I was proud of my accomplishments until one of my students stared at me funny and asked, "Shows, why are you all wet?"

The years have passed, and I now make a tidy income from my silversmithing skill amongst other talents. But I will never forget that two weeks of the gorilla-smithing intensive. Never in my wildest dreams would I have anticipated the future results. Eventually, I was also able to realize purchasing a vinyl apron would most certainly cure my wet pants problem.

PTA

To many the parent teacher's organization provides an exceptional conduit for parents and teachers throughout the year. Meeting the teacher twice a year, person to person, provides a window into a student's progress and tells us hopefully how little Johnny is doing. These interviews might not provide all the answers to improvement, but at least it implies someone might give a damn. After all, teachers need all the faith they can muster for their continuing confidence.

In 1975, in our sparkling, new Pine Hill High School, we prepared for our first parent teachers meeting. All teachers were to be present at the same time throughout the school for the entire evening.

Our school and community were unfortunately too small for staggered appointments like large public schools. The distances traveled on their reservation made even that option impractical. Some parents would have to travel up to 60 miles from a job in Gallup or Grants, and then also drive to the school that night. So, our little one-night stands serviced all equitably.

The parents at the time were mostly traditional Navajo or Nazarene faith-based and didn't speak much or even have the English to speak much. So, there was a lot of smiling and presenting of paper classwork and descriptions of students' progress, no one followed or understood anyway. As teachers we were flying on good intentions mostly.

In my brand-new art department, I showed parents students' work, took them on a tour of the new equipment, and actually felt like I was more a PR person then a teacher.

There was one mother, who had wire rimmed glasses that were badly bent. I gestured to a silversmithing bench and presented the tool drawer. Pointing to her eyeglasses, I asked to see them. Within moments I had straightened the frames, adjusted the nose guards, and corrected and reset the ear wires. The smile on her face told me I had done good, and we were both happy. The rest of the evening ran smoothly, and we teachers were released at nine o'clock to go home to beddie bye. It had been a very successful evening.

When the spring came in 1976, we continued our improvised PTA, and again parents showed up. We were again enthused by their attendance. I was running a little late, and when I finally arrived at my classroom, there was actually a long line at the door. I was certainly impressed. It seems word must have spread of the fine art education this invariably talented, brilliant, once in a lifetime artist was bestowing upon these needy students.

I was the hero of my own delusion and rightfully so because as soon as I opened the door, I spied hands clutching damaged eyeglasses. I repaired a dozen pair of glasses that night. Some I even had to solder to save and restore them. I was the last teacher to leave. My principal was certainly impressed at the attendance of my parents. Little did he know.

I taught some leather smithing that year to include with our crafts regimen. Somehow, one day I found myself repairing a boot heel for a smaller student who was struggling in school. I was able to place the boot in a vice and after generously pasting leather glue in the heel wedge, I was able to hammer four nails to hold it. Miraculously, the repair held, and our little waif was off to the races.

Surprise, surprise, at the next PTA I had twice as many parents attend my little art department's open house. Word had spread from one little repair. I also was in the shoe repair business now it appeared. There were three pairs of boots and a clunky pair of old woman's shoes. Three pairs of eyeglasses showed up at the end also, surprise, surprise.

As the head art teacher, I oversaw the department including all crafts and fine arts plus silversmithing. We even had a Navajo weaving teacher upstairs, Betty Henio. This entire department at the time was a wet dream for any school on any reservation in the state. I should be quite proud for all we'd accomplished.

Still, in the end, I believe I did more good for the community showing my willingness to do simple repairs that no one had the tools for or the money to have it done in town. I could joke and say it was my own fault to become the handy Andy of Pine Hill, but in retrospect these Navajos had to have been pretty desperate to trust a tall blonde, know it all, with their most precious belongings. After all, at the time, only a lame, blind man should trust an artist from Baltimore, and that's if he's asleep.

Substitute Principal

The monies that supported school budgets in the 1970s were created by appropriating funding from state or federal tax resources, and as a result they supported necessary educational programs. Once this funding was approved, the school board and then administrators had control of these funds that they then doled out to the proper departments who then appointed said monies to classroom teachers in the form of purchase orders.

At least that was how our school system structured it. Though the printed budget asserts to these directed allocations of funds, somehow, these monies could often magically disappear during their journey to the much-needed classroom. Misappropriation of funds, just plain greed, misdirection by sleight of hand, who knows how the disappearing act of funding occurred. All I knew, was having a copy of the approved budget, was the only paper trail and recourse we teachers in the trenches had to defend our meager class resources.

In the fall of 1976 our principal was investigating other employment possibilities in Albuquerque for a move there with his new wife. When he was away and had interviews, he needed someone to fill in for him. Bill, our principal, knew there was no one who could handle the kids better than that crazy old art teacher.

I loved my students all, but I also knew how to half-Nelson a ruffian if it proved warranted. Mostly an act of humor and play was all that was necessary to quelch a problem. Whenever Bill left for his interviews or some legal or school board assigned meeting, he appointed me principal. I know you can't believe it, be honest, that's what you're thinking, but he did.

I'd go over the daily schedule with him before he left and accepted that this was also going to be double duty having to carry on my own classes as well. The one cardinal point Bill would always make, as he was departing the doors was an emphatic, "Whatever you do, do not sign purchase orders."

I always responded to Bill, "You betcha, Bill, don't you worry."

Now, as soon as Bill's car left the parking lot, a note was sent to all teachers that I was in the office. Any purchase orders, that needed signing, were to be expected within the next hour. As acting principal, my signature was valid, and all the poor teachers desperately in need of supplies, formed a line down the hall to have their POs signed. They were practically in tears of relief from all the delays these needed materials had cost their classrooms. Bill wouldn't sign purchase orders; the administration wouldn't let him.

Where was that money anyway? After all, it was all in the budget. I've always thought Bill's hands were tied, and the situation only made his job harder and earned him distrust from the staff. I'd be looking for another principal's job also, if it was me. Anyway, he had an out with the administration. He could always blame that crazy art teacher for signing those POs while he was out conducting proper school business.

If you are ever placed in a similar situation where you can inadvertently do the right thing for the right reason, just remember the golden rule, "When the rooster's away, the chicks can play."

Ladies of Ojo de Gallo

The community of San Rafael was originally known as *Ojo de Gallo* (eye of the rooster). As a village it had also been the site of Fort Wingate, a very significant military location of the west's Civil War conflict. From this site Kit Carson and his militia began the roundup of almost all the Navajo tribe. It was this action that eventually led to the Navajos "Long Walk" to Fort Sumner. The name of San Rafael was bestowed on the village of Ojo de Gallo in honor of a Franciscan priest, who came in 1863. He was Father Jose Rafael Chavez, and through some odd twist of events would later be defrocked.

Fort Wingate was later moved east of Gallup. Eventually, a new railroad created a western hub in what would become the town of Grants, next to San Rafael. San Rafael itself was bountiful in natural springs, meadows, and rich grazing land and, as a result, it set the stage for prize cattle country and later with the railroad hub, in addition, great commerce and western decadence were soon to follow. See, you just can't stop progress.

Stories have traveled down the pike of many notorious characters in this region of the state. One was a Texas rancher who acquired a huge spread in San Rafael. Within a short ten years, he produced a concern so lucrative he decided someone as successful as himself should travel to Pari, France. Why not investigate a place called Europe while you're at it? Well, you know the French; they're not stupid, and they could smell the rancher coming across the Atlantic and prepared a gracious reception. Within a year this individual of impeccable cow-patty etiquette was inevitably flat broke.

The Texas rancher returned to San Rafael, hang dogged, packed his belongings, and skedaddle back to the Lone Star. I'm sure the bank took possession of the ranch. The rancher's great mansion, well, mansion in the eyes of the citizens of San Rafael, somehow became the residence of a flowering professional women's business concern.

Please, keep in mind the delicate details of their operation of entertaining men were all simply rumor and conjecture. Maybe they were teaching the fundamentals of bridge playing, who knows. Anyway, the girls got down to their bridge tournaments or whatever it was they were doing, and life went on.

As always time breezed by, and the house quietly stayed in business seamlessly secluded in the shadows of the village. History moved on also as WWI led the farmers in Grants to discovering carrots did quite well in this unusual western type of sand. Grants became the carrot capital of the United States. The railroad shipped their orange bounty everywhere rails would take them. Well, then World War II jumped up, and New Mexico fell smack into the middle of the hydrogen bombs inception. Guess what, the same sand those carrots loved in Grants was the same sand uranium loved also. No wonder those carrots were so so orange.

Anywho, the ladies of Ojo de Gallo were still there in San Rafael, servicing the carrot farmers. Eventually, the uranium miners and, of course, the local constabulary (pro gratis), of course, and anyone else who walked through the door. In my heart of hearts, I know this was these fine ladies' way of supporting the war effort. Everyone had to do their part or parts.

Well, when the war finally ended, and peace was realized throughout the planet, The US government decided they'd better create as many hydrogen bombs as they could make to keep the world at peace. Good idea, huh? So, mining replaced carrots, and Grants became a big hole in the ground glowing with shiny uranium. Glory, glory Hallelujah.

The Ladies of Ojo de Gallo were still able to carry on thanks to new commercial hair dyes and beauty accessories delivered by train. The old house, mansion, was finally showing her age also, but she still stood proud and indignant to all the snide social innuendos. But the late 1950s and early 1960s were eventually catching up with the girls, and business not being what it used to be, a sign advertising green stamps was placed in front of the house.

Green stamps and top value stamps at this time had a trade in value of one cent per stamp, and you traded in books of these stamps for prizes such as kitchenware, house products, etcetera. This promotion is nonexistent now, but at the time it was all the rage.

Who can say if the stamps were in fact part of transactional commerce with the ladies, but if it was, I believe it was a brilliant innovation. Just imagine the wife of a miner going through his clothes the next morning and finding a wad of green stamps and wondering. Then being relieved to find out later that the miner's favorite bar was starting to give out stamps for purchases, and her generous husband brought them home just for her. Who can say. Really.

The El Rancho and the Wigwam

The El Rancho Hotel was built in 1936. Gallup was finally grown up and discovered Hollywood and Vaudeville and anyone else who needed to stay on this rail stop and required a nice place to rest. The director, John Ford, along with more than a score of others and producers were pleasantly relieved to find this sparkling new western respite close enough to filming shoots to give a relaxing retreat to the day's end. Many a movie was shot literally across the street, then over the railroad tracks, and onto the open range with sandstone cliffs for backdrops already in place. Yes, the El Rancho was made for western movies, and many found the ideal facilities were just what the doctor ordered.

There were many Friday and Saturday nights, when as teachers in the 1970s, the El Rancho played a big part in entertaining and feeding us with its novel, old western-themed environment and menus. Dances were set up in the lounge, and guests of any Native background joined in on frolicking weekend music reviews.

But what really made this hotel and the Wigwam Motel famous, was the automobile. None of these roadside wonders would be here today without the one sole purpose of their existence, the car.

The Wigwam Motels were patented in 1935 and went on to be one of the first motel franchises in the United States. These concrete cones resembled their namesake and were planted along highways coast to coast. The automobile necessitated the need for this hostel industry as the highway became the lifeline of the expanding industry, commerce, and even national tourism.

The Wigwam Motels have now disappeared across present-day America. The one in Gallup was demolished twenty years ago. The city built a monument on the site next to the I-40 exchange. But many of us still have old pictures of this wonderful memorial to the commercial Old West that once bedded us down for the night under the stars.

Fortunately, the El Rancho is still in existence. My wife and I got stranded there once during a blizzard that we were lucky to escape. The guest rooms of the hotel are named after old movie stars. We were grateful to appropriate the Lee Remick room. It was tiny with a warm old radiator clanking peacefully in the corner of the room. We had dinner downstairs, and I swear to you, nothing has changed with the menu or authentic atmosphere, since they built it in '36. Although I am certain air conditioning was a new feature.

Why write about these old respites of the highway? Because nothing has really changed in nearly 100 years, has it? Even though we have air travel, which is becoming more and more unreliable and even though railways are chronically busy, they're busy with the movement of industrial commerce not of passenger transport. All these innovations to engage us in more relaxing forms of travel have failed to do the one thing we needed—to get us to anywhere we needed to go on time and in one piece.

The invention of the motel was a uniquely American innovation created through the necessity of getting us from point A to point B and along the way finding some rest and food.

So, the next time you're sitting in an airport waiting for a flight you paid for and find canceled and are left to sleep on a concrete floor for the next flight twelve hours from now, remember this one thing. With all the hours involved with parking, waiting, line jamming, and every other inconvenience the airport can throw at you, you could have been driving like a sane person across the United States of America and getting to your destination cheaper and on time. Also keep in mind, that club sandwich you just paid for in the airport cost you thirty dollars and a bottle of water, water was ten.

ZUNI BASEBALL

Springtime in Ramah brought, of course, flowers blooming, birds mating as well as everything else mating. Hell, even the low careening elk were open for business in the many canyons and ridge tops, which surrounded us. It was time to go outside and confront mother nature head on. It was time for baseball.

Softball was my forte, so in a call of wild enthusiasm, I attempted to enlist players for a friendly league of baseball enthusiasts. Surprisingly, the response to my invitation was instantaneous. Many teachers and school administrators answered energetically, and soon a league was formed. Now, somehow, I had envisioned a fun group of adults, embracing a game of softball in the spirit of relaxed camaraderie. But as it turns out, nothing was further from their minds. This group of fellow teachers and peers had obviously been baptized into the Church of Baseball one time or another in their academic careers and were devout to the seriousness of the call, play ball.

New Mexico has a long history of the game, starting with army bases scattered across the territory in 1868. Santa Fe became the first of these leagues. Eventually, like a spreading epidemic, the game blossomed throughout the New Mexico landscape and became an involuntary integration force. Teams of every tribe, ethnic group, and color thronged to the umpire's "batter up." Spectators of these small league enterprises were doggedly loyal and found in the game a new unity of spirit, previously unknown to their social consciousness. Baseball was democracy.

There were many great local teams to take note of, but the Madrid Coal Miners, a particularly rambunctious, hard playing bunch, made the game competitive on more than one level. Some players always carried bail money with them.

Roswell was another great league, and the town had Negro leagues as well. These teams were tough, probably the toughest in the territory. As an aside note, it should be known in the late 1980s a television program, called "The X-Files," played an episode involving an old white Roswell baseball player from the 1940s. He looked up the FBI Detective Mulder and reveals to him an unusual story, involving a black teammate he became close to during the playing season of 1947. This particular ballplayer was incredibly good and an asset to the team, but he tended to keep to himself except when playing on the field. The young white player so admired this more mature black player that he attempted to befriend him. It wasn't until the very end of the season though that the older Negro player opened up to the younger team member. He revealed to him he wasn't from this planet. He was an alien, and he had been assigned to observe our species for a time. Eventually, he concluded, after years in observation, that humanity was a total waste of life and time.

Then, somehow one day he studied a baseball game. As he watched the balls hit, bases run, and slides to home plate, something happened. This stranger from another galaxy was bitten by the baseball bug, and it held him tight. So, the alien decided, in an unusual state of otherworldly passion, that he wanted to be a baseball player. He borrowed the body of a Negro league player and worked his way up to the mixed leagues. His passion and ability for the game garnered him the eventual awe and respect of his fellow players. The result was a state of camaraderie. This emotional concept though, purely human, affected him deeply. All this the alien told the young white player. With the season ending he felt a need and longing to express his secret on contemplating his own personal mission.

He told his whole story to this young man as implausible as it sounded, shook his hand in friendship, and then he was gone. Wouldn't it have been nice to imagine that some hostile alien race could be considerate to our survival through the validation of baseball alone as our salvation. Play ball, could be the rallying cheer of our survival.

In Ramah our baseball season took off. We practiced it felt like nearly every day. A bag of hard balls was brought to the field, and no more softball was tolerated. We were going to be a baseball team, and that settled it. So much for my idea of a little fun. I never considered that these old boys could have been baseball stars on their high school leagues, but there you have it. We were going to be a tight knit team. Hell, we even appropriated a manager, a manager. His name was Floyd Curly, and he was a sweet, young Navajo man married to a Zuni girl. He was also my assistant teacher in silversmithing.

Floyd somehow was able to arrange a game with the league in Zuni four months from the present time, and all the gun-ho high school ballplayer veterans were salivating in anticipation of crushing the Zuni ball club.

I'll be honest, at practice I was old four eyes. I am not an overly, aggressive player due to owning only one pair of eyeglasses, and the repair shop was two hours away in Albuquerque. Ground balls were mostly the problem, of course. One bounce into the face, and I'd be blind until my frames were repaired. They only had glass lenses back then; plastic lenses were for the future. Anyway, I still felt I had a right to play, after all it was my idea to organize a ball team in the first place.

So, we practiced, and practiced, and practiced and the big day finally came. We were ready, it was our time. Arriving at the Pueblo, the ball field in Zuni was a professional affair. There were new bases, bleachers, benches for the teams, and even a hot dog vendor. The baselines were laid out in lime, and everything was measured and walked off to the game's specifications. These guys were serious. We had been playing on the dirt field behind the old, delinquent high school in Ramah, weeds and all.

Getting situated on our side of the bases, Floyd assigned positions of which I was not included, I was to be a benchwarmer, really guys. But that was that I was mortified humiliated, and ashamed. I was out of the mix, the sideliner, so I bought a hot dog.

The game started off well enough, and our team looked alert and prepared. While consuming my hot dog though, I noticed something. The Zuni team were youngsters; I'd gauge between 18 and 24 years old. It was obvious they'd been playing every season since they could hold a bat. Oh no. Being smaller Pueblo Indian players meant nothing in the eyes of experience. These guys were hot dogs, and they knew it.

The score by the second inning was three to two, their favor. By the fifth inning it was twelve to two. This was not in our teams' expectations at all. We had practiced so much, what went wrong? We knew what we were doing, right?

By the ninth inning the game was thirty-eight to two. It was apparent a bunch of middle-aged teachers and bureaucrats were no match for this youthful regular team of Zuni champs. The Zunis, I truly believe, finally struck out, out of boredom and pity for us. We were an embarrassment.

Returning home to Ramah, we never played another game of baseball after that, and no one ever mentioned Zuni baseball ever again. If I learned anything about baseball from that experience, it was that fresh hot dogs at the ballpark are delicious but cold, old hot dogs don't cut the mustard.

A Bear Story

Once upon a time there was a very young Navajo boy, who joined his father for a deer hunt up into the Shiprock Mountains. The youngster was too young to handle any sort of firearm, but he was excited to accompany his father anyway. They carried their lunch in a pack, and a trusty canteen would quench their thirst. Up, up they climbed on hidden trails only the father knew. He had traversed these mountain slots since he was a boy himself.

Somehow, having stopped to remove a stone from his shoe, the youngster lost all track of his father. He didn't cry or shout, knowing he would scare the deer away, and he was confident his father would eventually recover him.

So, with that youthful reassurance, he wandered on his own to a shadowed side of some cliffs. There was grass here and squaw berries, so he laid down and rested a bit awaiting his father. While resting, the boy heard some faint mewing/moaning sounds in the distance. In time the sounds got closer until around the cliff appeared a small bear cub all alone.

The two eyed each other hesitantly, wearily, oh heck—the way youngsters on the playground eye each other for the first time anywhere. They were both small, probably similar in size, all in all. As kids will do, they finally decided it would be more fun to play than just stare. As luck would have it, they both like to wrestle. So, tussle they did in that solitary spot of grass under the cliff. Oh, the fun they had—bear wrestling.

Soon there was a shout in Navajo of the boy's name. The competition stopped, and the small cub skedaddled. The boy suddenly realized the tribal taboo he had broken. Bears were the brothers of the Navajo, and they were not to touch a bear hide or represent its image in jewelry or any other craft. The bears were sacred.

The boy heard his father calling and responded to him. The father eventually located his son. Then he became curious why the child was scratched up, but he took it for granted the boy had acquired them while lost and never asked.

The years rolled by, and the child grew up. Then the youngster completed school, and he also married a wonderful woman. Later the two had a child, a little girl they named Laurie. But through all those years, he would disappear for short periods of time, and on returning he never revealed his whereabouts.

This good Navajo man did not drink, so this was never a consideration. He just disappeared in sporadic moments and would reappear a couple of days later. Time went on, and the mystery became eventually unbearable. Something had to be done.

The family hired a healer—a costly endeavor but necessary. At this point this good father, husband, was not eating. As a result, he was also losing weight and slowly becoming listless. He was seriously troubled.

The healer took the father to a quiet corner of the hogan. Then he prayed over him, gave him many blessings, and shared traditional chants with him through the ceremony he was assembling within the confines of this home. They spent many hours together, following this routine until the father cracked open with his story.

"For years I've been going to Shiprock Mountain and visiting the bears. They knew my scent and accepted me as one of their own. I would just wander around with them, becoming part of their world. It was so natural for me, and I was happy. But I cannot live in two worlds any longer. It is killing me. I cannot live two lives anymore; I must choose." he said.

The healer now understood the problem. This was a good man who had crossed lives with a bear and become lost. "There is a reason you needed to avoid contact with this brother. His world is not yours." said the healer.

After the sing the healer explained all this to the father and made him comfortable with the concept of one world, one life. There was no forgiveness necessary only the lesson learned. The family had attended every step of this healing process, and now they knew the secret to the mystery. Laurie's father was a wonderful man and a great husband, but he needed to stay away from those damn bears.

Laurie told me this story her senior year at the Pine Hill School. I almost didn't believe it for all its outrageous unlikeliness, but who was I to doubt such an obtuse recollection. It was a story concerning her father, her father, how could it not be true. The only thing I never learned from the story was, was that small cub possibly a female and had she seduced that poor man cub and trapped his heart in her world. Fortunately, for me I'll never know. Laurie's father passed over some time ago. Maybe he's in the bear's spirit world now, who knows. But he did leave me a lesson learned, when it comes to fur, feathers, scales, or skin, love is love, so what are you gonna do.

Retreads

In the fall of 1976 and the spring of 1977, my then wife and I were saving all my paychecks to purchase eighty acres of property, which butted up against the Zuni reservation and BLM (Bureau of Land Management) land. This unknowingly created a stressful economic turn of events, which meant every penny had to be assigned to every specific need. So when new tires were beyond necessary for Ole Blue, there had to be quality compromises to this necessary goal. The tires had to be cheap.

The Nichols brothers were local Mormons, and one of them opened a new mechanic shop and service station on the last hill before you descended into the Ramah Valley proper. Of all the brothers, this was the only one who proved to understand the concept of hard work. His gas prices were what they had to be, but affordable, and oil, brake fluid, transmission fluid, and any other fluid your vehicles circulatory system required was available.

The most extraordinary and unsuspected surprise of this service station though, was a rack of mint-new, retread tires from Mexico for sale. Now I've heard horror stories about retreads but, what the hell, fifteen dollars was in my price range, so I bought a set of four, hot dog.

The first week was a dream with my new black, rubber beauties. The second week was sweeter than the sweetest rose. Ah. But the third week, on one return trip from school, I heard an explosion and felt a heavy, jolting bounce. In shock, looking through my rear-view mirror, I saw a wide short, black snake fly in the air off the truck's rear as I was barreling down the road. Pulling over and stopping, I slowly backed up and opened the door to inspect this unusual and unheard-of phenomenon. Walking to the rear area of the truck, I discovered the entire surface tread of my brand-new tire, I mean all of it, spread across the road. The remaining tire was so bald you could see the rayon belts showing through. This was not good, not good at all. I didn't even make it home before I had a flat tire two miles from the house. I changed the tire with one of the old tires I had as a spare. The Nichols brother, who sold me this set of deceitful rubber imitations, was sympathetic, but he had only one solution for me. It seems he was selling brand-new tires now, and he was taking the trade-ins and reselling them for fifteen dollars. That is what I now bought.

As the weeks went by, I became immune to the sound of exploding retreads and got pretty damn good at speed-changing a tire. But one night, near Tinaja bar, while I was changing one, I felt the hair on the back of my neck rise. I stopped what I was doing and looked around. There was nothing. You must understand this was a country of wild legends. Ghosts and Skin Walkers and even a sighted hairy Bigfoot were normal observations to some folks. Hell, who knew what was hidden up in the Oso Ridge Mountains.

It wasn't that, but I still felt it. Slowly I looked up, and lo and behold, a big bright star was shining overhead. Well, so what, there are lots of stars. The problem was it was a cloud-filled night, and this light was not far above me. So what are you going to do? You finish up with the tire and go home. There are more UFO sightings on the western side of New Mexico then there is roadkill. I'd like to drop this subject, but two weeks later changing the last retread, again my hair on the back of my neck had a repeat performance. Sure enough, there was the UFO again—brighter than ever and even closer. Suddenly something occurred to me, I had neglected to comprehend. The reason these aliens were not interested in beaming me up was the simple fact that they were too entertained, observing the hilarious stupidity of a two-legged wonder who was changing tires for weeks all because he bought retreads to save a few bucks. Who in the f...ing universe is stupid enough to do that? Humph, I wonder.

The Lost Sword

In the spring of 1976, I was doing quite well with extra income coming from one consignment gallery on the south side of the plaza in Santa Fe. My wood-cut painted panels sold frequently in the front windows of the store and garnered extra attention for it drawing in the public. The gallery was an unusual business to say the least. The owner was an older woman of Santa Fe origins, who was well established particularly as an antique book dealer.

She dealt with her initial business interest while also being fully aware the Santa Fe tourist draw had much broader interest than just books alone. So, she expanded into a few antiques and a couple of artists whose work complemented the direction of the gallery/antique bookstore. I was one of them.

One day while delivering a new round panel of a Navajo girl holding a lamb while seated in the grass, I spied a bent sword and scabbard, newly hung on the wall behind the checkout counter. I knew what it was, hell, there wasn't a kid in America who watched old movies involving the US cavalry of the 19th century who didn't. I asked the owner to see it and held this relic of U.S. Army Indian Wars in my hands.

Was it the sword's energy or was it the absurdity that I could admire this piece of history that was symbolic of the subjugation of the very people that I now taught? Was this an enigma wrapped in a dilemma, who knows, but I knew one thing, I had never seen one of these rare representatives of that ruthless military machine call the US cavalry before for sale. I had to have it.

The price was sixty dollars, a princely sum in 1976. I had it deducted from my latest commission check, and we were square. Then I asked the owner the provenance of the sword and where it came from. The gallery owner informed me a high school history teacher from Socorro, south of Albuquerque, had discovered it with a metal detector. It appears this quirky individual's hobby was researching old army battle maps of pre-civil war Indian engagements. These were battles that the army lost, and there happened to be quite a few.

Back then as things were heating up back east for an imminent civil conflict, the army was depleting its western garrisons of men in this expectation. As a result, the numbers were on the Indian's side, and they took full advantage of it. At the time B company of the 4th US Cavalry was pressed way beyond rational expectations and eventually would be thrown full throttle into the civil war's overwhelming threat as well.

The trooper who possessed this sword did not come home, most likely was not buried after his squad's massacre. Time and the elements took charge of his mortal remains and returned him from whence he came until a shy history teacher from a Socorro high school discovered his bent sword and marked his squad's resting place on a map finally. It turns out this same teacher put his son and daughter through college with his weekend journeys into the lost past. I was honored to be supporting his efforts.

Returning early Monday morning directly to school from my girlfriend's home in Albuquerque, I brought the old bent sword to class to straighten it on the silversmithing vice. I described its history and shared the history of the battle lost by the US Cavalry engagement before the civil war with my Navajo students. They were fascinated by the long knife, the name the Indians had given this lethal device of war. Together we all pondered its history.

Now straightened, the sword fit perfectly into the scabbard just as it probably did 120 years before. They were finally reunited as one.

I still have that sword and scabbard; I look at it every day in the hallway of our house. It is a constant reminder of New Mexico's harsh military existence's past, but it is also a reminder of the future irrelevance of the weapon called the sword. The Indian campaigns would be the last direct mass employment of this antiquated tool of war in the United States.

Deep into human prehistory the sword has been the primal weapon of choice in human conflict. Untold millions have fallen under its deathly domain. It's relevance, an unpleasant reminder of our species' enduring unpleasantness. But now, hanging on my wall, with all its symbolic threats a memory of the past, it is simply another object demanding my feather duster when I get time.

Alcohol and Pentecostals

In 1953, Congress finally repealed prohibition for Native Americans. All previous congressional acts toward Native Americans were for the prevention of alcoholic consumption. The first such act was enacted in 1802. That's a total of 145 years ago. The resulting laws associated with these acts were focused on jailing any Indian caught with an alcoholic drink in his or her hand anytime and anywhere in these United States of America.

Newly arriving on the Navajo reservation, I was aware that only 21 years had passed since Native Americans were in a position finally to not get jailed for simply having a beer in public. This was the legacy of the generation of parents whose students I would now teach.

Their generation had survived extreme disproportionate discrimination, and all the rest of our nation's antiquated social baggage that was directed at them. Many Native Americans died from alcoholism. Some were victims of the bad booze of reservation stills, and some were from the cheap bar's back doors in Gallup. They would trade saddles, jewelry, rifles, any possessions they had, and the trading posts were there to give them as little as possible to facilitate their next drunk. It was an endless cruel dead-end cycle.

For those who would finally recover from this interminable disease, religion would often fill the gulf of the addictive need. It would become the new crutch just like their white counterparts. They would search for a hope or redemption in recovery that would send them down the road, looking for that something that would fill that hole that alcohol had left.

The Catholic Church would try to convert the Navajos, but they never really made major headway with these nomadic people. The Mormons had already taken their best lands, and they were out for themselves anyway. So eventually, along came the Pentecostals.

The Pentecostals not only baptized and preached to the Navajo, but they also ordained individuals as Native ministers. This was an incredibly brilliant move. This holy roller church most certainly thrived in Navajo land beyond anyone's expectations. They had made all the right moves.

Later still would come the tent revivals. One morning a huge tent would spring up like a toad stool after a rain. For the next week or two, tents would be lit up at night and arriving Navajos would be singing God's favorite hits all through the night. It soon became known that anyone with some silver could be saved. As a result, after a few evenings there wouldn't be a ring or bracelet or a squash blossom or concho belt left to their owners for miles.

Eventually the tents would be broken down and packed away as if nothing had ever occurred. The circus was leaving town. If you listened carefully though, while he was driving away, you could hear the preacher in the distance shouting, see you next year, same time, and God bless you. Praise Jesus. And then he disappeared into the Holy Spirit, Amen.

Christmas Candy

Not long after the 1974 Christmas festival, where I fortuitously ran to save the lives of some of our smallest students by realizing within a microsecond about a hundred pounds of rock candy falling from a gigantic pinata could possibly kill or main one of them, I heard we were having more discipline problems than usual with the elementary school kids.

The gym, when not in use, was the place we used for the student detention area. It was out of the way and served the purpose quite well. Even so, why were so many students acting up? This had been going on for months now.

Finally, through astute observation and the keenest sense of insight, one of our teachers instead of grading papers while observing detention, actually watched the kids. She revealed to us in devastating detail, the solution to this most uncanny mystery. It was simple, after the waterfall-rain of a hundred pounds of raw rock candy, the remains had scattered all through the gym and in every possible direction. This having been the location of our past Christmas festival, it never occurred to us this candy temptation was still in residence.

It turns out there was candy hidden in every nook and cranny of the gym, and no amount of sweeping was going to get it all. The kids knew it. We did not, so detention for them was a small price to pay for thirty minutes of a candy treasure hunt under the bleachers when a teacher was pre-occupied. Think about it, the closest candy store was fifty-five miles away, so wouldn't you?

Fortunately for the faculty the school year was soon ending, and we would be moving to our new school buildings. But I'd bet there are kids who would still sneak into the old building, follow the floorboard corners carefully, and try to discover a lime green or cherry red sucker. I know I would.

OLD MAN MIRABAL

One weekday afternoon when regular school was on break and summer school hadn't started, I stopped by Tinaja Bar for a beer. It was a nice day, and in two weeks I would be teaching summer school. I taught every summer school since there was no plan in place for year-round payroll for teachers at this time. I didn't mind, there was still a two-week break after summer school for a vacation.

Upon entering, as always, Pat was behind the bar, and I was the only one at the moment in on this weekday. As I sat there with my Budweiser, which he had served me, contemplating my belly button, three Hispanic geezers walked in. They were all pretty-rugged looking, and one of them wore the greasiest sheepskin vest I'd ever seen. Pat knew them and proceeded to converse with them in Spanish. Then he popped open three beers for them. The four of them talked for a while, laughed, and it felt like there was catching up with what was going on. Eventually, it appeared to me the shorter man, who wearing the greasy vest, seemed to be dominating most of the conversation. I suddenly became aware I had seen him around the area in an old beat-up green and white Chevy pickup truck, nothing curious, just around. Soon the trio of old farts were done and bid Pat—"Hasta La Vista" and were gone.

Pat stared at the door after they left, just stared. I guess out of boredom, he walked over to me and informed me, that that was old man Mirabal, the richest man on this side of the state.

I said, "Which one?"

Pat returned, "The one in that raunchy sheepskin vest."

I said, "Really, how?"

Pat, playing the part of the storytelling bartender to the only customer in the joint, proceeded to fill me in on this one-of-a-kind character, Senor Mirabal.

The story started when Pat was fifteen years old around the year 1930 in Grants, New Mexico. Those were bad years, the depression, and rural New Mexico was suffering the worst. People would sell their souls if they could get any money for them. Things were bad. Somehow, Pat found employment in a barber shop, where his job was giving shaves. He was young but hardworking and ambitious. One day a Hispanic rancher, a regular, walked in from San Rafael and asked for a shave. Pat attended to him and also knew him as Senor Mirabal, a very successful local rancher. Doing a good job as always, Senor Mirabal was handed a mirror by Pat, saw his reflection, and grunted approval to the shave. He stared at Pat a moment and finally said, "Pat, you do good work and give a good shave so I'm going to do something for you. You see that bank across the street?"

Pat responded, "Yes."

Mirabal then asked him if he had any money in it?

Pat said, "Yes Sir."

"Well, I'll tell you what Pat, I'm going to take my time here a few more minutes, and I suggest you go and get any money you have out of that bank now."

Pat didn't hesitate. He excused himself from the barbershop and did just that. He passed Senor Mirabal on the way back. Then, back in the shop, he watched as Mirabal entered the bank. Within ten minutes the bank locked its doors, closed, and never reopened again.

Pat's story continued, he told me old man Mirabal only hired Mexicans, which he placed in line camps. They ran the cattle with horses and no vehicles. The only vehicle was Mirabal's truck. Once a month he brought them beans and coffee and a few stores. They were permitted to take one stringy old cow from the herd once a month. If he ever caught them with a good one, he docked the entire crew a month's pay. Senor Mirabal knew these Mexicans weren't going anywhere without his help, and he used them as a somewhat indentured workforce.

Mirabal was a brilliant land baron also. He bought small homesteads for nothing since it was the middle of the worst part of the depression. Once he had surrounded the village of Tinaja, the place the bar was named after. He fenced in the village and just waited for the residents to leave without paying them a single centavo. It was a sheep herding village, and he had trapped them. Without grazing access, they were finished.

Albuquerque's population grew exponentially, due to these land grabs in the 1930s. Big ranchers saw a chance to eliminate small landholders back then, and they took it. Were it not for the railroad and the sawmills, there never would have been opportunities to support these stranded families.

Senor Mirabal was the unspoken king of San Rafael; his word was law. Outside of his family I doubt he had any real friends—only those Mexicans who had to work for him and a few Navajo cattle rustlers who sold him hot beef on the hoof. Mirabal even bought the old Texas rancher's house, who had lost everything at the turn of the century. I believe he purchased it from the professional ladies, who resided there for decades. And no, they weren't secretaries. Eventually, his family moved into the mansion and started renovating. Mirabal died and would never see the work completed.

Pat finished and asked if I wanted another beer. Then he moved on to the carry-out window as a customer honked his horn. I skipped the beer and took off.

I thought about those poor Mexicans stuck out on the *malpais*, watching the *rico's* cows and thought of how desperate they must have been to take such employment. The only blessing was what little they got paid, which they didn't receive until they left. Since they had no chance to spend it on the range, they had it all.

Mirabal accumulated his wealth through stealth and anonymity. No one outside of San Rafael was ever even aware of him, but I had been. At least I was curious, who that old Hispanic was, wearing that ratty old sheep's vest. Eureka. It suddenly occurred to me like a bolt of lightning, this man was a wolf and like a wolf he had no fear, so he studied his environment and his competition and using the camouflage of his victims, he dressed as a sheep, pretending to fit right into the landscape. Who would know, and that's what he did.

So, be aware of wolves in sheep's clothing, no matter how much you want to believe they're sheep at heart. They're wolves, and they're wolves because they want to be.

RAMAH LAKE

The lake is not a lake, it is a reservoir. The Mormons dammed this Zuni Mountain watershed, and the Zunis have been pissed off ever since. The mountain snows that feed this brook system are from the Oso (bear) Ridge part of this extended range. All this mountain chain is part of the great Continental Divide and peaks out usually at about 9,000 feet. There are ghost towns and old logging camps, now abandoned, lying hidden amongst the nooks and crannies of this miles long mountain complex. There are even waterfalls up McGaffy Road, roaring furiously throughout the spring thaw.

The secret of Ramah Lake's bass fishing is a coveted one. Many old New Mexicans feel the secret may only be bestowed on those who truly deserve it. The lake is a New Mexico treasure, one of the few independent water sources sustaining wildlife, cattle, crops, and two-legged intruders.

Visiting the lake for the first time with another teacher, I was takenback by its beauty and splendor. The lake itself is crowned on the north side by what can only be called Neapolitan ice cream stripes of sandstone. The red, pink, yellow, and cream coloration showing off in reflection into the lake's waters consumes the imagination. In the late afternoon from the south lakeside the view can only be described as no less than breathtaking. Following this discovery my first summer, I promised myself I would bring Socrates, my dog, and we would take to the rocky tree covered cliffs and then in the warm summer heat jump to our hearts desire into the slightly cool waters of Ramah Lake. We would quench our bodies thirst-full needs. Well, that was the plan anyway.

So one fine beautiful afternoon, with the sun shining bright and barely a breeze blowing, I grabbed my trunks and told Socrates it was time. Then I grabbed a towel from the bathroom, and we hauled off into the truck and drove a couple of miles, which meandered north through the village on past the rodeo grounds and then ended in a dirt parking lot adjacent to the reservoir. Soc and I jumped from the truck, full of anticipation and unbridled joy. We were ready.

We scoured the sandstone cliffs for the perfect spot and found it. Hidden behind a tree I changed into my trunks. Socrates had decided on his birthday suit. I climbed to the top of a high projecting rock with an inner state of expectant ecstasy and jumped twelve feet out into the beautiful, still waters of our dear *madre*, Ramah Lake.

The shock of the lake's waters rocked me. There are no words to describe. When my breath finally returned, after what seemed hours, I ever so slowly became aware I would continue to sink if I didn't begin to move my frozen limbs. I eventually fought my way to the surface and in a giddy moment of realization discovered the top foot of the lake offered a sustainable temperature for the human anatomy. Floating on my back, I slowly recovered my senses and finally remembered my bathing partner.

I could see Socrates scampering on the rocks and awaiting my evaluation of this extraordinary opportunity. He eyed me carefully, examining my every expression. He was always a smarty pants. Finally, concealing my honest opinion of the situation, I called to him, "Come on buddy, you're going to love it, you need a bath anyway." He could hear the treachery in my voice. He whimpered and jumped around and came up with what seemed every excuse he could dream up. He could even wait till next time, okay?

Finally I'd had enough, "You know your mother was a water dog, and besides that she was a girl, and she wasn't afraid of anything." Oh, the humiliation, I immediately regretted my words, but hell I had no other recourse.

In a total act of frustrated desperation my good buddy ran and jettisoned into the welcoming arms of the waters. Socrates eventually recovered and swimming toward me, he gave me a look I will remember to this day. I'm sure it was, "You Bastard." He paddled around me obviously planning some covert retaliation, but then suddenly you could see a light switch on in that brilliant mind. The decision was made.

He swam to me, With the use of superior dog telepathy, he demanded that I grab his tail, and he would drag me back to shore. Then we would get the hell out of here. He hesitated and added a final comment. "If anything happened to you, who do you think was going to feed me?" He was always the smart one in this relationship.

Helicopter Johnny

My cousin Nancy lived in Tucson, Arizona, with her husband John and two kids. John was stationed at the Davis Mothan Air Force Base there and was a flight mechanic. His expertise was a background in a wide variety of aviation technology. Now this particular air force base was the prime resting place of obsolete and aging aircraft, row after row of them. Essentially it was an aviation museum.

After a pleasant visit with the family in Tucson once, Johnny explained to me what he did and also that acquisitions were also carried out on the base itself—need a bomber (sin) bombs, come on down. You're a foreign government who needs some Korean War fighter jets—come on down. Don't like transport jets and prefer props like DC threes—come on down. I was shocked at first, and then I realized, why not. Even if everything was old, Johnny and his crew could get it running. Why not? This was amazing.

Back on the reservation, my mind was wandering one day and I thought about the local ranchers and the problems of rounding up lost strays. They were perpetually on the dirt roads and trails, searching for one calf or another, praying that coyotes or mountain lions hadn't gotten them. Now what if these ranchers had a helicopter. They could hop in, cover their vast stretches and look for lost herds, here and there, and be back home in time for tea. Well that just sounds nuts. Really? Why?

So after some cogitation, during a trip to Gallup. I used a payphone and called my cousin Nancy. She got John on the phone, "John, you said anyone can buy obsolete aircraft, right?"

John replied, "That's correct."

I asked, "So John do you have cheap old helicopters?"

He said, "Yes we have row after row of Korean War ones, why do you ask?"

So I laid out my total remarkable scheme to him of selling vintage helicopters to the Mormon ranchers.

After thinking about it, John said "Why not."

Two days later using the phone in the new school when no one was looking, I called him again. John had researched the antiquated Korean War units that we would be interested in and informed me for $100.00 each we could buy them, with a minimum lot order of ten, of course. John figured with age, hard use and deteriorated parts, we could still put five usable helios into the air, and we could sell them for no less than $5,000.00 each.

Hot dog. I was going to be the used helicopter king of New Mexico. Only a genius could come up with a plan like this. "Howard Hughes, move over and make room on the couch."

I didn't mind sharing my brilliant plan with others. After all, no one else had Johnny in their back pocket, so I mystified many other teachers with my intentions of being a used aviation tycoon. You could see their envy. The sky was now the limit. Watch me now.

"Are you going to ensure test flights? Do you have a test pilot? Are you licensed in New Mexico For these types of sales? Will there be a limited warranty on these helicopters? What makes you think they will even fly after so many years?" These were questions other teachers surrounded me with. Tut, tut, there was so much jealousy and envy around me. It was starting to wear me down. Why couldn't anyone see the big picture? This was the future.

After a week of this, I called Johnny and asked about the acquisition plans of our copters. Johnny coughed, heed and hawed, and then reluctantly informed me that he was given the opportunity for an early muster to his retirement. My cousin, Nancy, insisted he take it, so they could return to New Jersey, the family home.

"But Johnny, what about our helicopters?" I said.

John said it was just impossible with this now short schedule and that he was sorry, besides, he wouldn't be around to even assemble them now.

I was shaken, my self-important esteem was crushed. Now I was just an art teacher on a small reservation in New Mexico, that's all.

I looked up into the sky that night under the stars, and after meditating I remember saying, "Thank you, God, for protecting me from another of my hair-brained schemes. That was really close."

THE AMERICAN BAR

The Navajo Squaw Dance is generally a dance for young girls reaching that post pubescent period of their life that demands recognition of their new place in womanhood. This event is private and traditional and has all the hallmarks of an initiation into adulthood and recognition by the tribe.

That was why my friend, Samson, was there—girls. He and some friends decided to ride their Pinto ponies up to the dance and participate in the celebrations. There was much dancing and praying and singing all through the night. The festivities were incredibly significant to the long legacy of this Navajo group. Sometimes, though, a little hanky-panky may also be a byproduct with this occasion, and the unexpected can result.

The next school day back at the house one afternoon, Samson showed up. This did occur irregularly as anyone was welcomed to our abode if they dared. He had a frown on his face and trying to look at me in the eye, which is hard for a Navajo, he asked, "Will you give me a ride to Black Rock hospital?"

"Why," I asked.

"I need to get a shot," he said.

"What kind of shot?" asked I.

"The kind of shot that will keep my spicket from dripping." he said.

"Oh," says I. "Tell you what, meet me at the school parking lot after the last bell, and we'll take off for Black Rock."

That's what we did. The drive one way to the hospital is twenty-five miles, not around the block by a long shot. I got the whole story about the corruption of his spicket minus the girl's name, of course. His studly pride was now tarnished by his painful awareness of reality's consequences. Ouch.

While at the hospital I sat and read Herbert's *Dune* while I waited for him. The time dragged by but eventually he awkwardly walked toward me and said it was done. So we left. The ride back was quiet, and I hesitated a tiny smile on my lips at someone else's expense. I just couldn't help it.

The rest of the school year went by with the drama so natural to a small reservation community in the middle of nowhere. Sometimes the most insignificant happenings to occur would reach the front pages of our minds and entertain us through the rest of the week. One such news story was this.

Driving west early one morning, someone found Samson hitchhiking on the side of the road, barefoot. He was in bad shape and smelled bad too. Ah, the travesty of life's misadventures. The driver, who picked him up, asked, "What happened?" Curiosity was killing him.

Fortunately, Samsom was still inebriated enough to spill the whole plate of beans. It seems he had gone underage into the American Bar which is located on Coal Avenue in Gallup.

Somehow, as he sneaked along the bar's shadows, he came upon a couple of Navajo cattle rustlers who were celebrating their most recent theft. They were pretty wasted by the time he showed up. Even so, they welcomed him into the booth and ordered him beer and whiskey. Lord knows how long this newly acquired, steadfast friendship traveled through the night, but late in early morning the bartender was cleaning up and found our friend Sampson passed out in the booth and bootless. His fast-made friends had stolen his boots and left him adrift.

It was a cold early spring morning, walking barefoot fifty miles back to Ramah. I'm sure the birds were chirping, and the deer were nibbling fresh grass shoots by the roadside. The early morning sunlight was glorious. Somehow I think none of these blessings occurred to my Native American buddy. I'm sure, with all of God's gifts surrounding him, as he struggled barefoot on the side of the road, there was only one question he needed answered. Do you know how much a new pair of boots are?

OLE BLUE

Ole Blue was a slant six, baby blue Ford pickup born in the year 1963. She had a straight stick transmission, positive traction axle, and to my mind, never once got stuck in the snow or mud in Ramah, and that's saying something.

Ole Blue had saved me from Black Angus, cars swerving into our lane, and more close calls then a soul deserves. If I fell asleep at the wheel between Grants and Ramah, she would travel along visiting lonely meadows looking for ruts to shake me awake, and together we would wander until we uncovered the blacktop road again. Yes, sirree, she kept an eye on my worthless hide, and I wouldn't be here today were it not for her inanimate maternal concern. I should have married that truck. But in the end, I think she preferred a sisterly relationship anyway.

One of the fortunate aspects of our relationship was the fact she was easy and generally cheap to repair. For instance, Ole Blue's brake line was corrupted by some cliff rocks that bounced under the carriage and severed the brass brake line. At that time, we barely made it home without an accident. Now, there are no parts stores any closer than sixty miles, so unless you have a very creative mind you are not going anywhere soon. Next to our old Mormon rental house were a couple of wrecked cars left, years past, by my landlord. They were both Chevys. Since my truck was a Ford that was a no go, or was it?

I crawled under the old Chevy Nova, made some measurements, and found it damn close to the pickup's measurements, so why not. Replacing the new brake line for the old, it actually worked. I had to use bailing wire in a couple of junctures to keep the Nova's brake-line in place, but it worked. The tiny drip from one of the wheel's unions was negligible, and I would just have to check the brake fluid level more often.

Ole Blue was coveted by many Navajos. There was just something about her, besides the fact that young Navajos loved every pickup truck they saw. They were too young to know the difference between love and lust when it came to horsepower.

Now don't get me wrong, at the time there were other girls, I mean cars. There was a redheaded Volkswagen, also I had a fling with a white 1975 MGB. But none of them lasted. My girl, Ole Blue, waited me out, and knew I'd return, and I did with a hanged-dog apology and my sorry excuses.

Later, Ole Blue and I moved to Albuquerque. There I met a real girl, and we made a family including her mother and later Jeremy, our son. My baby blue sister was there through it all. She helped me renovate our first house on Palo Duro and accompanied me to the city dump quite a few times. But Sis was getting up in years, and soon she just rested on the corner of our lot and listened to the birds chirping. She was retired.

One day there was a hard knock on the front door. My mother-in-law, Alice Marie, went and opened the door. Standing there, well swaying, were three Mexican "Wise Men." Well, it was close to Christmas and they were holding a bottle of Tequila and asking the *madre* of the house if that gorgeous blue pickup outside was for sale. Mom came and found me about the house, and I proceeded to the front door. Now, these three gentlemen were roofers, and they had had a big payday. As they were driving by my house, they saw my sister and fell in love with her.

"Would you sell the truck, senor? We can give you two hundred dollars cash right now."

Now this was a lot of money back then, and I realized this was manna from heaven, so, guilt ridden though I was, I said, "Yes." I found the title, and we signed it, I grabbed the cash, then picking up the keys I said,

"Would you like me to start her up and back her out?"

The three Mexican wise men stared at me with bulging eyes and sang in chorus, "It runs?"

You never saw three Tequila-soaked brains sober up so fast. "Sure, senor, that'll be great." You could see they'd gotten the deal of a lifetime. They couldn't leave fast enough.

But as they were departing, I mentioned checking the brake line often. Also, I told them this truck had been very good to me, and I thought of her as almost a sister.

They stared at me pathetically, I can almost hear their departing last words, "Crazy Gringo. *Feliz Navidad.*"

Satellite Dish

In the Spring of 1977, an earth-shattering, mega occurrence happened at our school. Many were not prepared for the universal ramifications of this cataclysmic event. No prophecy could have divulged the major significance of this singular movement toward the future. That's right, maybe you guessed it, satellite TV came to the special education building. This was the very first television on all our little reservation.

The satellite dish itself was the size of a medium, children's swimming pool. When it was in full operation, it appeared as a giant toad stool, leaning upside down facing the sun. The true miracle was that it actually worked. I stopped by the special education building on my class break and investigated this wonder of American know-how and was not disappointed.

"The Gong Show" was on, and a few other teachers joined me. Since the classroom, where the TV was located, was not in use, we introduced ourselves to the American culture we had not participated in for a few years.

Chuck Barris did not disappoint. The show was offensive, stupid, trite, amusing and absolutely brilliant. Gene, Gene, the dancing machine, and the unknown comic, with a paper bag over his head with eyes and mouth cut out, were instant favorites. The hilarity and laughter were unrestrainable.

Somehow, I knew the earth had moved that day the satellite had been erected. This was a shift through technology that would permanently change the concept of isolated reservation life. Native Americans were now able to connect with the viewing nation at large, like it or not.

So much would now change their thinking. Prices for goods in commercials would be compared with those in the trading post. The cheaper price of trucks in Albuquerque would hammer the Gallup dealerships, who were used to gouging Indians for 40% down payments. But most of all, English would become the dominant replacement for Native speakers.

Within the first year of Satellite TV's springing up on our little reservation, I heard rumors that students were refusing to speak Navajo at home. English was television, a language all kids wanted to know. The transition of evolving change in language-dominance followed me through my three years, three years of teaching at Ramah Navajo school. My first year I heard Spanish as well as Navajo. My second year it was only Navajo and English, and the third year English was circumventing Navajo. Maybe this was my own warped personal observation, but there it is.

The future had invaded our little reservation, and its name was assimilation. All this was spinning through my mind; what would be the consequences? The realization was my life had already been molded by television. Who was I to talk. I was a "Howdy Doody" kid.

So knowing the Navajos the way I did, understanding their incredible sense of humor through the twist and turns life throws at them, I had little doubt they could survive The "Gong Show" and even Chuck Barris.

SOCRATES

Socrates was my friend, and I loved him, though I know he loved me more than I could ever reciprocate. His examples in loyalty and dedication only magnified the high intellectual capacity apparent in nearly every decision he made. He may have been the smartest being I was ever privileged to share space on this planet with. I am often in awe of the opportunity of that friendship and the guidance as he accompanied me in what time we shared in this life. I pray he allows me a reunion on the other side to share past memories and experiences.

Knowing Socrates, he will just look at me with those all-knowing eyes, see my pain, and approach me with that big ole tongue of his and lick my tears away. His love was always unfathomably dedicated.

Socrates was born in a manger, literally. His siblings and he resided in a hole between the legs of an old mare. She acted as their nanny when their mom was swimming, always swimming, in the reservoir in Gallenas Canyon, north of Las Vegas, New Mexico. Mom was one of the largest of the breed, Labrador Retriever. She easily weighed 140 pounds and was all muscle. She was sleek and black and the envy of every canine female for miles. She was just magnificent.

Now dad was another story. It seems he was a rolling stone of sorts; he was a Weimaraner. Those damn Germans just can't seem to keep it in their pants. Anyway, after he had his way, he was never heard of again.

Almost all the pups favored mom, but in a corner in the manger, when they were crawling around was the runt who favored both parents. Now nanny always kept close watch on these kids and would snort and whinny at any misbehavior. She allowed me visitations, but it was apparent I must remember my manners and address her with respect before I inspected the litter of pups. She was highly protective of her charges.

The runt stole my heart. I watched as he tried to join in sibling games of tuff and tumble, but it soon became obvious that he was a thinker.

When we were finally permitted into the sacred bonding of a man/dog union, after the completion of the weaning process, of course, we stared into each other's eyes and swore an unfailing friendship. Next to the river under a canopy of stars, in the eyes of God and all the Saints, I then proclaimed his name to be Socrates. After all he was a thinker.

Socrates was with me through the hardest most turbulent years of a young artist's life. Also, the country was trying to recover its self-confidence and self-respect following a misguided war and a struggle to accept its own multicultural identity. Through all that, Socrates never judged me. He was entirely aware of his and my surroundings and dealt with problems as they came. We were a team, and two is more than one. For a year after graduate school, I was forced to live in Baltimore as an amusement park designer in Pikesville, Maryland. During that year we shared an old iron factory building with another artist who worked as a bar back for James Brown's Baltimore restaurant. The area, in which we lived, was inner city sketchy and adjacent to the University of Maryland hospital.

While we lived there, there was an instance when Socrates, sensing a disturbance at the window, demanded to be outside. On two separate occasions this Labrador/ Weimaraner hero saved two nurses from the assault of rape. Hearing loud shouting we ran to follow him behind our building and found some poor disheveled young, exhausted nurse staring up at us in shock and said she thought she was a goner for sure. Socrates would then lick her to reassure her she was okay and now safe.

Eventually, Soc and I made it back to our beloved New Mexico. We had suffered so, contending with gray skies and crowded cities of the east.

Though the new job was a temporary teaching position on a small Navajo Reservation in western New Mexico, we didn't care. We were going home. The new position was fine by me, but it was a hardship on Socrates. The Mormon community I lived in had warned me about unleashed dogs. The ranchers would shoot any dogs they saw. They would tolerate no threat to their stock and took carte blanche to eliminate any supposed threat. This meant, outside the house, Socrates had to be chained like the prisoner of Zenda. He hated it, but he was alive.

Once, I left him off the chain, feeling a false sense of confidence that the community now knew us and had found my loyal companion somehow acceptable. I was mistaken. Socrates didn't return home that night. Where was he? After two days, I returned home from class to find a miserable dirty pile of bones by my back door. It was Socrates. I carried him inside, washed him and following a blood trail to his head, discovered a large hole above his eyebrow. He had been shot, but somehow the bullet traveled the surface of his skull an exited through the back scalp of his head. There is no luck to describe how close this dog came to death. I cleaned his wound and jammed three Bufferin down his throat. Three days later he was like new except for a funny little scar over his eyebrow.

The years at the reservation school went by, and Socrates and I survived many misadventures and adventures together. There were relationships with other friends and even a wife, but our bond outlasted them all. We had seen a lot together. It's not often in life you get to meet your soul mate, and he happens to be a dog. Well, so what, I've seen worst. Besides, he ain't heavy he's my brother.

Wrestling in Ramah

All the world's a stage and we are but a select few of its raunchy spectators. These are the words I think about when I'm referring to, what else, but the great "Sport?" Of wrestling. Wrestling was the greatest cultural integrator in the history of the state of New Mexico. At least it appeared to be so to me in the 1970s. Back then you might not know your senator or congressional representatives' names ,but you sure as hell knew the roster of wrestlers performing Saturday morning on Channel 5 TV.

The sponsor for Saturday morning wrestling was the one and only "La Copita Wines." A wine superfluously famous in possibly every alley and gutter in old Albuquerque and exclusively sold in pint bottles only. Mike London, the local wrestling promoter, was the presentator of this fine beverage for many years and did a damn fine job. This sponsor saw wrestling through the best of the sport's imaginary history. Shakespeare himself would fare relinquish his literary crown to the brilliant absurdities of this wrestling ring on Saturday mornings. The sheer joy of adolescent invention was a cornerstone in every performance.

I first saw Channel 5 wrestling on a lonely Saturday morning in Las Vegas, New Mexico, in 1972. My friend Eileen had traded me two months free rent for some construction work when I first got to graduate school at New Mexico Highlands. Later she would throw me out. She needed money. I had none and as a result I ended up on the floor under the student union building of the university. Nothing personal Andy, just business. I understood, Eileen had a family to support.

Any who, while I was there, I would watch this black and white TV production out of Albuquerque and wonder to myself, Is this serious ?

Then after watching the TV audience I suddenly realized, yes it is, like a heart attack. I had entered the "Real" TV world of New Mexico. The place where reality would go to die.

The names of these wrestling characters were as unique as the spectacular personalities they projected. There was Randy Romero, Mill Mascaras, TNT, El Hacon, The Shiek and of course Angel Blanco, just to name a few. On Saturday mornings, these men were gods (as long as they didn't drink La Copita). They were most possibly the best known and identifiable personalities in the state until the last advertisement and it was time to turn the TV off. Come on, it's Saturday morning, get a life.

In the fall of 1975, the school would occasionally employ a rotating circuit of performers to entertain the students and staff. One of these particular entertainments was a troop of visiting Albuquerque wrestlers. Now I immediately recognized Randy Romero and realized how difficult this venue was for him and the rest of the retinue. It had been three years from when I saw them last. Channel 5, in 1975, was not featuring Saturday Morning Wrestling anymore, did La Copita bail? Was the cartoon cartel finally addicting the vulnerable minds of younger viewers seducing them with the likes of "The Little Train that Could" or "Deputy Dog"? Albuquerque wrestling had been abandoned by Saturday morning prime time and would have to make its own way through signal free valleys and mesas of the western reservations and any other opportunities for live action performances throughout the state. These wrestlers were now as disenfranchised Ronan in search of a contract or hopeful temporary employment.

The day Randy and crew presented themselves in the gym of the school, you'd have thought the gods of Olympus had just dropped by for a visit. The kids were speechless, these men had been their heroes and still were. When their parents had travelled to Albuquerque visiting a relative who had moved there, these kids remember those Saturday mornings watching wrestling. These same kids were now in awe. These wrestlers were not just wrestlers they were superheroes before there were superheroes. The kids were gobsmacked.

After setting up, Randy and the Sheikh came forward and introduced one by one all the kids' heroes. The kids were in rapture. This was certainly the greatest experience of their lifetime. The gang had mats down and prepared and proceeded to demonstrate shoulder holds, hand locks, back flips and any other famous maneuver they were known for. The kids were shouting, cheering, jeering, and were generally enthralled by the whole show.

Toward the performance's end Randy asked for volunteers from the peanut gallery to step up and try their hand at a takedown or two. One or two went up and after a few falls too many, begged off and returned to their seats.

The afternoon's splendid entertainment was now nearing its conclusion. Our principal profusely thanked this fine entourage of Randy's, and after all the applause that would wake Godzilla himself, the students filed out shaking the wrestler's hands who stood in line as they exited.

In the parking lot while they were packing up, I stopped and visited a few of these fine men. I told them I remembered them in the heyday of the 1972 broadcasting season. They laughed, and said, "Oh yeah, the old days" and then explained they might not have had much physical fortitude remaining anyway. Even for all the show, the wrestling act was a physically dilapidating experience. They felt lucky they had gotten this far, besides, now they got to travel the state they did not know from sequestered TV studios. They now had a chance to meet adoring kids, like their own at home, who needed a little dose of famous superhero stardom right there in their own sleepy little reservation in the middle of nowhere.

I realized these men truly were heroes. Not the wrestling part, but the fact, even with their strained economic circumstances, they performed because they really loved the kids. Their smiles and cheers were all these men needed and that in itself was worth the price of a tank of gas to anywhere.

Mexico With Stan

Stan Lawrence had been my brother-in-law. He has since passed, God bless him. He was a brilliant musician and most times a good friend. In 1976, it was decided one Spring break, that he and I would sojourn down to San Carlos, Mexico and release our teachers' angst of the difficult past winter's months. This trip was well deserved and his sister, my wife at the time, supported the gesture. She even supplied her Volkswagen for the journey.

Driving through Show Low, Arizona, on the way down we happened upon a second-hand junk store with an abundance of items left along the street curb. This is where I spied a magnificent pair of elk antlers, a matching set. Since I was driving, I pulled over and liberated them from their lonely ordeal. Now if you know how large elk horns are, you can imagine the room it took in my wife's little red Volkswagen. Well, I never owned a rack like that before. How could I leave them?

Continuing on, the trip went smoothly, and we arrived on the "Catch 22" beach in San Carlos, Mexico. The beach's name was from the fact that the actual movie "Catch 22" and later the original "Mash" were filmed there.

The weather was beautiful, heck it was perfect. During the day whale pods cruised by and showed off their babies. The trip at this point was picture perfect. I read Hemingway while sipping Tequila under a makeshift lean-to on the beach. It felt good how time slowed down and let me relax and relish the afternoons.

Later Stan and I would play chess. Stan likes to win, like his dad, and I took joy throwing in every unpredictable move he'd never expect. He was still going to win; I just wasn't going to make it easy for him.

Near the end of our stay, we decided to explore Guaymas, the city next door, and maybe catch a movie. In town we were in luck, and the movie feature looked almost worthwhile. Into the theatre we went, seated with maybe half the population of the city. This was going to be a night to remember and all in Spanish.

After the previews and other introductory features, the movie came on. Within a few minutes, Stan and I sensed something was wrong, and soon it became obvious this was a bottom of the barrel Spanish-dubbed American porn flick. It was so bad it became farcically comical, so we sat through it.

Amazingly, there was a follow up feature, "The Life of San Martin de Porres." I kid you not. Only in Mexico could such an oblique, absurd circumstance of fate occur. Later, I would remember this entire segment of this wondrous saint's life story; he was indeed a mystery.

After the movie Stan said he'd drive back to the campsite, so I went to sleep. In a while the car stopped, and I was rudely awakened and realized we were at a police roadblock. These civilian-dress officers were looking for drug smugglers. After questioning us and preparing to let us through, one of them spied the elk antlers. This particular police officer wanted them, well so did I. We were forced to remove them from the back seat. After much admiration the police informed me they were dangerous and needed to be confiscated.

I could only imagine, running into a bank saying, "This is a holdup." Threatening with a dangerous rack of elk horns, the bank was going to pass over the money just like that? I don't think so, so I said, "No, you can't have them, and I want names." After that the police led me over to the side of the road, forced me to my knees, and held the rifle barrel to the back of my head. Great move, Andy.

The police then proceeded to take the car apart. Under the back seat next to the car battery, they found "one" seed of marijuana. Holding it with a tweezers, he shoved it under my nose, and then in English said, "Senor, in Mexico this is jail."

Stan was over by the car with a look of, "I knew you'd be trouble," and just stared. Suddenly another car appeared at the roadblock. There was a pleasant exchange with the occupants and the police, and then in a flash they suddenly hit the gas and took off.

It was pure chaos, the police jumped up, jumped into their Federal van like the keystone cops, and with guns out the windows, they speed away after their assailants.

Now it was just me on my knees and Stan by the VW, alone. "Well, I guess it's time to go home," I said. We packed up my beloved, elk horns and made for the campsite.

The next morning we broke camp and started for the border. There were no problems except something, every so often, something didn't feel right with the car. We stopped in Tucson, saw my cousin Nancy and her family, and then continued on through the night to get home. Travelling along the treacherous Salt River Canyon road, the car was beginning to swerve. Halfway up the Canyon at night with Stan driving, I saw a wheel roll by us and suddenly we were dragging our rear axle. We were royally screwed.

Somehow, there was just enough starlight to climb down into the Canyon. I was able to locate the wheel and carry it up the cliff and back onto the pavement. It was two o'clock in the morning. I investigated and uncovered the cause for the calamity.

We had had a new brake job on my wife's car done in Grants. The repair shop was run by a teacher who hired his students to do the work—kind of a work study. One student had obviously not been trained about the purpose and significance of the cotter pin, an object that holds the wheel onto the end of the Volkswagens axle's spindle, so we were stuck.

Ah. But there are miracles. A pickup truck stopped to see what was up—just a couple of drunken cowboys. I told them of our predicament, and they said "Sorry, but would a flashlight be of help?"

I said, "Sure." They handed it over and said goodbye and good luck, and then drove off.

Thanks to them, I could see now an inventory in my mind and the impossibility of what was needed for this repair. I loved Stan, but he was useless for this. He was a musician and a dreamer above all things. The second miracle had been the hubcap of the wheel had kept the large axle nut from disappearing.

Suddenly some police lights appeared over the hill. Oh no, I thought. The squad car pulled up and out stepped a middle-aged cop. I told him, "If I only had a wrench, I could rethread the axle spindle and eventually could probably get the wheel back on, and if I only had a nail for a cotter pin with the nut rethreaded I was certain I could get us back home."

This police officer was obviously exhausted, double shifted, but still he smiled. He went to the trunk of his squad car and after fumbling around, returned with a channel lock and a nail of all things. I told him he was my third miracle, and I just couldn't thank him in any words. He smiled and said good luck and drove away into the night.

It took me an hour. With Stan holding the flashlight, I slowly rethreading the ground off edge of the spindle with the nut and using the channel locks, I achieved success and we were on our way. The dawn through the Zuni valley was magnificent that morning. The shadows of the mesas were mixed with early morning mists, giving rainbow refractions at each curve of the road. It was the beginning of a beautiful day.

Now if you ever travel to beautiful Mexico and for some reason observe a pair of magnificent elk antlers on the side of the road, for God's sakes, don't stop, keep driving.

THE ONE THAT GOT AWAY

No, this story is not about a fish, though he was slippery as one sometimes. This story is about a student of mine and his name was Chee Dodge Martine, and he was the brightest, orneriest, cleverest, dumbest genius God ever created. Sometimes I believed he was my friend, little brother and student, and other times he was the greatest nemesis any teacher ever had. Because, you see, with all that potential, Chee was not going to be broken by the love and consideration of all those who surrounded him and cared for him. I loved Chee Dodge, and there was nothing I could do to help him except watch his acts of self-destruction and shake my head in hopelessness.

When I got to the Ramah Navajo summer school in 1974, Chee was one of my first students. He was obviously talented as an artist and quite a brilliant conversationalist when he wanted to be. His old music teacher and I accidentally brought up his name one time, and she informed me he was a certified genius. She had Chee in class the year before and watched him learn to read music almost entirely without her help. He then taught himself to play the guitar within three days. Three days. When he left her class, he never touched the guitar again and moved on to something else.

You see that was Chee's conundrum. He was so intelligent and talented that boredom and the slow pace of day-to-day life on the reservation just crushed him. But Chee did have a big ace in the hole, a gift only God almighty can bestow upon very special individuals who share their limited time with us. Chee Dodge Martine was the funniest Navajo ever created and I'm not mincing words.

I watched Chee one afternoon, slouched down next to the school with four other young boy students, proceed to tell jokes about an old Navajo woman crossing the street. He had those kids in tears of laughter from his verbal antics, and that was just about an old woman crossing the street. Chee was constantly telling jokes. His mind never stopped, there was always something to articulate about. Chee could make a dog taking a dump into a twenty-minute soliloquy of hilarious proportions. His cleverness dominated his intelligence though, and no one was going to get past that.

Is the child the father of the man? I always thought that was a Yeat's quote, but I'm probably wrong. Still, I've always believed in the premise of the quote. Whatever formed the childhood of an individual would eventually be responsible in some way for the future developments of said individual. I don't know what happened in his early childhood, I never met his parents either, but something happened to force him to hide behind that thick emotional armor of comedy. I knew no one close to him. I knew no girlfriends of his, and yet Chee was loved by everyone.

Like every Navajo boy in school, I knew he wanted to be a famous bull rider. Chee wore an oversized, wide brimmed, black cowboy hat with the traditional toothpicks stuck in the band. It was old and dusty, and I am certain that it had never ridden a bull either. Chee was full of cow patties, and everyone knew it. It just added to his clownish behavior.

For some reason Chee Dodge Martine had a fight in school five days before he was to graduate, and he quit. Just like that he quit, didn't come back, and I never saw him again. We had been through much in the three years that I knew him, and I even took him to Mexico for three weeks in an outrageous journey through the Yucatan in which he proved to be the most contentious plotter of mutiny than even Captain Bligh had to contend with. Chee and I had been through a lot, and neither of us had killed the other yet.

Two years after leaving Ramah to strike out on my own as an artist in Albuquerque, I got word that Chee had found an old fiddle and locked himself in a hogan until he had taught himself to play. Not long after he joined a Zuni-Navajo band, and they played in a Tinaja bar and other venues available to young starters. After that I lost contact of any info about what he was up to.

In the meantime, I met my future wife and moved into the back of her studio on 6th Street off Central Avenue in downtown Albuquerque. We had renovated the back area into a studio room apartment. We shared a twin bed. We were a lot skinnier then. Anyway, my Turza is gifted in many ways; she is multi-talented and sensitive. One night as we were sleeping, she was disturbed and opening her eyes was staring directly at a dim pillar of grey light. It shimmered standing there and then in time, suddenly departed out the back of the studio. Turza thought it odd but was able to go back to sleep.

The next morning she told me of her experience and asked me what I thought. I had nothing. We had some breakfast, and then we went to work in the studio. About 10:30 there was a phone call. Turza said it was for me. Answering I found Bradley, my old sheep thief buddy, on the line. "Yat ta hey."

"Yat ta hey yourself, you white demon," Bradley said. "I thought you'd like to know, Chee Dodge died last night."

Quite shaken I asked, "How'd he die?"

Bradley said, "He drowned in six inches of water at Tohachi Hot Springs—too drunk to save himself. His two drunk buddies just stood in the dark totally unaware of his drowning."

I asked Bradley when he thought this had happened.

Bradley thought between one o'clock and two in the morning.

I thanked Bradley, hung up the phone and just stared at the floor. I was devastated.

Sometime later Turza asked me when my friend had died.

I told her the approximate time.

She said, "That's about right then."

I asked what she meant.

She said, "No matter how difficult your relationship with Chee was, he found it important to say goodbye to you before he left."

Now I understood. I understood at that point there are those we want to save, and they break our hearts, but it is their life and their choices that matter. Respecting that and accepting them as they are is called love. I wanted more for Chee, but it was not my life, it was his. I miss you, old buddy. See you on the other side.

My Heroes Have Always Been Teachers

This book is dedicated to teachers, the greatest heroes of human history. What record of human achievement on this planet would even remain without them? Put simply, without teachers we do not exist and for that matter we'd have no history. Period.

Teachers are the first of humanitarians. It is the idealism they possess that leads them to endeavor to make the world a better place. No teacher enters this profession to get rich. Lord knows we are beyond needing to compensate them better. The majority of teachers are in it to share knowledge, do good work, and direct us with their efforts to make better decisions and more positive outlooks on the future.

Many a troubled student recalls one particular teacher, who pulled them aside and ask them simply, what's wrong? That simple question has probably saved many lives unknowingly by its timing and significant care. Often there is no one else in a kid's life but a teacher and that teacher is frequently their lifesaver.

We are all students; every good teacher knows that. A teacher's job is simply to present a map of life, explain its purposes and pitfalls, and refer to authors who have recorded their own impressions of the journey. Sometimes teachers share, through discussions, their own opinions in order to inspire debate with students for their own engagements into the unfathomable. The teacher's objective is to prepare students for the eventual events in their own lives.

Once they graduate, these students often forget those incredible individuals who guided them into that future. They deceptively imagine their endeavors are theirs alone—their achievements, their own personal reward.

Pray don't forget those few who lit the fire of curiosity, hope, and challenge under your chair. Just stop for five seconds every so often and thank that special teacher who was there when no one else was and said, "You can do this."

About the Author

Teaching on a small Navajo reservation in western New Mexico, surrounded by cowboys, Mormons, Mexicans and Zuni Indians was quite the cultural banquet to a boy from Baltimore. This was not the sleepy reservation experience I was expecting. It was so much more. It was a celebration of diversity, individualism, and Native tradition. Even after all these years, I am still in awe and reminded of the treasury of experiences I was allowed thanks to the opportunities presented me by the Ramah Navajo people.

www.ingramcontent.com/pod-product-compliance
Lightning Source LLC
Chambersburg PA
CBHW011744220426
43666CB00018B/2891